Capitalism and Class in the
Gulf Arab States

Capitalism and Class in the Gulf Arab States

Adam Hanieh

First published in 2011 by
PALGRAVE MACMILLAN® in the United States – a division of
St. Martin's Press LLC, 175 Fifth Avenue, New York, NY 10010.

Where this book is distributed in the UK, Europe and the rest of the world,
this is by Palgrave Macmillan, a division of Macmillan Publishers Limited,
registered in England, company number 785998, of Houndmills, Basingstoke,
Hampshire RG21 6XS.

Palgrave Macmillan is the global academic imprint of the above companies
and has companies and representatives throughout the world.

Palgrave® and Macmillan® are registered trademarks in the United States, the
United Kingdom, Europe and other countries.

ISBN: 978–0–230–11077–9

Library of Congress Cataloging-in-Publication Data

Hanieh, Adam, 1972–
    Capitalism and class in the Gulf Arab states / Adam Hanieh.
        p. cm.
        ISBN 978–0–230–11077–9 (hardback)
    1. Persian Gulf States—Economic conditions.   2. Capitalism—Persian
Gulf States.   3. Gulf Cooperation Council.   I. Title.
    HC415.3.H36 2011
    330.9536—dc22   2011001631

A catalogue record of the book is available from the British Library.

Design by MPS Limited, A Macmillan Company

First edition: July 2011

10 9 8 7 6 5 4 3 2 1

Printed in the United States of America.

Contents

List of Tables

Preface

This book has its genesis outside of the Gulf. From 1997 to 2003 I had the privilege of living and working in the Palestinian West Bank. During this time, I was struck by the immense influence that the Gulf region had on the Palestinian political economy. Gulf-based companies owned large stakes in major Palestinian companies and financial institutions, Gulf governments played an influential role in Palestinian politics, and many friends and relatives spoke of time they had spent as workers in the oil and other industries in the Gulf. It was clear that Palestine (like the rest of the Middle East) was profoundly affected by this connection. Yet, paradoxically, there had been little written on the political economy of these regional links and their relationship to the nature of capitalism in the Gulf—the Gulf was the core of Middle East capitalism but the dominant perspective seemed to downplay the regional scale and treat the Middle East as a simple agglomeration of distinct nation-states.

What this book aims to do is to contribute some essential first steps in thinking through these problems of the region's development. In order to appreciate how the Gulf is penetrating the broader Middle East, we first need to grasp the processes at work within the political economy of Gulf capitalism. This means taking seriously the Gulf states as *capitalist*—not simply monarchies that sit atop an oil spigot—and incorporating the process of Gulf regional integration into our analysis. From this starting point, we can hopefully begin to better understand how Gulf capitalism helps to form the broader hierarchies of the Middle East.

There are very many people who contributed to bringing this book to completion and in stimulating my ideas and thoughts on the region. I would particularly like to thank Gilbert Achcar, Greg Albo, Sam Gindin, Eberhard Kienle, Jerome Klassen, Thomas Marois, David McNally, Ananya Mukherjee-Reed, Sabah Al Nasseri, Leo Panitch, Alfredo Saad-Filho, Omar Al-Shehabi, Ahmad Shokr, Abdel Takriti, Issam Al Yamani, Anna Zalik, and Rafeef Ziadah who all read drafts or excerpts of this book. I greatly appreciate the extensive time these individuals gave to seriously engage and offer criticisms and comments. I would also like to thank Robyn Curtis at Palgrave Macmillan, who was a pleasure to work with throughout the entire writing process.

Many of the ideas in this book originate in my PhD dissertation, completed in 2009 in the political science department at York University, Toronto. I thank all the faculty and administrative staff that made my time at York such a pleasure and an exciting learning experience. There are very few academic institutions that truly encourage critical thought in a contemporary university setting—the York political science department is one of these and it was a privilege to work alongside an exceptional group of faculty and graduate students. In particular, I would like to thank Greg Albo, my dissertation supervisor. Greg remains a wonderful intellectual mentor and friend who taught me an enormous amount about understanding the world and working to change it. This book would not have been possible without him.

While writing this book I spent 18 months in the Gulf carrying out research and teaching at Zayed University, Dubai. Faculty and staff at ZU were generous with their time and friendship. I learnt a great deal from this experience, particularly from the opportunity to engage with many of the wonderful students at ZU. I appreciate the critical and thoughtful insights that these students often brought to our discussions on Gulf politics and the Middle East more generally—and I hope some of this is reflected in the pages that follow.

There are many other friends in Toronto, Montreal, Ramallah, London, and Adelaide that made the last few years of research and writing possible and from whom I continue to draw inspiration. In particular, I would like to thank deeply Rafeef Ziadah. She has been there from day one, both at an intellectual level to discuss many of the ideas contained in this book and as a dear friend and emotional pillar. I hope one day to repay the debt. My family has also always been there for me—perhaps slightly puzzled by my interest in the Gulf—but nevertheless a wonderful source of love and support. Finally, this book is dedicated to my father, Ahmad Hanieh, who passed away as it was being written.

CHAPTER 1

Approaching Class Formation in the Gulf Arab States

An oft-used representation of recent changes in the Gulf Arab states is a pair of photographs comparing a 20-year old snapshot of the main thoroughfare of Dubai, Sheikh Zayed Road, to the same stretch of road today. In the space of just two short decades, the pictures reveal a remarkable transformation. The older shot shows a few solitary buildings, surrounded by vast expanses of desert and a dusty road. The more recent picture portrays a stunning panorama of glittering lights and towering skyscrapers. Science fiction analogies are often used to describe this sight—the world's tallest buildings defy architectural logic as they jostle and twist in the skyline. Up until the puncturing of Dubai's construction boom in the wake of the 2008 global financial crisis, a widely quoted (although probably exaggerated) rumor put the number of cranes at work in the city at one-quarter of the world's entire stock.

Dubai's prodigious development boom is paralleled across the Gulf. All the states of the Gulf Cooperation Council (GCC), a regional bloc of the six oil-rich Arab monarchies—Bahrain, Kuwait, Oman, Qatar, Saudi Arabia, and the United Arab Emirates (UAE)—have been transformed over the past decade into a tangle of highways, skyscrapers, and fanciful projects. For much of the 2000s, the GCC was the world's largest market of "megaprojects"— huge construction and industrial schemes that attracted the leading engineering companies across the globe. The world's tallest building, biggest shopping mall, and largest aluminum, plastic, ceramics, and petrochemical complexes are all located or under construction in the GCC. With the arguable exception of coastal China, there is no other region on the planet that has seen such a remarkable transformation in so short a period of time.

What lies behind this dramatic development of the Gulf? The obvious answer is, of course, the judicious use of oil revenues—particularly in the wake of the large rise in the price of oil from 2000 to 2008. At the peak of this price rise, the GCC's nominal Gross Domestic Product (GDP) climbed to over $1 trillion, just under 2 percent of the world's total of around $61 trillion. In 2008, the GCC was the fourteenth-largest economy in the world (with a size about the same as Australia) and registered a per capita GDP three times the world average. Yet while hydrocarbon wealth is clearly key to the economic transformation of the recent decades, this book describes a different side to the GCC's development. It argues that—much like its desert cousin, the mirage—what visitors actually see in the region's oil-fueled boom is not the full picture. The concrete and steel are physical embodiments of a much deeper shift—a fundamental transformation in the political economy of the Gulf. The GCC has become a major node of world capitalism, a position that has precipitated changes in the socioeconomic relations that typified the region for many decades. This evolution of Gulf capitalism—its linkages with the world market and the development of the domestic political economy—is the analytical focus of the chapters that follow.

The key contention of this book is that in order to fully comprehend these changes it is necessary to understand and map the process of capitalist class formation in the Gulf. The Gulf capitalist class has emerged rapidly and in "hothouse" fashion—from state-supported and family-based trading groups in the 1960s and 1970s to the domination of a few massive conglomerates in the contemporary period. Most significant—and the key characteristic of the region's political economy examined in this book—is the pronounced *internationalization* of Gulf capitalism over the past decade. Large Gulf conglomerates now conceive their profit-making activities across the entire GCC rather than solely within its individual member-states. They own stakes in a wide variety of industrial, financial, and retail firms located throughout the region. The patterns of accumulation crystallizing in the GCC embody a new set of internationalized social relations and thereby represent a process of class formation—described henceforth as *Khaleeji Capital*. The Arabic word *khaleej* is literally translated as "Gulf" but goes beyond a geographic meaning to convey a common pan-Gulf Arab identity that sets the people of the region apart from the rest of the Middle East. Throughout this book, Khaleeji Capital is used to describe those capitalists whose accumulation is most thoroughly and consistently grounded in the internationalization of capital across the GCC space. Khaleeji Capital in no way means a loss of "national" identity, but rather an orientation and per-spective toward accumulation at the pan-GCC scale. As this book shows, Khaleeji Capital is hierarchical-structured around a Saudi-UAE axis, with other capital connected in a subordinate fashion to this core. It represents the development of an emerging space that reflects a shift in the social relations underpinning accumulation in the Gulf—a process of class formation located within, and occurring through, the internationalization of capital. This process of class formation is intimately linked to the rapid development of the Gulf economies and the physical transformation of the Gulf cities. It is the real untold story of the Gulf—the reality behind the image—and holds immense importance to an understanding of the contemporary Middle East and the world market as a whole.

Colonialism and the Origins of the Gulf States

With close to one-fifth of the world's total conventional oil reserves, Saudi Arabia dominates the GCC. The country holds around two-thirds of the GCC's total population and makes up over 80 percent of its landmass. It also contributes nearly half of the region's GDP, although its growth rates have lagged behind Qatar, Kuwait, and the UAE whose smaller populations mean that their GDP per capita is much higher. These aggregate figures should be interpreted with some caution, however, as a low-paid migrant workforce constitutes the majority of the labor force in all GCC states and the polarization of wealth between citizen and noncitizen residents is extremely high.

The political structures of the six GCC states bear strong similarities. The power of the ruler is effectively hereditary, concentrated in a family that controls the state apparatus and large tracts of the economy. Although limited political contestation exists in elected legislatures in two GCC states—Bahrain (*majlis al-nuwab*) and Kuwait (*majlis al-umma*)—voting rights are restricted to a small proportion of the resident population and the rulers in both states have the power to dissolve parliament. The other GCC states have even more limited "consultative councils" with little effective power to challenge the ruler. Political repression—ranging from tight control over media through to imprisonment and exile of opposition figures—has been commonplace in all the GCC states.

The significance and recent trajectory of these political and economic characteristics will be further explored in the pages that follow. But in order to set the framework for this discussion of capitalism and class formation in the GCC it is useful to have a broad appreciation of the historical origins of these six states. Much of the later developments bear the imprint of the particular configuration of class and state forged in the colonial era. What follows is a necessarily abbreviated description of the region from around the 1900s, at a time of direct colonial domination. Many of these themes that accompanied the region's emergence from colonialism will be revisited in later chapters (particularly Chapter 3).

Table 1.1 Basic characteristics of the GCC states

	Population (million, 2008)	Land size (Thousand Sq. Km.)	GDP (current, billion US$, 2008)	Real GDP Growth % (1992–2001 average)	Real GDP Growth % (2008)	GDP/ capita (2008, '000 US$)	Crude oil and gas as % of GDP (2007)	Migrant % of labor force (2008)
Saudi Arabia	24.807	2,000	475	1.9	4.2	19.15	48	51
UAE	4.5	83.6	261	4.3	5.1	58.27	35.9	92 (2006)
Kuwait	2.7	17.8	148	8.9	5.5	54.26	54.5	84
Qatar	1.3	11.6	71 (2007)	7.9	25.4	62.45 (2006)	56.6	94
Oman	2.8	309.5	60	4.4	12.8	21.65	45.2	68
Bahrain	1.1	0.7	21	4.9	6.3	19.8	13.6	74
GCC Total	36.88	2,423	1,037	–	–	28.28	–	69

Source: World Bank Statistics, GCC Secretariat General, http://www.gcc-sg.org, Accessed 10 October 2009.

At the end of the nineteenth century the region that was to become the GCC was firmly embedded in Britain's colonial empire (with the exception of the areas known as Najd and Hijaz—the future Saudi Arabia—and some recalcitrant Arab and Iranian tribes along the coastal areas). Throughout the region, Britain encouraged the concentration of power within the hands of individual rulers who were connected to a wider ruling family, and could trace their origins back to one of the Arabian Peninsula tribes. With their rule sanctioned and supported by the British, the ruler drew wealth from taxes on pearling, trade, as well as some agricultural activities (in particular, date farming and fishing). Britain's major concern was the exclusion of other colonial and regional powers from the Gulf region, and the continued profitable engagement with pearling and other trade. These interests in the Gulf were subordinate to a broader colonial framework centered upon enduring control over India.

As a result of this economic subordination to British-controlled trade, the ruling *shuyoukh* (pl. Sheikh) along the Gulf's coast were largely dependent on British support for their survival. The British were fully cognizant of this fact, and pursued a clearly articulated policy of divide-and-rule within the region—breaking the territory into many small sheikhdoms that would be reliant on an external power for their survival—and embodied in a treaty between the ruler and the British. The numerous border disputes that persist to this day within the Gulf—between Kuwait and Iraq, Iran and the UAE, Saudi Arabia and emirate of Abu Dhabi, Qatar and Bahrain, the emirate of Ras Al Khaimeh and Oman, and so forth—are partly a legacy of this British policy (accentuated in the modern day, of course, by the potential oil and gas reserves that lie within these borders). It is important to emphasize that through much of the Gulf the notion of territorial demarcation was a foreign import—borders were artificially imposed from the outside and the region's large nomadic population viewed geography through ever-shifting tribal influence rather than fixed boundaries.

Within this general framework, however, there was significant internal differentiation between the states that eventually came to form the GCC. Most notable was the exception of the Najd and Hijaz areas, which had a much greater degree of independence from Britain than the Gulf coastal areas. Except for a brief 12-year period from 1915 to 1927, neither Najd nor Hijaz held a treaty with Britain and their status alternated between a somewhat loose Ottoman suzerainty and the claims of rival tribes originating from within the Najd interior.[1] The dynasty that eventually emerged victorious in the struggle to control the Najd and Hijaz, the al-Saud, drew its wealth from a structure more akin to feudal tribute from nomadic tribes rather than the tax on merchant activities that was common along the coastal areas. Towns, however, played a critical role in providing the key nodes of control for the al-Saud—as points of centralized power, wealth, and domination over other tribes—and supplemented through the proceeds of warfare (Sharara 1981, p. 58). This perpetual drive to war was ideologically justified through the militant doctrine upheld by the Islamic sect, the *muwahiddun,* which sanctioned conquest in the name of religious zealotry. The religious-military symbiosis at the core of al-Saud rule gave the embryonic state a powerful expansionary character. Weaker neighbors—Kuwait, Qatar, Bahrain, Oman, and Abu Dhabi—were thus further compelled to draw closer to Britain in the face of this predatory power.

Kuwait, in particular, was precariously sandwiched between the forces of an expanding al-Saud, the Ottoman Empire, and British colonialism. It had a relatively prosperous merchant class, based largely on settled families originally hailing from Najd. By virtue of its location at the apex of the Gulf, where it formed a crossroads to the overland trade through Iraq, the merchant class prospered through the activities of pearling, shipbuilding, and entrepot trade. Standing over this class was the al-Sabah family, which, by the late eighteenth century, had become preeminent following the departure of its two rivals, the al-Khalifa and al-Jalahima families, for al-Zubara in Qatar (and eventually Bahrain). The relative strength of the merchant class vis-à-vis the al-Sabah, who relied upon the merchants for much of its import duties, meant that Kuwait's pre-oil political history was largely punctuated by successive waves of conflict and reconciliation between the al-Sabah and the merchants (and, up until the early 1900s, often conducted through the threat of migration by the merchant class) (Crystal 1995; Fattah 1997). It was partly in response to claims from the merchant class, and partly due to pressures from the neighboring al-Saud and the Ottoman Empire, that the al-Sabah pursued a very close alliance with the British government, particularly in the lead-up to World War One. This intimate British-Kuwaiti relationship continued following the discovery of oil, and (as is discussed in Chapter 3 in more detail) Kuwait's "recycling" of its oil revenues through the British sterling zone was an important step in the development of Kuwaiti financial institutions.

In the coastal areas in the South of the Gulf, British warships had definitively ended any challenge to their control of the sea with the defeat of the Qawasim, a tribal group based in the coastal area of Ras Al Khaimeh in 1819. Britain codified its policy of divide-and-rule through a series of treaties signed with all the Gulf sheikhdoms from 1820–1945 and seven "Trucial States" emerged (Abu Dhabi, Dubai, Sharjah, Ras Al Khaimeh, Umm al-Quwain, Fujairah, and Ajman—named as such because they came into being through the treaty process). In these states, the British sponsored seven individual ruling Sheikhs, forbidding them from entering negotiations with any foreign power other than the British, and preventing them from building up their naval power. Indeed, British control was so extensive that no foreigner could enter any of the Gulf states without explicit British permission (Zahlan 1998, p. 21).[3] Through the treaties, Britain blocked any move toward internal unity between the seven sheikhdoms, which were unable to negotiate with each other without British mediation. Britain also used the inevitable conflicts between the seven sheikhs as a way of setting themselves up as an external referent and power broker (Kazim 2000, p. 151).

From the early 1900s, Dubai became particularly important to British colonialism as a key trading route and port of call for the British India Steam Navigation Company following Iranian cancellation of British leasing and tax rights in the port of Lingah, located on the western side of the Gulf (Davidson 2008, pp. 73–74). Strengthened by the decision of Dubai's ruler Sheikh Rashid bin al-Maktoum to grant protection and tax-free status to Iranian merchants leaving Lingah, Dubai became strongly orientated toward trading activities with a flourishing merchant stratum that benefited from the city's tax-free incentives. Following the discovery of oil in Abu Dhabi in the 1950s, however, Dubai was soon eclipsed by its wealthier neighbor. The seven Trucial States joined together as the UAE after British withdrawal in 1971.

In Qatar and Bahrain, the relationship between rulers and the rest of society was markedly different. In 1766, the aforementioned al-Khalifa and al-Jalahima families had settled in al-Zubara on the west coast of Qatar after they had left Kuwait. These families set up a prosperous pearling and trading center in al-Zubara, linked to tribal connections back in Kuwait. The other main clan present in Qatar were the al-Thani, who originally hailed from Najd. Qatar, however, was of minor importance compared to neighboring Bahrain, which, at the time, was under the control of Iran.[4] In 1783, in the context of several years of rivalry with the Matareesh (an Arab tribe who ruled Bahrain and owed fealty to Iran), the al-Khalifa and al-Jalahima conquered Bahrain and moved their pearling and trading operations there. Qatar was relegated to a collection of minor pearling and fishing towns and was viewed by most as a dependency of Bahrain. One of the consequences of this was that the al-Thani (who remained after the departure of the al-Khalifa and al-Jalahima) became a relatively poor ruling family situated within a much weaker merchant class. Qatar's small population also meant that the broader al-Thani tribe constituted a very large proportion of the entire population—by some estimates half of the indigenous population of Qatar in 1900. The weakness of the merchant class, and the relatively large size of the al-Thani, has meant that political disputes in Qatar have largely originated from within different factions of a fractious ruling family (Crystal 1995). A tiny handful of merchant families, notably the Darwish and al-Mana, remained close to the al-Thani and evolved to be an important component of the Qatari capitalist class today.

The al-Khalifa and al-Jalahima alliance broke apart soon after the conquering of Bahrain in 1783, and the al-Khalifa emerged as the unchallenged rulers of the island. Bahrain was a key location for trade and merchant activities in the Gulf.[5] It formed the major port in the trade of Indian goods between Basra (in modern-day Iraq) and Muscat (Oman), and was one of the most important pearling centers in the Gulf. The defeat of the Matareesh by the al-Khalifa gave a very important socioeconomic distinction to Bahrain in comparison to the rest of the Gulf. Unlike Qatar, Kuwait, or the sheikhdoms that eventually became the UAE, the ruling elite of Bahrain, the Sunni al-Khalifa, joined an existing Sunni community that was much smaller than the Shia majority who hailed from Arab tribes that had been settled on the eastern side of the Gulf. These sectarian differences were reflected in social divisions—the Sunni constituted the bulk of the merchant and ruling elite while the poorer Shia were concentrated as rural date farmers and in fishing. Shia farmers were required to pay a poll and water tax to the al-Khalifa—similar taxes were not placed on the Sunni population (Khuri 1991, p. 48). Over time, a stratification began to emerge within the Shia as some were given the positions of *wazir*, a minister or secretary, and thereby obtained the right to redistribute land and collect rent. This social structure meant that the key division in Bahraini society emerged between the al-Khalifa, allied Sunni tribes, and a small layer of Shia on one hand, and the bulk of the mostly poor Shia on the other. While Bahraini politics should not be interpreted as "Sunni vs. Shia" and Bahraini opposition groups have historically been careful to build across sectarian divides, the imprint of this early history on the country's class formation remains important to this day.

Of all the states in the Arabian peninsula, Oman was perhaps the most affected by British colonialism (although it was never officially a British colony or protectorate). In the eighteenth century, Oman had been the center of a vibrant trading system in the Indian Ocean, dominating much of the trade between East Africa, India, and the Arabian peninsula. The key to Oman's prosperity had been its control over the East African island of Zanzibar, which acted as the chief trading intermediary between the precapitalist African interior and an industrializing European capitalism (Sheriff 1987). Virtually all the lucrative East African trade in slaves, animal products, and raw materials passed through Zanzibar on its way to Europe via India. As Britain and France fought to assert their dominance over the Indian Ocean during the early 1800s, this trade was largely halted but replaced by the extremely profitable production of cloves, once again under the control of Omani landowners. In the 1860s, however, Oman lost control over Zanzibar and its East African possessions following British mediation of a succession dispute within the Omani ruling family. The British came to dominate Oman, intervening militarily to support their main ally based in the country's capital Muscat, Sultan Taymur Ibn Faisal, against threats from tribes in the interior of the Arabian peninsula[6] (Al Naqib 1987, pp. 55–70). The country was rapidly impoverished, with the main concern of the British being the tight control over the strategic entrance to the Gulf, the Straits of Hormuz. The Omani armed forces were run by British officers, decisions of the Sultan were largely directed by British representatives, and in 1891 a treaty was signed that forbid Oman from relinquishing territory except in British favor (Kaylani 1979, p. 570). Omani Arabs were prevented from participating in commerce, and travel outside the country was next to impossible for them. Indians who were protected by the British largely controlled merchant activities. Moreover, the British brought Baluchi Sunni Muslims, originating from an area now part of Pakistan, to serve in the country's military.[7] In contemporary times Baluchi still make up a significant part of the Omani population (around 12 percent in 2002) and an important family in the contemporary Omani capitalist class, the Zubair, is said to have Baluchi origins (Peterson 2004).

In short, at the cusp of the oil era that began to emerge from the 1920s onwards, most of the Gulf remained tightly inserted in the British colonial system (with the important exception of Saudi Arabia). Each of the future GCC states was controlled by a ruling family, which—to varying degrees—relied upon a network of powerful merchant families and colonial backing. Many of these early merchant families, alongside new groups that emerged with the onset of oil, were the proto-class that came to underlay Gulf capitalism. They form the social substratum that was transformed through a complex process of development in the subsequent oil era into contemporary Khaleeji Capital.

Theoretical Approaches to Class Formation in the Gulf

Analysis of state and class formation in the period following these colonial times has been largely dominated by rentier-state theory, a theory that has been described as "one of the major contributions of Middle East regional studies to political science" (Anderson 1987, p. 9). The Iranian economist Hossein Mahdavy is usually credited with developing the concept of the rentier-state in relation to Iran prior to the Revolution of 1979.[8] He defined rentier-states as countries "that receive on a regular basis substantial amounts of external rent [which are] rentals paid by foreign individuals, concerns or governments to individuals, concerns or governments of a given country" (Mahdavy 1970, p. 428). In addition to the revenues of oil producing countries, other examples of external payments identified by Mahdavy included rents for pipelines or transportation routes (such as the Suez Canal in Egypt). Oil revenues, however, were particularly significant according to Mahdavy because their size did not depend upon production in the country itself but from "differential and monopolistic rents that arise from the higher productivity of the Middle Eastern oilfields and price fixing practices of the oil companies" (Mahdavy 1979, pp. 428–29). Mahdavy described the period from 1951 to 1956 as a turning point in the Middle East because the rising nationalist movements meant that several states were able to gain a greater share of the oil revenues that had previously accrued to foreign oil companies. Crucially, this enabled the Iranian government to embark on large-scale public expenditure programs and other state spending without having to resort to taxation. Mahdavy described this as a "fortuitous étatisme" in which the government became an important—and perhaps dominant—factor in the economy.

Mahdavy's theorization of the Iranian state carried both political and economic implications that were frequently echoed in subsequent literature. He explicitly linked the rentier-state to the high possibility of social stagnation and political inertia. The revenues of the government were derived from external rents rather than from exploitation of the population, thus relieving the government from any pressure to implement political reform. Moreover, because part of the population experienced an increasing prosperity from oil revenues, mass movements for social change were less likely to emerge. Furthermore, the government possessed large capacity to bribe or coerce pressure groups and thus forestall any fundamental change. These distortions in the political structure were paralleled at the economic level. Mahdavy believed that the economic policies of rentier-states were predisposed to myopic, short-term reliance on rent flows with little incentive to diversify. He argued that Iran needed to consciously lessen its reliance on these flows and implement plans for industrial diversification.

Mahdavy's concept of the rentier-state was further developed in an edited collection on the theme published by Hazem Beblawi and Giacomo Luciani in 1987. This work has become a main reference point for debates over the nature of the state in the Gulf monarchies. In it, Beblawi and Luciani argue that the rentier-state needs to be distinguished from the rentier-economy, with the former a subset of the latter. The rentier-state is a mediating link between the national and international economies. Through its control over the flow of rents, it shapes the economic development of the country as a whole. The analytical focus of Beblawi and Luciani's work thus revolves around an examination of the size of the state and its linkages and role vis-à-vis the economy as a whole. They also introduce a more specific definition of the rentier-economy *ideal-type*, based on four characteristics: (1) the rent must be external to the economy, that is, it comes from foreign sources; (2) rent must be a predominant economic activity (defined by Luciani as 40 percent of revenue); (3) the majority of the population are engaged in the consumption and redistribution of rent rather than its production; and (4) the principal recipient of the rent is the government (Beblawi and Luciani 1987, p. 86–88).

Using the framework advanced by Beblawi and Luciani, much of the subsequent debate has focused on the relationship between the state and other social groups in Gulf societies. Three key political and economic characteristics of the rentier-state have been highlighted. First, following Mahdavy, numerous authors have postulated a link between rentier-states and autocratic regimes (Skocpol 1982; Beblawi and Luciani 1987; Ross 2001; Jensen and Wantchekon 2004). Michael Ross, for example, has argued that rentier-governments are able to relieve "pressures for greater accountability" by relying on low tax rates (thereby short-circuiting claims for representation), fostering patronage networks, and blocking the formation of groups that might challenge the dominance of the state. He infers from this that these regimes tend to be more autocratic in nature (Ross 2004, p. 332). Second, it is argued that the rentier-state has a pronounced degree of autonomy in economic decision-making, and is thereby able to determine which social strata to promote and support. Third, there is supposedly a bias in rentier-economies toward the service sector rather than value-added production. States find it easier (and possess the fiscal resources) to import goods to satisfy consumer demands and increasingly sophisticated tastes, rather than produce those goods domestically (Niblock 1980; Abdel-Fadil 1987).

These three characteristics have typically been used to explain the development of the private sector and merchant classes in the Gulf in the post-colonial era. The allocative decisions of the state mean that certain elites are able to benefit from the redirection of oil revenues. This does not happen through direct involvement in the oil sector itself, which remains under the exclusive purview of the state (and hence the ruling family). Rather, no longer reliant upon the merchant classes for financial support, the state/

ruling family's coalition with the leading merchant families is reworked in the wake of the large influx of oil rents. A key strategy emerges in which, as Jill Crystal has argued in the cases of Kuwait and Qatar, "the merchants were bought off, by the state, as a class." The state did this in both a direct and indirect manner, through mechanisms such as land grants and providing money and monopoly concessions to the old trading families (Crystal 1995, p. 8).

The rentier-state framework has certainly provided some useful insights into postcolonial development of the Gulf states (as well as those in other similarly rent-financed states in Africa and elsewhere). At a comparative level, it has helped to distinguish different outcomes dependent upon the particular configuration of state institutions and their relationships with other social classes. Much of the historical analysis in the following chapters draws extensively upon rentier-state narratives of the Gulf state in the early periods of state formation. This book, however, departs in a number of distinct ways from the methodological assumptions of rentier-state theory. The most fundamental of these differences concerns the nature of the state and its relationship to class. As noted, rentier-state theory relies heavily upon a notion of "relative autonomy," in which the state is seen as a distinct sphere of the political economy with a high degree of latitude to maneuver and deploy economic strategies free from the constraints of the capitalist class. A main argument of this book is that this approach is highly misleading, because it views the state as a separate object—severed from the class relations of Gulf society—with politics interpreted as the struggle over this object. This is reflected in the common use of phrases such as "capturing the state" in much Arabic-language commentary on the state or, as a prominent Lebanese sociologist puts it, "the state was given birth as an external force . . . holding the reins of government, political institutions, the means of production and the official ideology" (Sharara 1980, p. 280). Within the rentier framework the analytical focus is typically placed upon the state (usually assumed to be opposed to an all-encompassing "society") with little attention given to capitalism as a social system. The class character of the Gulf economy is seldom tackled with any theoretical sophistication and the term "capitalism" often absent from these accounts. The category of "merchants" is typically used as a synonym for "bourgeoisie" or "capitalist class"—terms that are (as Luciani has noted in regards to Saudi Arabia) rarely encountered in scholarly work on the region (Luciani 2006, p. 145).

In contrast, this book conceives the state not as a "thing" or collection of individual social actors, but rather as a particular expression of class formation—with the latter understood as a set of social relations that is continually in the process of coming-into-being. This methodological approach draws from a range of Marxist understandings of the state, in which the key point is to understand the state as an alienated form of the social relations that exist within society. Seen in this manner, the existence of the state is ultimately an expression of the fact that social reproduction occurs within a society divided into classes yet, simultaneously, *is* a society—that is, these classes are mutually interdependent. The state is the form taken by this social relation—the contradiction "between universal and particular interests" (Marx 1844). Marxists describe this materialization of social relations in the form of the state as fetishism, in which the "relationship between people takes the character of a thing and thus acquires a 'phantom objectivity,' an autonomy that seems so strictly rational and all-embracing as to conceal every trace of its fundamental nature: the relationship between people" (Lukacs 1968, p. 83).[10] The state is therefore not a thing, but rather a *relation*, or, as Bertell Ollman has put it, "the set of institutional forms through which a ruling class relates to the rest of society" (Ollman 2003, p. 202). These institutional forms allow the ruling class to actually *be* the ruling class (in the political sense).

It is important to understand the particular manner in which Ollman uses the notion of "relation" here. Ollman employs an epistemological approach that emphasizes Marx's "philosophy of internal relations." According to this perspective, the relations existing between objects are not considered external to the objects themselves, but are part of what constitutes those objects as they actually exist. Any object under study needs to be seen as "relations, containing in themselves, as integral elements of what they are, those parts with which we tend to see them externally tied" (Ollman 2003, p. 25). In other words, objects are not self-contained; they are constituted through the relations they hold in their stance with the whole. Thus the relationships in which things are embedded do not exist "outside" of these objects but are internal to their very nature. The state, therefore, is "part of what it means for a ruling class to rule, that is . . . an essential feature of the class itself" (Ollman 2003, p. 202). It is not a distinct or separate sphere that is external to the ruling class.

For this reason, care must be taken when speaking of the "autonomy" of the state. In capitalist society, the state apparatus acts to articulate and manage the interests of the capitalist class. This is true both economically, in the sense of securing the conditions that best facilitate capitalist accumulation, and politically, in the sense of ensuring that there is no challenge to the power of that class.[11] Because production and exchange under capitalism is anarchic, in which individuals are set against one another in pursuit of their private interests, it is difficult for a common capitalist class interest to be articulated directly. The capitalist state thus acquires (and *requires*) a certain level of autonomy from individuals and factions within the capitalist class, in order to mediate the "common good" of capital as a whole. This is more pronounced the more developed the capitalist economy, and is well illustrated by the vital roles of the modern state: regulating the function of the market and labor, arbitrating disputes within the capitalist class, securing the necessary infrastructure that no single capitalist could profitably provide, and managing the inevitable periods of crisis that emerge. But autonomy should not be understood in the sense of "independence" or "separation" from the ruling class; rather, it as an actual aspect of ruling class power itself. It is precisely in the appearance of "relative autonomy," that the state is able to represent the interests of the dominant class as a whole.[12]

Moreover, if the state is conceived as an "internal relation" of the capitalist class—part of what constitutes it as a class—the conceptual division between class and state should not be seen as a rigid boundary. Class lines shift as capitalism develops, and it is critical to remember that class formation is a process in which social relations emerge over time.[13] Understanding the state as an institutional relation of class thus implies that many of the individual personnel related to the institutions of the state can simultaneously be considered part of the capitalist class. This is a pronounced feature of the way that capitalism has developed in the GCC and, in many cases, the "capitalist class" should be understood as inclusive of state personnel and individuals from the ruling family. From this perspective, notions of relative autonomy as they are typically employed by rentier-state theories are misplaced. This book will note many cases in which members of the ruling family who hold high-ranking state positions should simultaneously be considered part of the "private" capitalist class and, in a related fashion, where prominent nonroyal private capitalists simultaneously serve in the state apparatus. This is not a novel observation, as Abbas Al-Nasrawi noted two decades ago in an interesting Arabic-language debate on the nature of the state and private sector in the Arab world: "The question raised is whether it makes sense to speak of the existence of different sectors in [the Gulf] . . . and whether the interlocking of the State and the private sector will make the separation between these sectors meaningless or, at the very least, give it a meaning different from that usually accepted in economic literature" (Al-Nasrawi 1990, p. 530). Indeed, the World Bank has offered the interpenetration of the state and private capital as one explanation for the "business-friendly environment" in the Gulf, remarking that the private sector in the Gulf "included mostly entrepreneurs either from the ruling families or close associates" and that the GCC's "political leadership (often their extended family members) are . . . large enough to develop the private sector country-wide" (World Bank 2009, p. 181).

Of course, seeing the state as an institutional embodiment of class power does not mean that the state is just an automatic or passive reflection of capitalist social relations. As the above analysis suggests, state formation is very much intertwined with class formation and plays an active role in the latter process. Marx noted the historical role that the bourgeois state played in providing the necessary fixed capital for the growth of capitalism; creating private ownership of land and a mobile labor force forced to sell their ability to work (e.g., the enclosure acts in England); restraining forms of capital accumulation that were threatening the very existence of the social structure (e.g., the eight-hour day, child labor laws); and, of course, enabling much of the initial primitive accumulation of capital through the state-orchestrated brutality of colonialism and slavery. Engels was also to write of the Russian state "breeding a Russian capitalist class" through the "emancipation" of the peasants (thereby creating a proletariat) and forcing the development of a bourgeoisie "as in a hot-house, by means of railway concessions, protective duties, and other privileges" (Engels 1890). Engels' phrase is apt and, as will be seen throughout this book, Gulf capitalism has developed in similar "hot-house" fashion with the critical assistance of the state.[14]

But integrating the Gulf state's active role in the development of capitalism is not a *causal* explanation of how and why class and capitalism formed in the Gulf. The Gulf state is an institutional reflection of a set of social relations that has developed within Gulf society. It is not the *reason* for those social relations—except in the narrow sense that it fosters the conditions that help them develop—and it cannot explain the specificity of capitalism in the Gulf (both spatially and temporally). The theoretical weakness of the institutionalist assumptions underlying rentier-state theory is found precisely in this point. To eschew the Marxian observation that "the conditions of existence of specific institutions are the wider social structures that they mediate, rather than institutions being determinant relations unto themselves" means to advance an explanation that is largely self-referential (Albo 2005, p. 74). The logic of much rentier analysis—where the development of capitalism is seen as the outcome of actions and decisions by state elites—needs to be turned on its head.[15] Specifically, the challenge becomes one of understanding why capitalist social relations developed and took the particular form that they did in the Gulf. Obviously oil revenues and the concomitant development of the state is a central feature of this narrative, but the deeper factors shaping class formation must be given analytical primacy. Capitalism did not arise ex nihilo and cannot be simply explained by the policy choices of the state.

What then explains the nature of class formation in the Gulf? This is the third major methodological difference between the theoretical approach of this book and standard rentier-state frameworks. The perspective adopted here is that Gulf class formation has evolved alongside and within the development of a global capitalist system, and is best seen as a specific reflection of the capitalist world market as a whole. This process took place in societies that were largely precapitalist, but which were rapidly integrated into the world market over a period of just a few decades. The focus is thus placed upon the evolving relationship between the social relations of the Gulf and those of the world market as a whole.

Seen in this manner, the GCC is not a sealed bubble that can be understood through a narrow focus on what goes on solely inside its borders (such as the deployment of oil revenues).[16] Rather, this regional space is constituted through the relations that exist between it and global capitalism as a whole (most importantly since the end of World War Two). This should not be understood as an external impact or "effect" on the Gulf (the standpoint taken—even if implicitly—by many rentier-state approaches). Instead, following Ollman's theorization of "internal relations," the global economy is part of the actual essence of the Gulf itself—the development of the global "appears" through the development of the Gulf. The Gulf materialized as a concrete spatial region alongside, within, and through the making of the global economy, and the process of class formation in the Gulf needs to be seen as a unique, spatially specific expression of the concatenation of tendencies underpinning the development of global capitalism. It is necessary to identify those tendencies (or at least their broad outlines) and trace the ways in which they appear in the making of class in the Gulf.

This conception of the Gulf as a region that materialized alongside the development of the capitalist world market implies a rethinking of the nature of the oil commodity. Oil is clearly the major factor differentiating the region from any other in the world and will undoubtedly form the central part of any account of the development of Gulf capitalism. But one of the main arguments of this book is that oil is not a "thing" but a commodity embedded in a set of (globally determined) social relations. Marx warned of "commodity fetishism"—an attempt to explain patterns of social development through the presence (or absence) of a commodity rather than understanding the significance given to that commodity by the social relations within which it is situated. It is these social relations that need to be identified and traced if the nature of oil is to be understood. This implies that a primacy needs to be placed on the wider motion and tendencies of the capitalist world market that confer a particular meaning to oil as a commodity centrally located within the reproduction of the system as a whole.[17]

Once again, it is important to emphasize that this methodological approach is not meant to deny the role of institutional factors or the decisions of state actors in shaping the particular form of the Gulf political economy—indeed, these will continually be highlighted throughout the analysis that follows. This book, however, does not claim to present a complete accounting of the institutional history or evolution of economic policy in the Gulf economies. Rather, the focus is placed on elaborating an analysis of Gulf capitalism—specifically the process of capitalist class formation—alongside and within the development of capitalism at the global level.

Class and Capitalism

Identifying the tendencies that structure the development of the world market and give the Gulf region a particular meaning requires a theory of accumulation. This book adopts a framework drawn from Marxian theory, in which the endless drive to accumulate is seen as the sine qua non of the capitalist system. Marx noted that human beings are distinguished from other animals through their repeated, purposeful application of labor on nature as a means of producing the necessary elements of survival. This labor is necessarily social, and the extension of this social labor presupposes and deepens the development of tools and language, as well as more complex social forms of organization. In this manner, the necessity of socially organized human labor underlies the development of human beings.

At a certain point in human development, the production of the means of survival through this metabolic interaction with nature posits the possibility of production that is greater than that necessary for day-to-day survival and reproduction. The existence of this increasingly permanent and predictable *social surplus product* is the basis for the development of classes (Marx 1859; Engels 1877; Engels 1884). As this social surplus increases through the development of more efficient tools and methods of social production, the struggle for control over it eventually leads to the development of classes and a state able to protect and secure preferential access to this surplus for the ruling group.

Marx's perspective is grounded in the fundamental observation that, in all human societies, labor is necessarily social and must be distributed between different productive activities (in other words, a division of labor) as well as appropriated in specific ways. The social relations that emerge between human beings in this process are the central element of Marx's theory of class. This is an important point to emphasize as it differs from the Weberian-inspired definitions offered by much contemporary academic work. According to Marx's perspective, class is not defined by a person's occupation, income level, or status. Rather, class is an antagonistic social relation. It arises through the relationship established between groups of people in the course of society's reproduction of itself and through the struggle over the social surplus product.

Classes do not come into existence ready-made. They crystallize alongside the formation of the set of social relations that come to typify a certain society, and hence the emphasis is placed on class formation as a *process* rather than as a static category. The methodological key to understanding this process is an emphasis on how the production and circulation of commodities occurs, thereby enabling a mapping of the social relations (and hence class structure) that emerges around these activities. Marx developed a particular heuristic tool for describing the motion of capital through different stages of accumulation, which he called the "circuit of capital":

$$M\ldots\ldots C(Mp + Lp) \ldots P \ldots C' \ldots M'$$

In this basic circuit, an individual capitalist starting with a sum of money (M), exchanges it for commodities, C, which includes labor power (Lp, or the work done by the worker) and means of production (Mp, raw materials, machinery, factories et cetera). Labor power and the means of production are combined in the process of production, P, to produce a commodity with an increased value C' that can then be exchanged for an increased sum of money, M'. According to Marx, this increased value is created by the worker (Lp) and appropriated in money form by the capitalist. The circuit thus captures the basic capitalist *social relation*—workers employed by capital in the production process, P, to produce a commodity C' with a value greater than C.

This is a schematic representation of a single capital with the arbitrary beginning point M (presuming, therefore, the existence of money and capitalist social relations prior to the beginning of the circuit). It is an abstraction, therefore, from any historically determined or concrete capitalism. The value of this heuristic tool, however, lies in the fact that it highlights the different moments through which the system as a whole reproduces itself and the points at which accumulation can occur. Specifically, there are three basic moments or subcircuits to this general circuit of capital, each of which corresponds to different capitalist activities. Some capitalists specialize in the production (P) of commodities through their ownership of manufacturing and other businesses. This is the *productive circuit*, which, broadly put, involves the creation of new commodities through the transformation of other commodities. Second, some capitalists specialize in the sale of commodities (C') through their ownership of retail outlets and other types of shops. This is the *commodity circuit*, which involves the realization of the value produced in P through the sale of commodities. Finally, a section of the capitalist class deals in money (M') through their ownership of banks and other financial entities. This is the *finance circuit*, and it has become an increasingly important feature of contemporary capitalism (see below). Of course, all capitalists are involved in all three activities to some degree, but this basic division of the general circuit of capital into three subcircuits— the productive circuit, the commodity circuit, and the finance circuit—is useful in that it describes the way in which capitalism reproduces itself, and the way in which classes form around this process. These three circuits form the basic framework used in later chapters to understand the character of the Gulf capitalist class.

The Internationalization of Capital

Based upon this understanding of accumulation, Marx was led to make a prescient remark on the nature of capitalism: "Thus, while capital must on one side strive to tear down every spatial barrier to intercourse, i.e. to exchange, and conquer the whole earth for its market, it strives on the other side to annihilate this space with time, i.e. to reduce to a minimum the time spent in motion from one place to another. The more developed the capital, therefore, the more extensive the market over which it circulates, which forms the spatial orbit of its circulation, the more does it strive simultaneously for an even greater extension of the market and for greater annihilation of space by time" (Marx 1973, p. 539). This conception of capital's tendency to overcome "every spatial barrier to intercourse" powerfully captures the pressures toward the *internationalization of capital*, that is, the ways in which capital seeks unrestricted, increasingly rapid, and free flows across the globe in order to "conquer the whole earth." In this view, space is not a property that can be understood separate from the time it takes to traverse it. The distance between spaces can be "annihilated" through revolutions in time. Internationalization drives the search for new markets, cheap labor, and sources of raw materials. It underpins the continual technological revolutions in the communication and transport industries. The conquering of space is something that springs immanent from the nature of accumulation itself—not a policy choice or a decision of states.

The motor-force of this drive to internationalize is the competition between different capitalists. Because the aim of production under capitalism is not human happiness or the satisfaction of needs but the pursuit of profit, capitalists are forced to compete with each other or face being swallowed by a more successful rival. Those capitalists able to engage in large-scale investments generally out-perform smaller capitalists—they have better ability to produce cheaper commodities, swamp markets, and engage in price wars. One of the effects of this competition is an ever-growing increase in the scale of production. The increasing amount of capital, however, is amassed in fewer and fewer hands—a feature of capitalism described by Marx as the concentration, and centralization of capital.

But the growing scale of production, as Christian Palloix pointed out in a seminal analysis of internationalization in the 1970s, means much more than the increasing traversal of capital across state borders. Such a definition would be "purely descriptive and not theoretical" (Palloix 1977, p. 20). Rather, internationalization means that "the process of converting the functional "money" form into the commodity form and into the productive form (and vice versa) can no longer be fully realized inside of a single capitalist social formation" (Palloix 1977, p. 20). The circuit of capital, in other words, can no longer be reduced to its movement within a national space. Due to the increasingly large scale of production, national markets become too small for the largest capitalist to profitably operate within. As a result, the production and sale of commodities is "conceptualized, produced, and realized at the level of the world market" rather than within the borders of a single state. This formulation of internationalization as a way of capital "conceptualizing" or "conceiving" its self-nature (i.e., the motion of its circuit) is one that is constantly reiterated throughout this book.

Internationalization implies that capital tends to push ever outwards, penetrating all spheres of life and knitting together all human beings and geographical spaces in a complex web of production and reproduction that extends across the planet. Behind the dazzling array of commodities that appear to represent competing products in the marketplace, ownership is distributed among a handful of massive corporations headquartered in the leading capitalist countries (typically based in North America, Europe, or Japan). The concentration and centralization of capital at an international scale means that some sectors develop at the expense of others, and the concentration of wealth and power takes on a geographical form—polarized both within and between states. Accumulation occurs within a single global system marked by profound unevenness and sharp hierarchies.

But the development of a single, deeply interconnected world market should in no way be taken to mean that individual nation states have lost their importance. Capitalism is certainly marked by the expansion of accumulation, the erasure of differences between national markets, and the creation of vast, interconnected chains of production and realization across the globe. Yet, simultaneously, the accumulation of capital demands "a certain 'coherence' and 'materialization' in time and space"—it must occur *somewhere* (Albo 2003, p. 91). This means that internationalizing capital is faced with the challenge of securing accumulation conditions (disciplining labor, protecting private property rights, ensuring adequate financial conditions and laws, et cetera) *everywhere* In other words, precisely because of the development of the world market, the state becomes more, not less, important for ensuring that accumulation takes place and that the conditions that underpin internationalization are satisfied across the globe (Panitch and Gindin 2003).[18] The tightly integrated nature of all spaces in the global economy means that the maintenance of the conditions of accumulation at each level of the hierarchy takes on an increasing significance—no "rogue" states can be permitted. This reinforces processes of state formation, with each national space compelled to align itself with the conditions set at the international level.

The relationships between states are thus contradictory. Capital pushes toward internationalization and is concentrated in a handful of large corporations, resulting in increasingly feverish competition between states over potential markets, raw materials, and sources of labor. Yet simultaneously, the leading capitalist states have a common interest in maintaining the stability and necessary conditions for internationalization across the globe. These states (and their various international institutions) are compelled to cooperate, direct, and maintain these conditions for the good of capitalism as a whole. International relations between the leading states are characterized, therefore, by dual tendencies of cooperation and rivalry. During the postwar period—as will be further explored in Chapter 2—the US state played a very specific role in mediating this configuration of power.

Finance and Internationalization

The deepening process of internationalization moves in tandem with another feature of accumulation, the growing importance of financial flows—credit, debt, and, later, more complex instruments such as derivatives—within the circuit of capital. Finance is, of course, as old as capitalism itself. It enables capitalism to take on a social character beyond the individual interests of the private capitalist, by, as Marx described it, bringing together the money resources that "lie scattered in larger or smaller amounts over the surface of society" (Marx 1992, p. 778). Different institutional forms such as banks, joint-stock companies, and other financial markets, gather together the capital held in a variety of hands and different classes, allowing it to be collectivized and redirected into the accumulation process through the credit system.

At the most fundamental level, the development of credit and other forms of financialization are consequences of capital's attempt to deal with barriers that inevitably emerge across the circuit of capital during the process of accumulation. In a typical example, a capitalist may borrow money to engage in production before the commodities produced in the previous round of production have been sold. In this manner, credit enables the system to temporarily overcome the barriers arising from the fact that production must necessarily take place over a particular time period (Rosdolsky 1977, p. 392). Another potential barrier is the difficulty faced by capitalists in mobilizing funds to engage in production. The growing scale of production means that a mounting share of total costs is represented by fixed capital (such as machinery, factories, etc., as well as the increased expenditure on the associated labor required to constantly revolutionize technology, e.g., R&D). The growth in fixed capital costs means that it becomes difficult for one capitalist firm, or even group of capitalists, to produce upfront the necessary financial outlay for modern industrial plants and technologies. These barriers to the circulation of fixed capital can be partially ameliorated via the credit system. Capitalists are able to resort to credit in order to raise the necessary funds for investing in fixed capital. In this case, credit "switches" an oversupply of circulating capital toward the fixed capital circuit and thus bridges branches of different circuits (Harvey 1999, p. 265).

Another important illustration of the potential barriers to the accumulation of capital can be seen within the moment of exchange. The growing scale of capitalist production means there is an increasing tendency toward the overproduction of commodities unable to find buyers in the market place. The problems presented by this tendency are accentuated due to the initial large outlays on fixed capital demanded by the production process (combined with the reduced turn-over time of that fixed capital and its potential devalorization, e.g., the obsolescence of machinery and technology) (Mandel 1983, p. 229). For this reason, the whole system becomes increasingly unstable and there is growing difficulty in ensuring the sale of an ever-increasing quantity of products in the market place. Credit plays a key role in overcoming these barriers to the realization of value by creating extra demand, either through an increase in individual consumer debt or through the state guarantee of profits by means such as military, infrastructure, and other government contracts.

The role of finance as a means of overcoming barriers to the motion of capital has been deeply reinforced by internationalization. In this case, finance subsumes barriers to space-time that emerge as capitalism "conquers the whole earth." As the geographical scale of accumulation grows, for example, the costs of doing business rise exponentially. This has generated the rapid increases in cross-border investments in the postwar period, as well as the global expansion of stock markets and private firms dealing in financial instruments—mechanisms through which companies can obtain credit at a global scale. Furthermore, the development of highly complex global production chains demands ways to link circuits of capital across a very large number of geographical spaces and time periods. This means dealing with potentially disastrous fluctuations in currencies, interest rates, and other variables, and is the origin of financial instruments such as derivatives, which enable capitalists to manage the risk associated with the fluctuations in value that occur across time and space (Panitch and Gindin 2004, p. 64). In short, financial flows ultimately act to create interdependencies between different moments of the circuit of capital across geographical spaces and periods of time. They act like "glue"—enabling internationalization to take place by interlocking the production and realization of commodities across different circuits, and tying together the past and future creation of wealth. As these circuits of capital intertwine across different spaces, the reproduction of capital within a specific geographical space becomes more closely tied to the reproduction of other capitals at the international scale.

Internationalization and Khaleeji Capital

The tendencies of internationalization and financialization are key concepts framing the argument in this book. In Chapter 2, the successive postwar deepening of both these tendencies at the global scale is outlined and used to situate the development of Gulf capitalism within the world market. These tendencies, however, are also critical to understanding the internal development of Gulf capitalism. Within the GCC, internationalization has led to an interlacing of each of the three subcircuits of capital (productive, commodity, and financial) across national borders. This does not simply mean an increase in pan-Gulf cross-border flows of money or commodity trade. Rather, behind these flows lies an elaboration of social relations that link Gulf capitalist classes across the GCC. The social relations underpinning Gulf capitalism are increasingly interlocked across the Gulf states, and capital comes to conceive its accumulation from the perspective of the GCC as a whole. There are various ways in which this may take place. In the case of relatively similar-sized capitals, the interlocking of the Gulf circuits of capital may manifest itself as the fusion of ownership within a genuinely multinational framework. Alternatively, in the case of significant differences in size and power, it may take the form of direct takeover of the subordinate capital by larger groups. At the most fundamental level, internationalization represents a new set of social relations forming around the interlocking of geographically dispersed circuits of capital.

In short, each of the Gulf circuits of capital is increasingly articulated at a pan-GCC level, reflected in the patterns of cross-border investment flows, intra-GCC trade, joint ventures, the establishment of branches and representative offices, and so forth. As the circuits are elaborated and interlocked regionally, the leading Gulf capitalists come to conceptualize and view their accumulation through the "regional" lens. As this proceeds, each GCC member-state becomes more and more aligned to the imperatives of regional accumulation. Concurrently, regional structures develop—examples include the common market and proposed monetary union (see Chapter 5)—that act to buttress the burgeoning pan-GCC nature of Gulf capitalism. In this sense, internationalization in the GCC has occurred through a process of *regionalization*. Regional integration has facilitated the internationalization of GCC capital through the regional space, and this new set of internationalized social relations embodies the process of class formation captured in the concept of Khaleeji Capital.

The Spatial Structuring of Class

In addition to the concepts of internationalization and financialization that underlie the analysis of capitalism advanced in this book, there is one further aspect to accumulation that needs to be highlighted—the spatial structuring of class. This concept captures the notion that accumulation does not occur in an abstract or undefined ether but is spatially concrete. As Henri Lefebvre, an early theorist of the relationship between space and accumulation, put it: "[W]hat exactly is the mode of existence of social relationships? [. . .] The study of space offers an answer according to which the social relations of production have a social existence to the extent that they have a spatial existence; they project themselves into a space, becoming inscribed there, and in the process producing that space itself" (Lefebvre 1991, p. 129).

Lefebvre emphasized that space is a social product that both reflects the nature of capitalism's social relations and can also be used as a means of control and hegemony. A range of interesting theoretical contributions during the late 1970s and 1980s built upon these ideas to stress the importance of analyzing how production is spatially organized. The British geographer Doreen Massey, for example, explored the spatial placement of controlling, managerial and administrative functions and how they exist in a mutually defining relationship with other controlled areas (Massey 1984, p.112). She described this mutually defining tension across a geographic space as a "spatial structure," and stressed that any regional analysis must theorize the functional division of labor at a regional level as well as its place within a wider system of relations of production (Massey 1988, p. 252).

Her empirical work attempted to examine the ways in which the British economy could be mapped through changes in production and the way that the structuring of space became an active strategy of accumulation by British capital. She argued that uneven spatial development arose as a consequence of the spatial structuring of relations of production based upon dominance and exploitation. According to Massey, "Different classes in society are defined in relation to each other and, in economic terms, to the overall division of labor. It is the overall structure of those sets of relationships which defines the structure of the economic aspect of society. One important element which any concept of uneven development must relate to, therefore, is the spatial structuring of those relationships—the relations of production—which are unequal relationships and which imply positions of dominance and subordination" (Massey 1984, p. 87).

Another geographer, David Harvey, has further explored this understanding of space and its relationship to accumulation. Harvey followed Lefebvre and Massey in arguing that the spatiality of capitalism is a reflection or product of tendencies and countertendencies within the circuit of capital. Capitalism depends upon the production of territorial complexes such as factories, transport routes, urban environments, communications networks, and regulatory institutions in order to expand and circulate capital. These socially produced spatial forms are necessary in order "to overcome space" (Harvey 1985, p. 145). A key contribution of Harvey, however, lay in his argument that capitalism could switch between different forms of these spatial structures as a means of averting, displacing, and overcoming crisis tendencies (Harvey 1999). He called this crisis-averting utilization of space a "spatial fix." The spatial structuring of capitalism acts to underpin (or "fix") accumulation for a period of time but, at a certain point, it becomes a fetter on further accumulation possibilities. Capitalism then faces a "switching crisis" as the old spatial structures collapse, and new forms of spatiality arise to underpin the flows of capital. A switching crisis can be seen, for example, in the collapse of the steel industry and other manufacturing activity in North-Eastern United States during the 1980–1990s as capital relocated to other areas in the United States and internationally (leading to the emergence of the so-called Rust Belt). Rather than conceiving space-time as a fixed constant, Harvey's approach affirms that the way human beings conceive of, utilize, and structure space is a product of struggles shaped by capitalist social relations. The production of space then acts reflexively on these social relations by placing limitations and shaping the process of capitalist accumulation itself.

This understanding of space and spatial fix is a key element of this book's analysis of GCC capitalism. Class, as a set of social relations, is located in concrete spatial configurations—it is spatialized through the relationships that are established between distinct geographical zones in the course of its formation. Subsequent chapters will discuss how the process of class formation in the Gulf has been spatially structured—institutionally reflected in the reliance on temporary migrant labor flows and an extremely restrictive notion of citizenship. This spatial configuration of accumulation has acted as an important spatial fix for Gulf capitalism, helping to maintain the enduring stability of the system as well as enabling a superexploitation of workers drawn from the peripheries surrounding the GCC. Most recently, the spatial structuring of class in the Gulf has facilitated the displacement of crisis—further strengthening the position of Khaleeji Capital and its tendency toward internationalization.

Understanding Class Formation in the Gulf—the Structure of the Book

Having outlined these initial methodological and theoretical perspectives, it is now possible to summarize the basic structure of the following chapters. This book is divided into three sections. The first section (Chapters 2 and 3) maps the initial process of class formation in the Gulf. Framed around the concepts of internationalization and financialization, Chapter 2 explores the political economy of postwar global capitalism from the end of World War Two until the early 1990s, with a view to understanding how the tendencies underlying the development of the global economy were reflected in the nature of class formation in the GCC. It concretely traces the successive deepening of capital's internationalization through this period, focusing in particular on the continuous expansion of accumulation, the intermeshing of production and consumption across the globe, and the growing significance of finance. These developments within the global economy are of pronounced significance to the nature of oil and its place in capitalist accumulation—they are the social relations in which oil is embedded as a commodity. Viewed in this manner, the story of Gulf class formation shifts from a focus on oil as such toward an understanding of how the social relations of the GCC formed as part of the deepening internationalization of the global political economy. It is this relationship between the global and the regional that must be excavated in order to fully understand the political economy of the GCC, and thereby map the process of class formation that forms the theoretical object of this book.

Utilizing this understanding of the global economy, Chapter 3 discusses the initial period of class formation in the Gulf states. It focuses on two specific characteristics of this class formation—the spatial structuring of class and the initial accumulation of capital through the state-directed use of oil revenues. The former acted as a spatial fix for Gulf capitalism, enabling the development of a privileged social layer of Gulf citizenry upon which a capitalist class developed. The actual development of this class throughout this period is examined through an analysis of the productive, commodity, and financial circuits in the Gulf. Within each of these circuits, a set of social relations formed that underpinned the rise of large, domestic capital that was closely tied to the state and earlier merchant classes. The way in which these circuits developed were, in turn, materializations of the broader tendencies of the global political economy to be described in Chapter 2.

The second section of this book (Chapters 4 and 5) turns to the formation of Khaleeji Capital in the subsequent period. Chapter 4 examines the development of the global economy in the decades following the collapse of the USSR and the integration of China into the capitalist world market. It focuses in particular on the post-2000 phase of internationalization and the critical role played by the financialization of capitalism in this process. The implications of this for the GCC region—specifically the shift in energy exports, the vital function of GCC financial surpluses, and the accelerating industrialization of the GCC—are examined from the perspective of the global economy and the rivalry between the major capitalist powers.

Paralleling the methodological approach of Chapter 3, Chapter 5 examines the evolution of the GCC circuits of capital given this development of the most recent phase of internationalization. Each of the GCC circuits of capital is explored with a view to understanding how accumulation takes place, who controls it, and where it is located. The focus is on understanding the pan-GCC nature of accumulation rather than attempting to present a comprehensive account of the political economy of each individual GCC state. Chapter 5 confirms the development of Khaleeji Capital within the GCC—an emerging capitalist class closely imbricated with the pronounced internationalization trends of each of the Gulf circuits. Of particular importance to this process is the finance circuit, which shows the most developed pan-GCC accumulation structures.

It should be noted that because this book is concerned with the development of class across each of the moments of the circuit of capital, and its process of internationalization in the pan-GCC space, the empirical analysis oscillates between two distinct levels. First, much of the data is focused on broad macro-level and sectoral trends shown through GDP, Foreign Direct Investment (FDI), import/export statistics, and the like. This data, however, only partially captures the nature of internationalization in the GCC and the development of specific sectors. In order to fully comprehend the changing social relations in the region, the other component of this book's empirical study is the micro-level analysis of firms and companies. In particular, much of the analysis focuses on the interpenetration of capitalist social relations as reflected through joint ownership structures and interlocking directorships at the company level. This micro-level analysis (involving an examination of over 500 GCC companies, financial institutions, and projects) captures the "fine" process of internationalization that is not revealed through typical macro aggregates. The book's appendices list some of the results of this study.

The final section (Chapters 6 and 7) examines the implications and future trajectories of Khaleeji Capital and Gulf capitalism. Chapter 6 develops the study of the internationalization tendencies at the core of Khaleeji Capital to examine its impact on the broader Middle East political economy. Throughout the Middle East, national economies have been strongly penetrated by both state and private capital from the GCC. This chapter looks closely at two specific examples of this penetration—the banking sectors in Jordan, Lebanon, and Egypt and the political economy of the Palestinian West Bank. In both cases, Gulf capitalism is rewriting the nature of accumulation through its ownership of key financial and industrial firms. The chapter concludes by raising some of the implications of this penetration for an understanding of the regional political economy.

Chapter 7 assesses the impact of the 2008 global financial crisis on the structures of accumulation in the Gulf. The crisis has had a sharp effect on the region, and its subsequent unfolding confirms the importance of Khaleeji Capital to a full understanding of the GCC political economy. The dominant response of the Gulf states has acted to strengthen the leading GCC conglomerates and the internationalization tendencies explored throughout this book. It has also further emphasized the significance of the spatial structuring of class to the patterns of accumulation in the Gulf. These trends portend a sharpening of the contradictions between the Gulf region and the surrounding peripheries. They will be a vital component of the future development of the world market and its attendant rivalries at the global level.

CHAPTER 2

The Political Economy of Postwar Capitalism and the Making of the Gulf

The "Golden Age"

The global economy emerged transformed in the decades following the destruction of World War Two. A key underlying cause of the war—encouraging both the rise of fascism and the clash of European powers—had been the period of stagnation and crisis that preceded the conflagration. The years before the war had been marked by low profits caused by the overaccumulation of capital—few profitable outlets for capital investment leading to intensified struggle between different world powers for control over markets and resources. War had a remarkably palliative effect. The leveling of factories, housing, and infrastructure across much of Europe and Asia served, in the words of David Harvey, as "the ultimate mechanism of capital devaluation," inaugurating one of the greatest economic upswings in the history of capitalism (Harvey 2001, p. 310). This economic boom—or "Golden Age" as many economic historians now describe it—had begun by 1950 and was to last until the late 1960s. One study of the US economy shows the profit rate rising from around 10 percent in the early 1930s to 45 percent in the postwar period, and remaining high (from 30–40 percent) until the late 1960s, from whence it began a secular decline (Duménil, Glick, and Levy 1992).[1] Growth rates in Western Europe and North America averaged 4 percent annually in the 1950s and 5 percent in the 1960s, way above the anemic 2 percent they were to fall to by the 1980s (Marglin 1991, p. 1).

The Golden Age was partly enabled by the massive destruction of capital throughout the war, which precipitated a postwar investment boom across Europe and Asia after hostilities ceased. From 1948 to 1952, the US

Marshall Plan directed US$13 billion toward reconstruction in Europe alone and industrial output expanded by 40 percent from prewar levels (US Department of State 2007). Cities, factories, transport lines, and infrastructure were rebuilt, and the production of basic consumer goods dramatically increased across all the leading capitalist markets. This stimulation of investments led to a rise in employment and production levels, buttressing the rate of profit. Although the "creative destruction" of capitalism had come at a colossal human toll, it nevertheless underpinned the transformation of the global economy.

Of course, the rising profit rates of capitalism's Golden Age were not preordained by some iron law of economics. The postwar situation may have evolved in a completely different direction—initially the mood was decidedly anticapitalist, particularly in those countries with organized antifascist resistance movements. In France, Yugoslavia, Italy, and Greece, radical ideas were in the ascendancy, trade unions were strong, and socialist and communist parties were held in high esteem due to their role in the resistance against fascism. Mass strike-waves occurred in Japan, Germany, and other European countries in the first two years after the war, with demands for the nationalization of factories and the adoption of government-led production plans in place of the anarchic decisions of privately owned companies (Armstrong, Glyn, and Harrison 1991, pp. 11–21). Widespread industrial action also occurred in the UK, United States, Canada, and Australia where governments were under enormous pressure to grant concessions to those who had fought in the war.

By the 1950s and early 1960s, however, these potential challenges had been largely neutralized through a combination of repression and incorporation into the new order. The leading role in this process was taken by the United States as the emerging dominant power. The United States had escaped any serious physical damage from the war and was thereby able to benefit from the reconstruction of Europe and Japan. Potential rivals had suffered enormous destruction and their grip on their colonial possessions was fast evaporating in a wave of anticolonial struggles across Asia, the Middle East, and Africa. By 1952, the United States held about 60 percent of industrial production of the advanced capitalist states, and over 73 percent of world equity market capitalization (Ikeda 1996, p. 45).[2] In 1960, United States trade was one-fifth of the world's overall figure and was roughly equivalent to the combined trade from UK, France, and West Germany—the three leading European economies (Winham 2008, p. 114). Furthermore, the 1944 Bretton Woods Conference had cemented the US dollar as the main currency of the international monetary system. All currencies outside the United States were assigned a value in relation to the US dollar, which,

= ascendency of dollar & Bretton Woods

in turn, was linked to gold at the rate of $35 per ounce. The dollar became the global currency of trade and commerce, with countries required to amass quantities of US dollars to cover their own international transactions. For all these reasons, the United States was able to take "undisputed leadership of the world system of institutions that was created in the 1940s and expanded in the 1950s" (Altvater 1993, p. 114).

As this postwar international system developed during the 1960s, it came to be characterized by three key aspects. First, despite the initial predominance of the United States, by the mid-1960s the global order was beginning to be marked by increasing intercapitalist competition and rivalry. As both Japan and West Germany completed their reconstruction after the war, they managed to industrialize at a level comparable to that of the United States (and, in some manufacturing industries, began to supply an increasing share of world production) (Brenner 2000, p. 16). Competition in the context of the profound postwar realignment meant that large capitalist firms in these countries struggled for ownership and control over markets and resources on the world scale. At the level of foreign policy, these economic interests compelled the leading capitalist countries to jostle for political influence across all areas of the world.

revival of competition

This rivalry unfolded, however, in the presence of the USSR, China, and other state-socialist countries—the second key feature of the postwar state system. Although these countries were noncapitalist (their economies were not driven by the pursuit of private profit) their foreign policies nevertheless sought to demarcate spheres of influence across the globe. The threat of countries pulling out of the capitalist world market meant that the extension of Soviet or Chinese influence inevitably generated rivalry with the advanced capitalist countries as a whole. The presence of this bloc, therefore, reinforced a deep unity of interest among the major capitalist powers. Indeed, the actual causes of the spectacular development of Japan and West Germany in the postwar period—much like the development of South Korea, Taiwan, and the so-called Asian Miracles in subsequent decades—had much to do with US concern to provide a counterweight to the state-socialist bloc.

cold war unity

Finally, the third key feature of the postwar international state system was the surge of anticolonial and nationalist movements in the wake of the war. These movements had a long history of struggle against colonialism, but the weakening of the major colonial powers in the war—particularly Britain and France—gave them new impetus. These nationalist struggles reflected a variety of inchoate emerging social forces in the colonized world, and unfolded within a world system defined by the previous two features—intercapitalist rivalry coupled with a simultaneous unity of interests against

Anticolonial National Lib.

the state-socialist bloc. In many cases, the anticolonial movements allied with the USSR or China as a means to maneuver against the major capitalist powers. This relationship, however, was often fraught with tension as the goals of the national liberation movements became subordinated to the foreign policy objectives of their sponsors.

These three interrelated features of the postwar state system reinforced the need for what the German economist Elmar Altvater has called the "hegemonic guarantor"—a power that could guarantee the stability and reproduction of the postwar economic order. As accumulation became increasingly global in nature, capitalism as a whole required harmonization of laws, regulations, and institutions that governed financial markets and other aspects of its reproduction. This required strong and coordinated state policies from within the capitalist orbit, able to confront the rivalry of the noncapitalist bloc as well as any potential challenges from anticolonial and left-wing movements. At the same time, the leading capitalist states remained in sharp competition over access to resources, markets, and influence. The fundamental mediating force in this duality of unity and rivalry was the United States. The United States both promoted the interests of US-based capital on the world stage while attempting to manage capitalism in its totality (Panitch and Gindin 2003; Bromley 1991, 2008; Stokes 2007). US dominance grew but at the same time played a system-supporting role, nurturing and sustaining the conditions that enabled the upturn in the rate of profit and the deepening global reach of capital. These two poles of US power were thus interrelated. The position of hegemonic guarantor depended on the consent of other rival capitalist powers, which flowed from its ability to maintain and deepen conditions of capital accumulation—and thereby its own strength—at the global scale. Rivalries certainly persisted but, as Leo Panitch and Sam Gindin point out, "only the American state bore the burden—and had the accompanying capacity and autonomy—to take on the task of managing the system as a whole" (Panitch and Gindin 2005, pp. 54–55).

Expansion and Internationalization of Production

The Golden Age was not only marked by a new international state system and a change in the structure of global political power. It was also characterized by a fundamental transformation in the nature of capitalist production. There were two key aspects to this. First, there was an unprecedented increase in both the quantity and variety of goods produced across the world market. This was largely enabled by the application of scientific and technological innovations (often based upon military research developed during the war period), which stimulated the development and generalization of new industrial sectors. Second, and very much related, was an extension in the geographical scale of production, with the rapid expansion in world trade and the international orientation of much productive activity becoming notable features of the first few decades of the postwar era.

A major example of the first trend, the transformation in the nature of production, was the petrochemical industry, which first emerged in the 1930s with the substitution of manufactured commodities such as plastics, synthetic fibers, and detergents, for naturally occurring materials such as natural rubber, cotton, and soaps.[3] A parallel and related development was the introduction and widespread use of inorganic fertilizers and pesticides in place of natural agricultural methods. These industries made possible rapid increases in productivity and output, as technology-rich manufacturing displaced human labor from the production of everyday commodities. Up until the end of World War Two the most advanced manufacturing of petrochemical products occurred in Germany, which had been forced to find alternatives to natural resources for its dye, fertilizer, and explosives industries because it lacked the extensive colonies of other capitalist rivals (Spitz 1988; Chapman 1991). Germany produced these products using chemical derivatives made from domestically sourced coal. At the end of the war, the center of gravity of the world chemical industry shifted toward the United States under the domination of large chemical companies such as Dow, Union Carbide, and Standard Oil. These companies benefited from the earlier technological advances made by the German chemical industry and, like their German counterparts, were intimately linked to the military industry (Spitz 1988, p. 33). A key feature of the postwar industry that distinguished US companies from their German competitors, however, was the use of petroleum and natural gas, rather than coal, as the feedstock used in the manufacture of synthetic commodities. This shift was made possible by technological developments in petroleum cracking that enabled the utilization of more reactive hydrocarbons and significantly cheapened the cost of production. Indeed, the nomenclature "petrochemical industry," which began to be commonly used in the late 1930s and early 1940s, signified the shift in feedstock facilitated by this new technology.

Another expanding sector of industrial production was the automobile. Although the US car industry had developed during the first two decades of the twentieth century, the period after World War Two saw a phenomenal growth in production levels. World automobile production quadrupled from 1939 to 1960 as the car became a widespread form of personal transport (Jones and Womack 1985, p. 394). The most significant feature of this expansion in automobile production was the emergence of mass markets in

Western Europe as factories were built under US-backed reconstruction plans. In Italy, the number of cars per 1,000 inhabitants increased from 9 to 32 during the 1950s (Fauri 1996, p. 181). The most important Italian automobile company, Fiat, became the "best known example" of a company that was rebuilt by Marshall Plan funds, with Fiat production during the 1950s expanding nearly seven times from that of the 1940s (Fauri 1996, p. 180).[4] Production levels in the 1960s increased by another factor of three. In Germany, the production of passenger cars by German manufacturers increased an average of 19 percent each year from 1957 to 1960. As automobile markets expanded so did the export-oriented nature of much of the world's car production—exports as proportion of global production increased from 9 percent in 1950 to 28 percent by the end of the 1960s (Jones and Womack 1985, p. 394).

As the growth in automobile exports indicates, underpinning the transformations in both the scale and scope of production was the second key trend in the global political economy—an intense deepening of the internationalization of capital (Palloix 1977). World trade grew by 6.6 percent per annum between 1948 and 1966 and a further 9.2 percent per annum between 1966 and 1973 (Waters 1995, p. 69). Exports became a vital element to the strategic orientation of the largest corporations. Partly enabling this orientation was the development of a new global institutional architecture for trade; from 1963 to 1967 the Kennedy Round of negotiations in the General Agreement on Tariffs and Trade (GATT) led to an average 35 percent tariff reduction, mostly on manufactured goods. Once again, this was a US-led process, with the political commitment toward trade liberalization indicated by a US congress authorization to President Kennedy to cut US tariffs by 50 percent if other nations reciprocated.

In addition to this growth in exports, large companies also began to internationalize production itself. Factories and other production facilities were located outside of their national markets, sourcing raw materials and labor from a variety of different geographical spaces and enabling companies to sell their goods to markets worldwide (a development reflected at the time in ubiquitous spread of the term "multinational corporation"). From 1959 to 1964, US companies set up international subsidiaries at the rate of more than 300 per annum, more than ten times the period immediately before World War Two (Grimwade 2000, p. 119). More than one-third of these subsidiaries were established in Western Europe, which emerged as the most important destination for the internationalization of US capital in the immediate postwar period (Grimwade 2000, p. 156). The beginnings of these global production chains further reinforced the development of the transport sector—commercial transcontinental flights using new jet airplane technology began in 1952 and rail networks expanded across continental Europe, the United States, and Asia. Another important factor in this growth in world trade and the international production networks was the standardization of container shipping in the late 1950s. Ports were designed to enable the rapid loading and unloading of standard aluminum and steel containers that were seamlessly connected to road and rail systems, a development that had a dramatic effect in reducing the cost of transportation at a global level (Levinson 2006). All of these changes signaled a qualitative leap in the internationalization of capital, which became a defining feature of the postwar economy through the Golden Age.

Oil and the Transition to US Power in the Middle East: 1950–1970

These postwar developments in both the economic and political spheres—the expansion in the scale of industrial production, the development of new industries and sectors, the internationalization of capital, and emerging US leadership/dominance of the capitalist world—were united by a common factor: the growing systemic centrality of energy and raw materials". And here too there was a shift. The new internationalized production regime was underpinned by a new energy regime—with oil and gas displacing the relatively energy-inefficient coal. Oil had become, in the words of Simon Bromley, a "strategic commodity" (Bromley 1991, p. 82). It had a greater energy density than any other rival energy source, and its relative ease of transport far exceeded that of coal, making it ideal for powering automobiles and airplanes. Oil was also considered "politically more reliable," as coal miners had been the backbone of powerful strike-waves through the decades before the war (Painter 1984, p. 361). Oil and gas were not just the key energy source for expanded industrial production and the new transport networks that underlay internationalization; they also formed the basic feedstock for new industries such as petrochemicals. Moreover, oil had become central to powering modern navies and armies—the US output of gasoline for military use at the end of the war was about 18 times greater than at the beginning, and that of aviation gasoline about 80 times greater (Baldwin 1959, pp. 10–11).[6] In 1949, oil and gas had accounted for 53 percent of all energy used in the United States. By 1960, this proportion had risen to 72 percent (EIA 2007). By the early 1970s, the global production of oil had increased tenfold compared to levels at the end of World War Two (BP 2007).

Some of the increased demand for oil and gas was initially supplied by ramping-up production in the United States and Europe. However, by the mid-1960s, it had become clear that the world's largest supplies of cheap and easily accessible oil and gas were to be found in the Gulf region of the Middle East—Saudi Arabia, Kuwait, Iraq, Iran, and the smaller Gulf states—where a wave of exploration and discoveries had occurred during the 1920s and 1930s. The region had always been viewed as a strategic location at the crossroads of the world (as Britain's carefully constructed system of control over the Gulf indicated) but the massive expansion of commodity production and the new technological developments that underpinned the internationalization of capital catapulted oil and gas to the center of the capitalist economy. By 1969 the Middle East had surpassed North America and Europe as the world's major oil provider. By the mid-1970s, the region's oil production would be equivalent to the combined totals of Europe and North America (BP 2007). Deepening internationalization thus depended upon the integration of the Gulf region into global capitalism and, for this reason, the underlying basis of US power increasingly came to rest upon domination of the Middle East and the incorporation of the Gulf states into a US-led global order.

Up until World War Two, control of the Gulf and broader Middle East had essentially swung between the ever-present rivalries of Britain and France and their struggle over the remnants of the Ottoman Empire. With the weakening of all these powers during the war, the United States began to emerge as the dominant player in the region—its foreign policy driven by the interventionist Truman Doctrine articulated by the then US President in a speech to Congress in 1947. Truman pledged the United States to intervene wherever necessary to shore up American interests and those of the "free world." Although his initial speech did not directly mention the Middle East, an earlier draft made reference to the region's "great natural resources of the Middle East which should not be under the exclusive control of any single nation," and the need to ensure the perpetuation of "free enterprise . . . in the other nations of the world," without which "the very existence of our own economy and our own democracy will be gravely threatened" (Jones J. 1955, p. 156; McCormick 1987, p. 77). The reality of these interests had been outlined earlier in a 1945 State Department memo, which called Saudi Arabia's oil supplies "a stupendous source of strategic power, and one of the greatest material prizes in world history" (US Department of State 1945). The shift away from British toward US power was reflected in the breakdown of ownership of these "stupendous" supplies—between 1940 and 1967, British ownership of Middle Eastern oil reserves dropped from 72 percent to 30 percent while American control grew from 10 percent to 60 percent (Harvey 1999, p. 20).

The emerging threat to these interests, however, became clear during the 1950s with the development of powerful anticolonial struggles in Iran,

Egypt, Iraq, and elsewhere. These movements were closely tied to mass communist parties, operating in an uneasy relationship with military officers and more conservative nationalist forces. In 1951, a significant blow to colonial interests occurred with the nationalization of the British-owned and operated Anglo-Iranian Oil Company (AIOC) in Iran by the newly appointed Prime Minister, Mohammed Mossadegh. Mossadegh, pushed by mass mobilizations across the country, expelled AIOC and took Iranian oil into state hands. Another major turning point on the other side of the Middle East was the overthrow of Egypt's King Farouk in 1952, led by the popular military officer Gamal Abdel Nasser. In July 1956, Nasser's government nationalized the British/French-controlled Suez Canal, a move that was met with wide popular acclaim across the region.

In the Gulf, one of the critical reflections of this growing assertion of national sovereignty was the attempt to exert control over oil resources.[7] Since the initial discovery of oil in the Gulf at the beginning of the twentieth century, the region's oil supplies had been controlled by eight international oil companies (IOCs). These were the so-called Seven Sisters cartel—made up of five US companies (Esso, Mobil, Standard of California, Gulf Oil, and Texaco), one British company (BP), and one Anglo-Dutch company (Shell)—and the French "independent" CFP (renamed Total in 1985). These eight IOCs were the outright owners of oil concessions in the region, from which they paid the ruler a royalty or tax from their production. The refining of crude oil—the critical step in turning it into a useable commodity—took place in North America or Western Europe, and was also controlled by these companies. Beginning in the late 1950s, however, political agitation grew across the Middle East aimed at taking control of the Gulf's oil reserves away from the IOCs.

The first steps in this process occurred with a series of unofficial meetings held between the leading Gulf oil producers and Venezuela (the dominant producer in Latin America). In April 1959, these meetings produced a secret agreement known as the Maadi Pact, signed between Venezuela, Iran, Iraq, Saudi Arabia, Kuwait, Egypt, and Syria—the latter countries not significant oil exporters but important transit points for oil and the centers of Arab nationalism at the time (Bromley 1991, p. 152). The Maadi Pact proposed the establishment of a Petroleum Consultation Commission, which would monitor and attempt to stabilize oil prices, establish national oil companies that would work alongside the IOCs, and attempt to locate refinery operations in the oil producing countries rather than in North America or Europe (Terzian 1985, pp. 27–28). The impetus for the agreement came from two individuals strongly affected by the rising tide of nationalist sentiment across the South—Perez Alfonso of Venezuela and

Abdullah Tariki of Saudi Arabia (dubbed the "red sheikh" by the IOCs due to his ideological leanings).

Although the Maadi Pact was not immediately implemented, it revealed the tensions building between oil producing states and the IOCs. Most oil producers in the Middle East received payments from the IOCs dependent on the "posted price"—the price at which oil was publically offered for sale. In times of excess supply (such as during the late 1950s and 1960s) the actual delivery price was less than the posted price. The discount came out of the IOC profit margin and thus led them to push toward a reduction in the posted price as a means of lowering their tax payments to oil states (Skeet 1988, pp. 4–6). IOC control over the posted price (due to their monopoly power) gave them the ability to squeeze producer states in this manner—in August 1960, for example, Esso unilaterally reduced the posted price by just over 7 percent causing consternation among the oil producing states in the Middle East as their tax receipts dropped (Skeet 1988, p. 17).

In an attempt to gain control over posted prices, Alfonso and Tariki built upon the initial relationship established through the Maadi Pact to convene a series of meetings of oil producing countries in Baghdad in 1960. The meetings resulted in the creation of the Organization of Petroleum Exporting Countries (OPEC), a grouping consisting of Iran, Iraq, Kuwait, Saudi Arabia, and Venezuela. Initially, the establishment of OPEC did little to affect the structure of oil ownership or the posted price system and, throughout the 1960s, IOCs maintained their dominance in the upstream and downstream parts of the industry (Fattouh 2007). OPEC expanded, however, during the subsequent decade to include Qatar (1961), Indonesia (1962), Libya (1962), Abu Dhabi (1967, replaced by the UAE in 1974), Algeria (1969), and Nigeria (1971). It was later to lead the creation of state-owned oil companies that replaced IOC ownership of upstream activities.

As the United States displaced Britain and France as the regional hegemon, it was forced to shoulder increasing responsibility for defending general Western interests against both Arab nationalism and any threats to the supply of oil from the Gulf. Despite the Truman Doctrine's commitment to military intervention and "active containment," US foreign policy initially rested heavily upon a continued British presence in the region. Albeit considerably weakened as a result of the war, Britain remained the dominant power along the Trucial Coast—a network of small Sheikhdoms in the Gulf that had been under British control since the early 1800s and eventually became the United Arab Emirates, Bahrain, and Qatar in 1971. British bases were located in two of these sheikhdoms, Bahrain and Sharjah, and much of the region's military forces, including those of Abu Dhabi, Kuwait, and Oman, were commanded and staffed by British officers.

By the late 1960s, however, a sustained British presence in the Middle East had become increasingly untenable as a result of the spiraling cost of maintaining overseas bases and troop levels in the context of a weakening British currency. In 1968, British Prime Minister Harold Wilson announced that the country would withdraw troops from Malaysia, Singapore, and the Gulf by 1971. Although the United States attempted to convince the British to maintain a strong presence in the area, the weakened Sterling made this an impossible fiscal burden. Partially in response to impending British withdrawal, the US government announced the "Nixon Doctrine" in July 1969 as a new strategic framework aimed at managing its interests globally. Nixon's strategy called for increasing reliance on local allies to support US interests both militarily and politically (reaching its apogee in the so-called Vietnamization of the Vietnam War). This was to have important implications in the Gulf.

The End of the Golden Age

Just as the United States was displacing Britain and France as the dominant power in the Middle East, the postwar economic boom was beginning to draw to an end. By the end of the 1960s, many of the factors that had enabled this boom to occur had begun to be undermined. First, two decades of expanding production had led to overaccumulation at the global scale—particularly following the entry of European and Japanese competitors into major manufacturing sectors who were able to benefit from low wages, long working hours, and the introduction of modern technological techniques (Armstrong, Glyn, and Harrison 1991; Altvater 1993; Brenner 2000).[8] The high profit rates that had been made possible by productivity rising faster than wages could not be sustained as better living standards during the boom stimulated expectations of further gains and the confidence to struggle for future improvements. The growing size and industrial concentration of the working class, and the expectations of continually rising living conditions engendered by the boom period, strengthened trade unions and worker organizations. Furthermore, the presence of the Soviet Union meant that an all-out assault on domestic living conditions in the advanced capitalist countries was not completely possible and some benefits needed to be granted in order to guarantee social stability. At a global level, the anticolonial and national liberation struggles of the postwar period (India 1947, China 1949, Egypt 1952, Iran 1953, Iraq 1958, Cuba 1959, Algeria 1962, Libya 1969, Vietnam 1975, and many others) challenged the dominance of the leading capitalist countries. Those countries that achieved some measure of independence from their colonial past (e.g., India, Egypt, and Algeria) appropriated some of the wealth that had previously flown to the core and redirected it into nationally focused development plans. In other cases, countries actually withdrew from the world capitalist market (e.g., China, Cuba, and Vietnam), shrinking the area directly circumscribed by capitalist social relations.

By the early 1970s, accumulation problems had begun to reemerge in the form of rising inflation and falling profit rates. The end of the Golden Age, however, did not signal a reversal of the deep internationalization tendencies that had marked the immediate postwar period. Indeed, from the 1970s onwards, the internationalization of capital became a profoundly significant feature of the world capitalist economy, with economic power clustered in three major blocs—North America, Europe, and East Asia. Each of these blocs embraced internationalization, with large conglomerates expanding production overseas, establishing regionally integrated production networks, and focusing on exports to overseas markets. By 1977 it would be estimated by the US Department of Commerce that more than one-third of all US exports consisted of intrafirm trade—a striking confirmation of the development of international production chains and the dominance of the global economy by multinational corporations (Grimwade 2000, p. 180).

This next phase in the internationalization of capital was facilitated by a further transformation in the nature of the world market—the rise of financial processes as a vital feature of the reproduction of the circuit of capital. Internationalization meant that companies were faced with the growing cost of doing business at a global level. Companies needed to raise debt in order to fund these activities, and they were required to do so across a variety of new markets with differing currencies, interest rates, and financial systems. The growth of credit instruments and globally integrated financial markets helped to reduce transaction costs, fund the necessary expenses that accompanied internationalization, and ameliorate the risk of doing business in a highly interconnected world (and later spawned derivatives, swaps, and other complex financial tools). Capitalism's financialization was, in this way, the backbone to its internationalization.

Two major shifts in the structure of the global monetary system linked this financialization with the internationalization of capital. The first of these shifts can be traced back to the 1960s, when a new set of financial markets had begun to emerge in Europe, known as Euromarkets. Euromarkets consisted of deposits in banks that were denominated in dollars rather than in the currency of the European country of deposit. These markets arose as a direct consequence of the internationalization of capital—US companies wishing to finance foreign investments were restricted by US government policies from exporting capital from the United States, so these new "offshore" markets allowed them to evade capital controls. Likewise, UK banks sought to move into the Euromarket to circumvent reserve requirements and thereby narrow the differential between lending and borrowing rates. From 1964 to 1982, the size of foreign assets held in the Euromarket increased at a remarkable 28.7 percent annually, a rate much faster than the growth of national banking markets in Europe or the United States (Gibson 1989, p. 5).

Uncoupled from government restrictions on lending and reserve requirements, Euromarkets permitted a dramatic expansion in global credit levels and also enabled multinational companies to interlock their activities across several markets and eliminate exchange and transaction costs. The extent to which the growth of these financial markets was connected to internationalization is shown by the role played by multinational corporations in Eurodollar borrowing—responsible for 50 percent of all Eurodollar movements in 1972 alone and increasing over the subsequent decade (Mandel 1975, p. 23). At the same time, the development of the Euromarkets spurred other "offshore" zones in the world market such as the Cayman Islands, where internationalizing banks set up in low-regulation environments in which they could conduct their dealings in the Euromarkets.

The second major shift that linked internationalization with financialization was the demise of the Bretton Woods system. This system had underpinned the international monetary order since its signing in 1944, and was structured around the pegging of international currencies to the US$, which was then convertible to gold at a price of $US35/ounce (hence its description as the gold-dollar standard). With the dollar established as the central currency for world transactions, the United States supplied dollars to the world system and other currencies were adjusted in value through an adjustable-peg exchange-rate regime overseen by the International Monetary Fund (IMF) (an institution created at Bretton Woods). By the early 1970s, however, the growth of financial flows in the world economy had made it increasingly difficult for the United States to maintain a fixed value of its currency in terms of gold. In 1971, US President Richard Nixon announced a decision to sever direct US$ convertibility with gold. By 1973, the leading economies had decided to end the adjustable-peg exchange-rate system and replace it by a system of floating exchange rates (formalized in 1976 when the IMF's Articles of Agreements were amended to legalize the new system). Under the new system, government restrictions on capital mobility were lifted and the size of cross-border capital flows were able to increase dramatically. Moreover, the removal of the convertibility constraint increased the capacities of central banks to fuel growth in liquidity, thus further stimulating financialization.

The Gulf, Financialization, and US Power

To a large extent, these overall trends in the financialization of capitalism were structured through—and enabled by—the integration of the Gulf region into the broader reproduction of the global economy. The reasons for this relate to changes in the structure of the international oil industry that had begun with the formation of OPEC in the early 1960s and continued through to the 1970s. The "red sheikh," Abdallah Tariki, had been exiled from Saudi Arabia in 1961 due to his increasingly radical calls to transform the Saudi monarchy and nationalize the country's oil resources (Vitalis 2007). Tariki had spent much of the 1960s traveling the Middle East advocating his position, which resonated strongly with the nationalist sentiments across the region. With the exile of Tariki, however, Saudi Arabia became the leading voice in OPEC advocating for a compromise with the IOCs. Backed by US oil companies, the Saudi monarchy had replaced Tariki with the lawyer Ahmad Zaki Yamani, who took a much more pragmatic position in favor of a phased transition away from foreign control—arguing for participation agreements between the IOCs and producing countries that "would be indissoluble, like a Catholic marriage" and would "save [the IOCs] from nationalization" (cited in Sampson 1976, p. 278). Yamani—in his position as oil minister in the world's most important producer—emerged as the primary interlocutor between the IOCs and the Gulf countries. His delicate negotiations between the IOCs and the more radical forces in the Middle East calling for nationalization coincided with growing worldwide demand for oil and sagging production capabilities in the aging oil fields of the United States and Europe—trends that further strengthened the Middle East's pivotal position as the world's primary source of energy. From 1970 to 1973, Yamani attempted to convince the American company that controlled Saudi oil concessions, Aramco, to give a share of the company over to Saudi Arabia. Instead of royalty and tax payments, the US oil majors that owned Aramco—Exxon, Texaco, Socal, and Mobil—would pay Saudi Arabia for the latter's share of the produced oil (the so-called buyback price). In the words of one historian of these negotiations, Anthony Sampson, Yamani's aim was to convince the Aramco owners that "what mattered in a growing shortage was not so much who owned the oil, as who was able to buy it" (Sampson 1976, p. 279).

Yamani's efforts were eventually successful. In early 1973, the IOCs agreed to give up 25 percent control of the established concessions in the six Gulf states (with an agreement to increase this to 51 percent by 1983) in return for a guaranteed buyback of the oil at 93 percent of the posted price. These shifts in the structure of the oil industry had a profound consequence on the price of oil. With the peaking of oil production in the United States in 1970, "spare capacity"—the ability to increase supply in order to meet demand—was no longer provided by Texan oil reserves but was instead located in the Gulf countries (principally Saudi Arabia and, to a lesser extent, Kuwait and the UAE). In 1972, the eight IOCs noted above—the Seven Sisters and the French company Total—had owned 91 percent of all crude supplies through concession agreements arranged with Gulf monarchies (Bromley 2005, p. 230).[9] By 1980, this control would be completely reversed, with IOCs owning less than a third of the crude oil located outside of the United States (Kobrin 1985, p. 5). OPEC's ascendancy thus meant that the Gulf states gained a much greater influence over the price of oil through their actual or potential ability to restrict supplies to the world market.[10]

With this newfound power, Middle East oil producers unilaterally increased the posted price of oil in 1973/1974 while also temporarily cutting supplies to the world market in the wake of Israel's October 1973 war with Egypt and Syria. The price of a barrel of standard Saudi Arabian crude oil rose from $2.59 on January 1, 1973, to $5.12 on October 16, 1973, to $11.65 on January 1, 1974.[11] The increase in the oil price, coupled with the changes in the structure of ownership in the oil industry, meant that Gulf states were suddenly recipients of huge amounts of oil revenues, which became known by the term "petrodollars." From this moment on, the Gulf's role in the global economy was not just tied to its hydrocarbon exports, but also linked to the ways in which its petrodollars were utilized in global financial circuits.

Petrodollar flows from the Gulf, particularly from Saudi Arabia, played a critical role in strengthening both the financialization of the system as a whole and the specific role of the United States as the dominant power. There were two particular components to this role, reflected in the different ways that the Gulf was integrated into the financial structures of the world market. First, much of the Gulf petrodollars flowed into North American and European banks (often operating in Euromarkets) where they were recycled as loans to multinational companies, governments, and other borrowers. Kuwait provides an excellent example of how these petrodollar flows helped to consolidate the trends of financialization. As oil prices increased, assets of Kuwaiti commercial banks tripled from 1971 to 1977 (Khouja and

Sadler 1979, p. 165). The massive amounts of funds accumulated by Kuwaiti banks were redirected into international capital markets through "consortium banks": joint partnerships between Kuwaiti banks and large foreign banks. The first of these was the FRAB Bank, established in 1969 between a group of Arab banks (mostly Kuwaiti) and the French banking giant Société Générale (Sherbiny 1985, p. 20). This was followed by Union des Banques Arabes et Françaises (UBAF) in 1970, the European Arab Bank (EAE) in 1972, and Banque Arabe et Internationale d'Investissements (BAII) in 1973. These consortium banks allowed foreign institutions access to the considerable levels of petro-capital amassing in the Gulf region, which was then recycled to borrowers around the world. Indeed, by 1978 the Kuwaiti Dinar Eurobond market was the third-largest sector in the Euromarkets, after the US dollar and Deutschemark sectors (Nashashibi 1984, p. 77).[12]

From 1973 to 1977, US$107 billion of OPEC reserves flowed into Euromarkets, constituting over 10 percent of the market's total dollar-denominated assets.[13] Over 40 percent of total OPEC reserve assets were held as Eurodollars from 1976 to 1984, a striking indication of the importance of the market for the oil exporting countries (CBO 1981, p. 35). Much of these petrodollars were to enter the Euromarkets from banks headquartered in Bahrain, which, in 1975, introduced regulations similar to those existing in the Cayman Islands and Singapore that allowed "offshore banking units" (OBUs). Offshore banks were exempt from all corporate taxes and were only required to pay a small fee to establish a branch on the island. This process coincided with restrictions that were placed on foreign banks in Saudi Arabia and the deepening of civil war in Lebanon, which had been the traditional financial center of the Middle East. By 1978, there were 48 OBUs operating in Bahrain reaching a peak of 76 in 1984 (Tschoegl 2002, p. 131). Citibank ran much of its Middle East operations from Bahrain and Chase Manhattan established its regional offices in Bahrain. Other major banks that followed suit included the Bank of Tokyo, the Canadian Imperial Bank of Commerce, Credit Suisse, Dresdner Bank, Societe Generale, and the Swiss Bank Corporation (Wilson 1983, p. 112). While many of these banks conducted business in neighboring countries like Saudi Arabia, a significant proportion of their holdings ended up flowing back into the international financial markets.

The second way that the Gulf was integrated into the global financial markets was more directly linked to the strengthening of US power. The US government made a special effort to ensure that Saudi petrodollars, in particular, were invested in US dollar-denominated bank accounts, equities, and treasury bonds. As the detailed research of David Spiro has shown, in

1974 an agreement was reached between the Saudi government and the US Treasury that saw Saudi Arabia deposit billions of dollars in the US Federal Reserve through a secret arrangement to buy US treasuries outside the normal auction for such securities. Spiro points out that "[h]aving agreed to invest so much in dollars, the Saudis now shared a stake in maintaining the dollar as an international reserve currency . . . dollars constituted 90 percent of Saudi government revenues in 1979, and . . . Saudi investments were, roughly at the same time, 83 percent dollar denominated" (Spiro 1999, pp. 122–23). At the level of OPEC as a whole, reserves held in US dollars increased from 57 percent of total reserves to 93 percent from 1973 to 1978 (CBO 1981, p. 35). The linkage between OPEC reserves and the US dollar was further reinforced by a guarantee from the Saudis that the world oil trade would be denominated in US dollars, thus ensuring that the American currency underlay trade in the world's most important commodity.[14] In return, the United States offered Saudi Arabia extensive military, and political support—with the Saudis using their influence as the world's largest producer to prevent OPEC from pricing oil in a diversified basket of currencies (Spiro 1999, pp. 105–26).

This tight linkage between US financial dominance and the US relationship with the Gulf states was mutually reinforcing. The huge influx of US dollar-denominated funds from the Gulf strengthened US political power through the numerous advantages that accrued to it under dollar hegemony. With the demand for dollars way in excess of any domestic needs, the United States could print dollars with the confidence that demand for the currency would be found at a global level. This meant that the United States was able to spend more abroad than it earned (on construction of military bases, for example) and avoid the balance of payments problems that constrained the spending policies of other countries. As financialization deepened and the rising tide of credit was provided in dollars, US banks and financial institutions became the main source for companies and governments seeking funds. In this manner, the centrality of the dollar also strengthened the size and weight of Anglo-American financial markets (Gowan 1999).[15] At the same time, the Gulf states came to share an interest in the growing strength of the US dollar and US financial power. With most of their reserves invested in US dollar-linked markets (whether the Euromarkets or directly in US securities)—and reinforced by the deep dependence of the Gulf's autocratic and unpopular monarchies on US military protection—the Gulf states were integrated as junior partners into the reproduction of the system itself. By the late 1980s, for example, Kuwait was receiving more income from its financial investments abroad than from its oil exports (Ayubi 1995, p. 226). Tied to an emerging global financial system, Gulf states were thus deeply implicated in—and acted to support—the specific role of the United States as the dominant power in this system.

Neoliberalism and the South

The changes in the structure of the world market through the 1970s and 1980s were reinforced through a common set of economic policies adopted by governments of all leading capitalist states at the time. These policies, which came to be known as neoliberalism, drew their intellectual roots from a range of sources including classical liberal philosophy and the Austrian school of economics. Everywhere it was introduced, neoliberalism meant an assault on working conditions and wage levels through privatization, cutbacks to social spending, the reduction of tariffs, and deregulated markets.[16] Capitalist governments attacked unions and other defensive organizations of the working class. Unemployment levels increased, work became casualized and part-time workers replaced full-time. Health and safety conditions, environmental protections, and the basic elements of the postwar welfare state were eroded. The main thrust of these measures was an attempt to reverse the economic gains won by workers during the latter years of the boom period, thereby enabling an increase in the rate of exploitation.

The turn to neoliberalism reflected not only a focus on domestic economic policies but also greatly facilitated the new wave of internationalization and financialization. By removing barriers to the movement capital across and through national spaces, and widening the spheres of human activities subject to the imperative of profit, neoliberalism aimed to ensure the conditions for capitalist reproduction at a global scale. Internationalized capital needed borders that were open to capital flows, the protection of private property rights, disciplining of labor, and consistency in financial conditions and regulations. In this way, investors could seek to exploit sources of cheap labor and other resources across the globe; gain ownership of businesses, factories, and land; and sell their products to a global market place. This trend could be seen, for example, in the proliferation of export-processing zones (EPZs) that enabled large corporations to parcellize their production and locate different activities internationally depending upon competitive advantages. Taiwan, South Korea, and Malaysia led the way in this respect—as US and Japanese firms sought out cheap labor and assembly platforms in EPZs across Asia. This internationalization was further reinforced by US policies that opened US markets to allies in East Asia and provided tariff-free exports for intrafirm trade between US multinational corporations and their subsidiaries.

The deepening of these internationalized production chains was predicated on the penetration of most states by neoliberal policies that lowered tariff barriers, lifted restriction on foreign investments, and ended subsidies of domestic industry. One of the fundamental mechanisms enabling this generalization of neoliberal policy was the weapon of debt—which was once again intimately related to the Gulf's particular role in the world market. Following the oil price rises of the 1970s (first from 1973 to 1974 and again from 1979 to 1982), much of the former colonized world was forced to seek loans from US and European banks in order to finance industrialization and meet the rising cost of oil imports. These loans were deeply connected to the petrodollars originating in the Gulf states, which were recycled to borrowers in the South through Anglo-American banks and the Euromarkets. In 1974, the Euromarket accounted for about 25 percent of total financing requirement of deficit countries in the South reeling under high oil prices. By 1979, this figure had risen to 50 percent of financing (Gibson 1989, p. 242). Other components of the global financial architecture also developed during the 1970s to complement the role of Euromarkets as an institutional mechanism for recycling petrodollars. In June 1974, the IMF established the Oil Facility, which channeled surplus oil revenues to countries facing pressure because of the increase in oil prices. Saudi Arabia was the major source of funds for the Oil Facility, consequently becoming the largest lender to the IMF and permitted to appoint its own Executive Director to the Fund.

With these debt levels growing during the 1970s, the US government suddenly raised interest rates in a move named the 1979 Volcker Shock, after Paul Volcker, then Chairman of the Board of Governors of the US Federal Reserve. Volcker's decision to raise interest rates to double-digit figures was a moment of consolidation of the neoliberal program—aimed at halting US inflation through precipitating a recession, thereby increasing unemployment and lowering wage levels. Volcker stated this goal bluntly, noting "the standard of living of the average American has to decline" (Rattner 1979, p. A1). Concurrently, the Volcker Shock helped to strengthen the position of the US dollar vis-à-vis other currencies as capital was attracted to the United States in search of high returns.[17] For countries in the South, the result was devastating. Because most debt was held in US dollars, the rise in interest rates meant a sudden increase in overall debt levels. Debt repayments sucked up wealth from the South and deposited it in banks and financial institutions in the leading capitalist economies. The fiscal demands on the South were extremely severe—the 15 most heavily indebted nations saw their debt levels increase from just under 10 percent of their Gross National Product (GNP) in 1970 to around 48 percent by 1987 (Ferraro and Roser 1994, p. 17).

Pushed to the brink of insolvency, heavily indebted countries in the South tried to renegotiate their debt schedules with US and European banks—and were surprised to find themselves faced with a requirement to gain consent from the World Bank (another institution set up at Bretton Woods in 1944) in order to alter the loan agreement. The World Bank insisted that countries embrace privatization, open themselves to foreign capital flows, and cut back on social spending in order to receive assistance to cover budgetary shortfalls. Likewise, in the case of the IMF Oil Facility, countries had to agree to avoid the use of restrictions on trade and payments and to demonstrate that they would develop medium-term policy to drop barriers to capital flows in order to receive support (Woods 2006, p. 32). In October 1985 at the annual meeting of the World Bank and IMF in South Korea, these ad hoc "conditionality" agreements were consecrated as the guiding feature of lending policy after the US government presented the "Program for Sustainable Growth" (dubbed the Baker Plan after the then US Treasury Secretary James Baker). These measures became the staple requirements of the so-called Structural Adjustment Programs—neoliberal economic plans imposed by the World Bank and IMF on debtor countries. Debt was thus the weapon used by international financial institutions such as the World Bank and IMF to compel indebted countries to open their productive, financial, and commercial sectors to foreign ownership and thereby accelerate the internationalization of capital.

Writing in 1989, the World Bank admitted that the debt crisis had massively facilitated the transfer of wealth from the South to the North, noting that "Before 1982 the highly indebted countries received about 2 percent of GNP a year in resources from abroad; since then they have transferred roughly 3 percent of GNP a year in the opposite direction" (World Bank 1989, p. 17). From 1979 to 1989, UNICEF estimated that per capita spending on education fell by 50 percent and on health by 25 percent in the 37 poorest countries in the world. The result was social devastation, with over half a million children dying because of poverty in 1988 and a massive plunge in income levels—by the end of the decade, Latin America alone had per capita incomes 9 percent lower than ten years earlier (UNICEF 1989, p. 16). *"lost decade"*

US Power in the Middle East

As the Gulf's pivotal role in both commodity and financial flows developed from the 1970s onwards, the United States placed a prime strategic emphasis on strengthening its relationship with its two key allies in the region—Saudi Arabia and Iran.[18] The Saudi monarch, King Saud, had long been reliant on US aid and military support following the arrival of US oil companies to the country in the 1920s (see next chapter). Through the 1950s and 1960s, this relationship grew even closer, as the Saudi regime came under pressure from more radical states in the region, particularly Egypt, as well as internal movements calling for reform of monarchical rule and a distancing from the United States. The close relationship was confirmed through the financial agreements described above, through which the Saudi regime pledged itself to support US global financial dominance and its regional hegemony, in return for military and political aid from the most powerful country in the world.

Particularly important, however, to US strategy in the Gulf, was the relationship with Iran. The United States had backed a coup against Mohammed Mossadegh in 1953, restoring full power to the Pahlavi monarchy over the nationalist and communist movements in the country (Abrahamian 2001).[19] Following the 1969 Nixon Doctrine's pledge to strengthen regional allies around the globe, the United States massively increased its military funding to Mohammad Reza Pahlavi, reaching US$1.7 billion under the first Nixon administration (1968–72), nearly three times the limit set by Nixon's predecessor Lyndon Johnson. A 1969 report by the Rand Corporation noted that Iran was a critical feature of US power in the Gulf because it could "help achieve many of the goals we find desirable without the need to intervene in the region" (cited in Stork 1975, p. 19). US military support to Iran skyrocketed from 1973 onwards, amounting to more than US$6 billion annually from 1973 to 1975. In addition, Iran received the most sophisticated weaponry available from the US military arsenal. Internally, the Iranian secret service, the SAVAK, built a vicious repressive apparatus with the close support of US government agencies such as the CIA.

However, just as the Gulf's position as a critical element to the overall development of the world market was being consolidated, US interests in the region received a severe blow. In 1979, a popular movement in Iran overthrew the US-backed Shah and effectively removed the country from the sphere of US influence. The new Islamist government would no longer act as the US' chief ally in the Gulf region, and US businesses were denied any involvement in the country. Not only did the United States and Britain lose direct influence over the large Iranian oil fields, the revolution presented a direct threat to the other Gulf states, particularly due to the large Shia minorities present in Iraq, Bahrain, Kuwait, Saudi Arabia, and the UAE. Uprisings inspired by the Iranian revolution occurred across the Gulf and explicitly targeted the role of the United States in the region.

Alongside the epochal shift in Iran's political allegiance, events in neighboring Central Asia had also begun to reinforce a potential challenge to US dominance in the Gulf. The coming to power of the Afghan communist party, the People's Democratic Party of Afghanistan (PDPA), in the 1978 Saur Revolution occurred a few short months prior to the Iranian revolution. Afghanistan bordered Iran, and thus formed part of the critical hinterland of the Gulf, and in late 1979 the Soviet Union entered Afghanistan in support of the new government. Both the Soviet intervention in Afghanistan and the Iranian revolution fuelled concerns of the United States over the future stability of the Gulf monarchies upon which their influence in the region largely depended. With these emerging threats, it became vital for the United States to ensure that the Gulf states remained within the orbit of US power.

In this context, US foreign policy shifted once again in 1980 under the then US President Carter. The "Carter Doctrine," as it became known, returned to the themes of the Truman era by stating that "any attempt by an outside force to gain control of the Persian Gulf region will be regarded as an assault on the vital interests of the United States" and "will be repelled by the use of any means necessary including military force" (Carter 1980). There were six main elements to the Carter security framework: increased naval forces and carriers in the Indian Ocean; access to military facilities and bases from friendly Gulf countries; use of bases further afield, primarily in Egypt; expansion of the existing US base on the island of Diego Garcia; creation of a rapid deployment force; and increased military exercises in the area.

The onset of a war between Iraq and Iran in 1980 provided an excellent pretence to test this framework and work toward an increased US presence in the Gulf. Both Iran and Iraq had large, well-equipped militaries and the ability to assert themselves as a regional hegemon in the Gulf. The United States seized the opportunity of the war to prevent this possibility, tilting overall toward Iraq as a means of weakening a sovereign Iran. Howard Teicher, who was responsible for the Middle East and for Political-Military Affairs at the National Security Council during the war, confirmed this support and noted that the United States "actively supported the Iraqi war effort by supplying the Iraqis with billions of dollars of credits, by providing U.S. military intelligence and advice to the Iraqis, and by closely monitoring third country arms sales to Iraq to make sure that Iraq had the military weaponry required. The United States also provided strategic operational advice to the Iraqis to better use their assets in combat" (Teicher 1995).[20]

At the same time, the United States capitalized on the conflict to strengthen military alliances with the Gulf states. Shortly after the war began, the United States encouraged Bahrain, Saudi Arabia, Kuwait, Oman, Qatar, and the UAE to establish the Gulf Cooperation Council (GCC), a regional integration project that had both economic and security implications. The GCC was formed on February 4, 1981, and quickly became a major ally of US power in the Gulf region. US strategy towards the new regional bloc was aimed—as Joe Stork remarked a few years after the GCC's formation—at "minimiz[ing] the need for direct US military intervention in the event of a coup or insurgency while at the same time maximizing the facilities and weapons inventories available for such intervention should it be required" (Stork 1985, p. 5).

The reality of "maximizing the facilities" became clear during the first few years of the GCC's establishment. In Saudi Arabia, despite the lack of formal basing rights, the United States convinced Saudi Arabia to host four US Air Force Airborne Warning and Control Aircraft (AWAC). The AWAC system provided refueling and servicing capacities for up to 70 US F-15 fighters (Stork and Wenger 1984, p. 45). At the same time, the Saudi government pushed other Gulf states to purchase air systems that could be connected with the AWAC network, thereby developing an air-based cross-Gulf network under US control. The United States also developed military bases in several locations throughout Oman with much military decision-making in the country delegated to US and British advisors. Indeed, until 1989 the Omani Chief of Staff for Defence was a British army commander. *Oman as UK proxy*

In addition to the stationing of military equipment in Saudi Arabia and Oman, the United States stepped up its naval presence in the Gulf. One way it did this was through "reflagging" operations, in which Kuwaiti ships were registered under US flags, and escorted through the Gulf under the protection of US naval forces. Also in 1983, two years after the formation of the GCC, the United States restructured the initial Carter-era Rapid Deployment Joint Task Force into a regional unified command known as US Central Command (CENTCOM). The command headquarters of CENTCOM was based on US navy ships permanently stationed at Bahraini ports that liaised with US embassies and nations across the Middle East (it later moved to Qatar). In the UAE, the largest man-made port in the world, Jebel Ali, was to become the US navy's number one overseas port.

The US alliance with the GCC states was based in particular on the continuing close relationship with Saudi Arabia, to whom the United States moved even closer in the post-1979 period. In addition to the hosting of AWACS and other military equipment, the United States relied upon Saudi Arabia to provide a supportive political pole in the Gulf and broader region.

One example of this was the encouragement of Islamist movements as a means of undercutting the Soviet presence in Afghanistan as well as other left and nationalist forces in the region. Invoking the notion of "leadership of the Islamic world" that had been cultivated in the 1960s, the United States encouraged Saudi Arabia to develop this ideological pole that was solidly anticommunist and thereby acted in conjunction with US policy objectives (Achcar 2002).

[handwritten: fomenting Islamist nutts via Riyadh]

The First Gulf War

The US strategy during the 1980s was largely successful. Bled by internal domestic pressures, the prolonged conflict in Afghanistan, and the spiraling cost of military competition with the West, the USSR and its satellite states underwent a dramatic collapse from 1989–1992. This placed severe pressures on those states and political movements that had used Soviet support to carve out some independence from the United States. In the Middle East, the United States seized the opportunity of its "unipolar" moment to further deepen its control over the Gulf region. Of particular importance to the United States was reassertion of its control over Iraq. Although Iraqi leader Saddam Hussein had long worked closely with the United States and had been a major recipient of weapons and funding during the war with Iran in the 1980s, he was considered an unreliable ally. Iraq's regime rested partly on a claim to Arab nationalism and, in 1972, the government had nationalized Iraqi oil resources, evicting United States and British oil companies from the country. The country was widely believed to hold the second-largest proven reserves of oil after Saudi Arabia and the largest unexplored reserves of any country. Not only did Iraqi oil present a major inducement to US oil companies that had been shut out since nationalization, bringing the country under US influence would provide a major lever over any potential rivals.

The first stage in what was to become a two-decades long attempt by the United States to dominate Iraq began in 1990. Since the conclusion of the war with Iran, Iraq had accused the GCC countries, in particular Kuwait and Saudi Arabia, of unfairly claiming Iraqi debts accrued during the war. At the same time, the Iraqi government stated that Kuwait was engaged in "slant drilling"—drilling for oil across its border—and deliberately colluding with Saudi Arabia to keep the world oil price low in order to further weaken Iraq's precarious postwar finances (Gause 2005). With these arguments offered as justification, Iraq launched an invasion of Kuwait on 2 August 1990—annexing the country for a total of seven months. In response, a US-led coalition began an aerial bombardment of

Iraq on 17 January 1991, followed a month later by a ground invasion. Around half of the entire US army was located in the Gulf during the war. Of the total $61 billion that it cost in military spending to remove Iraq from Kuwait, $36 billion was paid for by GCC states (Freedman and Karsh 1993, p. 361). Although the Iraqi government was not ousted by the US-led attack, the country was cut in three by "no-fly zones" imposed by the United States and UK. Over the next decade, its industrial and social infrastructure was devastated by a wide-ranging sanctions regime, with UNICEF noting that "if the substantial reduction in child mortality throughout Iraq during the 1980s had continued through the 1990s, there would have been half a million fewer deaths of children under-five in the country as a whole during the eight year period 1991 to 1998 (UNICEF 1999). US President George H. Bush utilized the occasion of the 1991 Gulf war to announce what he described as the "New World Order." This new vision implied more than just an untrammeled US military supremacy. More fundamentally it signaled a new phase of internationalization and financialization—the story of which will be resumed in Chapter 4.

Conclusion: The Global Political Economy and Gulf Class Formation

One overriding impression emerges from this account of the development of postwar capitalism: throughout each phase of internationalization and financialization, the Gulf region has become increasingly central to the functioning of the overall system. The Gulf has formed as a region nested within global hierarchies—essential to the broader development of postwar capitalism and its transformation into a tightly integrated world system. Capitalism's tendencies toward unbridled accumulation, internationalization, and financialization are materialized in the making of the Gulf region as a key node within the world market. Precisely for these reasons, control over the Gulf became a defining element of power in the global economy. As US power developed through the postwar period this relationship has been strikingly elucidated: the first entry of US oil companies into Saudi Arabia in the 1930s and 1940s; the displacement of British influence in the Gulf; the evolution of US policy through the Truman, Nixon, and Carter Doctrines; and the linkages between Gulf petrodollar flows, US dollar hegemony, and the emergence of neoliberalism. Each of these features of the global political economy are indicative of how the Gulf was a central constitutive element of US power in the postwar period.

The following chapter explores in detail how the centrality of the Gulf to the overall elaboration of global capitalism shaped the initial process of class formation in the region. At this stage, some general points can be made that help signpost the subsequent argument. First, the development of Gulf capitalism occurred alongside—and as part of—the region's ascension as a core zone within the global economy. For these reasons, the Gulf's embryonic capitalist class and state was integrated (as a junior partner) into the regional construction of US power. This is not to imply that there were no separate interests or rivalries between Gulf capitalism and US capital. Nor does it mean that this relationship will continue unchallenged for the foreseeable future. Rather, it merely indicates that the formation of the Gulf capitalist class has been subordinated to—and integrated with—the extension of US power at the regional scale.

Class formation is not just a process of accumulation by a handful of owners of capital. It is predicated on the formation of a laboring class that produces (and reproduces) capital itself. The centrality of the Gulf to the structure of the global economy means that the working classes of the Gulf (and, by extension, the Middle East) present a significant potential threat to capital accumulation at a global scale. This observation partially explains the peculiar character of working class formation in the GCC—overwhelmingly constituted by temporary, migrant workers with no citizenship rights. Class formation in the Gulf has occurred through its spatial structuring, and this feature is linked to the role the region plays in the global economy.

Moving beyond these general characteristics of Gulf capitalism and its overall position as an element of US power, the making of the Gulf capitalist classes have also been shaped by the region's location in the global tendencies of internationalization and financialization. First, a clear implication of the Gulf's role in the global economy is the significance of hydrocarbon production to domestic capitalism. Propelled by spiralling levels of global production in the postwar era and the development of new commodities such as petrochemicals, the production of hydrocarbons overshadows all other productive activities in the Gulf. The Gulf's productive circuit materialized in this context, structured from the outset around externally oriented production not domestic or national needs. In this sense, it has become an elemental link in the global productive circuit, underpinning the internationalization of capital at a global scale. Gulf capitalist classes have formed around revenues arising from this circuit—not through direct ownership of oil production but rather through related activities such as construction and services explored in the following chapter.

One consequence of this bias toward hydrocarbons and its weight in the global economy was the relatively undeveloped nature of non-hydrocarbon sectors. Consumer commodities and industrial machinery tended to be imported from outside rather than manufactured in the Gulf At the same time, the large amounts of available liquidity, rapid industrialization, and the expansion of infrastructure and other development activities meant that the size of the region's markets (particularly on a per capita basis) was significant relative to other areas outside of the advanced capitalist core. For these reasons, the Gulf became heavily reliant upon foreign imports to satisfy demand for consumer items, high technology, and industrial goods. This import trade provides another route for capital accumulation through the Gulf commodity circuit.

The third major route of domestic capital accumulation was shaped by the pivotal position of petrodollar flows in the financialization of the global economy. The importance of the Gulf financial sector to the making of the global economy and US power far exceeds its role in satisfying domestic financial needs. The very large levels of surplus capital available in the Gulf place significant pressure on the financial sector to develop markets and institutions capable of linking the Gulf with the global economy. Consequently, finance occupies a disproportionate weight within the overall circuit of capital—relative to the productive and commodity circuits—and is very significant to the formation of the leading sections of the domestic capitalist class. Through involvement in banks and other financial companies (although often subordinated to state capital), Gulf capitalists capture part of the value of these petrodollar flows and became closely linked to the overall financialization of the global economy.

CHAPTER 3

The Development of Capitalism in the Gulf Cooperation Council

As British hegemony in the Gulf underwent a slow decline from 1930 to 1970, the Gulf sheikhdoms were able to negotiate an independent status with their old colonial master. Britain recognized the Sultanate of Muscat and Oman's independence in 1951, followed by Kuwait in 1961 and the remaining Gulf states—Bahrain, Qatar, and the seven "Trucial States" that became the future UAE—in 1971.[1] Saudi Arabia, a remote and inhospitable area surrounded by desert, had managed to retain a relative independence from British control during the apex of colonial rule. With the unification of the kingdoms of Najd and Hijaz in 1932, the country in its modern form was born. The accumulation structures underpinning capitalist class formation across the Gulf date from this period of state building.[2]

Significantly, these four decades also coincided with the discovery of oil in the region and the commodity's growing centrality to the world economy described in the previous chapter. Oil concessions had been granted to various US, British, and French companies from 1923 onwards but it took until 1931 before oil was first discovered in Bahrain. Full-scale production in the Gulf began immediately after the war in Saudi Arabia, Kuwait, Qatar, and Bahrain, and by the early 1960s in the UAE and Oman. The importance of oil at a global scale meant that processes of state and class formation were firmly tied to US-British rivalries in the Gulf, as well as their shared interest in avoiding any popular control of oil resources by the region's people.

Initially, Britain's hold on Kuwait, Bahrain, Oman, and the Trucial States precluded any enduring US alliances along the coastal areas. Instead, the US entry to the Gulf occurred through Saudi Arabia, which, during the 1930s and 1940s, had been in urgent need of external support following the collapse of religious tourism in the wake of the Great Depression, and the outbreak of World War Two. Utilizing these fiscal crises, the United States cemented its alliance with Saudi Arabia by providing loans and other aid to the Saudi monarch Ibn Saud, in return for exclusive American access to Saudi oil. A 1943 memorandum from Standard Oil, one of the US oil companies controlling Aramco at the time, neatly encapsulated the rivalries with Britain and the logic driving American aid: "Concern is felt over the rapidly increasing British economic influence in Saudi Arabia because of the bearing it may have on the continuation of purely American enterprise after the war. Direct aid from the United States government to the Saudi Arab government . . . would check this tendency and give some assurance that the reserve of oil in Saudi Arabia will remain under control of Americans" (cited in Vassiliev 1998, p. 324). The US Department of State expressed precisely the same sentiment in a memorandum to President Truman in 1945, noting that Saudi Arabia's oil resources "will undoubtedly be lost to the United States unless this government is able to demonstrate in a practical way its recognition of this concession as a national interest by acceding to the reasonable requests of King Ibn Saud that he be assisted temporarily in his economic and financial difficulties" (United States Department of State 1945, p. 45). The Department estimated that "some money—about ten million a year for the next five years—would be necessary to obtain economic stability in that country sufficient to give reasonable security to American interest in the vast Arabian oilfields" (p. 47).

Saudi Arabia was not alone in feeling economic crisis. The collapse of the highly profitable pearling industry during the 1920s—precipitated by Japanese mass production of cultured pearls—compounded by the plunge in trade and tourism as a result of depression and war, provoked a series of internal divisions within the coastal Gulf sheikhdoms. These divisions were reflected in different forms. In Qatar, for example, some merchants left and attempted to find opportunities elsewhere in the Gulf. In other areas, different social forces clamored for greater representation and access to the ruler's revenues. These preexisting internal divisions—merchants against rulers (notably Dubai, Kuwait, Bahrain), struggles within the ruling family (Kuwait and Qatar), and disenfranchised Shia against Sunni rulers (Kuwait and Bahrain)—are the social backdrop through which to interpret the sudden flood of wealth resulting from the discovery and production of oil.

Initially, as the previous chapter outlined, the exploration and production of oil was largely controlled by foreign multinationals that paid royalties and other rents to the ruler. The potential profit for foreign oil companies operating in the Gulf was huge. Aramco, for example, had an average net return of 57.6 percent on the capital it invested in Saudi Arabia from 1952 to 1963 (after taxes)—way in excess of the 10–12 percent that was the average for operations in the United States (Vassiliev 1998, p. 332). But despite the vast profits accrued by foreign oil companies, the inflow of revenues to the ruling families in the Gulf precipitated a dramatic increase in their personal wealth. In addition to profligate spending on cars, palaces, swimming pools, and other luxuries, the ruler would negotiate the redistribution of part of these revenues between different factions within the ruling family, allied tribes, the merchant class, and other social groups. Britain (and the United States in Saudi Arabia) oversaw this process, providing military backing to any ruler that appeared under threat and switching allegiances to other factions in the ruling family if their interests were so suited.[3]

Crucially, the decline of British hegemony and the beginnings of oil production coincided with the rise of anticolonial sentiment across the Middle East. Even though it has been largely erased from the official state histories of the region, the anticolonial and left-wing impulses of the 1950s and 1960s found strong echo within the Gulf states. In Qatar, Kuwait, and Bahrain a series of powerful strikes occurred through the 1950s—fusing anti-British sentiment, solidarity with movements in neighboring countries (Palestine and Egypt in particular), and a yearning for a greater control over oil resources. In Saudi Arabia, Ibn Saud's semifeudal regime—and close relationship with the United States—was threatened by the rise of revolutionary and nationalist movements during the 1950s and 1960s. Symptomatic of the popular mood, an October 1955 editorial in the Saudi daily newspaper, *Al-Bilad al Sa'udiyah*, accused the wealthy elite of the country of "shortsightedness, laziness, and lack of self-confidence" and called on them to invest in the country's development rather than "locking their money in bank safes and building edifice after edifice abroad" (cited in Badre and Siksek 1959, p. 108). From 1962 to 1966, a range of strikes and demonstrations rocked the Saudi oil fields, led in part by Saudi workers with strong leftist leaning or inspired by nationalist movements in Egypt, Iraq, and Yemen. Opposition groups were established—the Union of the People of the Arabian Peninsula, the National Liberation Front, the Revolutionary Najdi Party, and the People's Liberation Front of Saudi Arabia—all of which expressed anti-Western sentiments and directly challenged the Saudi monarchy.

Each of the Gulf states responded to these movements with a wave of repression—often overseen and advised by Britain and the United States. The opposition movements were reinforced by the overlapping of class divisions and religious distinctions: Kuwait, which had a sizeable Shia minority; Saudi Arabia, where the oil fields were mostly located in the Shia-populated Eastern Provinces; Bahrain, where a Shia majority had long-held grievances against the Sunni Al Khalifa rulers; and Oman, where a guerilla struggle based in the Dhofar region emerged during the 1960s. In each of these states, leaders of the strikes and other political movements were arrested, exiled, and—in some cases—killed.

Repression, however, was not the only response to these struggles. At a more general level, each of the Gulf states settled on a particular *spatial strategy* as they emerged from independence. Class was constituted through its spatialization—an acute reliance on temporary migrant labor flows came to overlay an extremely narrow definition of citizenship. Across the Gulf states, citizenship was restricted to a tiny minority of the population who were provided with varying levels of access to the benefits accruing from oil revenues. These ranged from cheap housing, education, and other state benefits for the average citizen, to massive economic grants, contracts, and "sustainers" for members of the ruling elite and wealthiest merchant families. Concurrently, the nature of the working class was transformed through its spatialization. Rather than native workers, those who did most of the work in the Gulf states were brought from outside the country as temporary migrant labor lacking all citizenship rights. Citizens moved up the ladder—taking jobs in higher-level managerial positions and the government sector.

The process of class formation during the first phases of capitalist development was thereby marked by two fundamental characteristics: a "spatial fix"—underpinned by the systemic reliance on temporary migrant labor flows—and, simultaneously, the development of a domestic capitalist class through the redirection of oil revenues to leading merchant families and other elites. These twin features of class formation enabled the Gulf regimes to construct a powerful system of control over the vast majority of the resident population, while consolidating and binding citizen allegiance to the ruling monarch upon which an indigenous capitalism could develop.

The Gulf's Spatial Fix

The spatial fix embedded at the core of GCC class formation needs to be seen in the context of the region's position in global hierarchies described in the previous chapter. The critical centrality of the region to the making of global capitalism (and US power) meant that the working classes of the Gulf presented a significant potential threat to capital accumulation at a global scale. Any attempt by labor within the Gulf to wrest control of the oil rents fiercely guarded by the ruling family could profoundly impact the stability of the world market. This was not just a question of nationalization of oil supplies. Most fundamentally, it concerned the emergence of a potential link between the control of oil (and its revenues), and the ability to use this control to reshape the politics of the region as a whole—moving it out of the gambit of US power or the capitalist world market. Gulf capitalism's spatial fix helped to protect against this outcome, securing not only the position of Gulf capital (based on the broader social layer of citizenry in the Gulf) but also the global hierarchies that the Gulf was so central to constituting.

The argument is frequently made that the Gulf's heavy reliance on flows of migrant workers stems from "population pressures in the areas of origin and of opportunities in the host areas" or a "lack of a local, well-educated and adequately experienced workforce" in the Gulf countries (Nijim 1985, p. 50; Kapiszewski 2004, p. 115). While these factors are clearly proximate causes of labor flows, they obscure vital questions—why are these workers systematically denied any possibility of becoming permanent citizens of the GCC states and how does this exclusion facilitate capital accumulation in the Gulf?[4] Citizenship and its attendant rights cannot be understood separate from the spatial structuring of class that came to characterize Gulf capitalism. This was not an accidental or haphazard outcome. Rather, it was embedded within the process of state formation itself, with early Gulf states each promulgating a series of laws that defined citizenship and nationality rights while circumscribing those of migrant labor.

In the case of Saudi Arabia, Robert Vitalis (2007) has traced how the labor camps of Aramco initially relied upon a Saudi workforce organized in a highly racialized fashion that closely resembled the institutions of South African Apartheid. Many of these workers (particularly in security and truck driving) were drawn from Bedouin tribes that had been sedenterised through a combination of compulsion and the restriction of grazing rights. Forced to enter the cash economy, they took up positions as workers in the oil fields (Dahir 1986).[5] Aramco figures from 1958 recorded that Saudi nationals constituted over 70 percent of the company's workforce (Badre and Siksek 1959, p. 37). In the economy as a whole, in the early 1960s, over 90 percent of the workforce were Saudi nationals according to figures from the Central Planning Organisation (Niblock 2007, p. 51). The series of strikes and labor actions noted above, however, provided the context in which Abdallah Tariki emerged as an advocate of nationalization and the removal of US oil companies from Saudi soil. As Aramco was taken over by the Saudi state, its leaders were "free to rebuild hierarchy anew . . . [with] migrant laborers from Yemen, Egypt and elsewhere" (Vitalis 2007, p. 272). Saudi workers were drawn into the state, with guaranteed job security and numerous privileges of citizenship. Unskilled and, in some cases, illiterate citizens were provided jobs that were essentially designed to do little more than collect a paycheck while noncitizen, migrant workers filled positions in the rest of the economy.[6] By 1980, migrant labor constituted a majority of the workforce (50.7 percent), with the actual size of the civilian workforce almost tripling between 1970 and 1980 (Niblock 2007, p. 91).

In Kuwait, the ruling al-Sabah family followed a similar process of delineating citizenship on a highly restrictive basis, thereby institutionalizing preferential treatment and privileges for those classified as Kuwaiti "nationals." A series of laws were issued through the 1950s and 1960s that deliberately aimed to "differentiate and differentially control Kuwaiti and expatriate labor," separating migrant workers from those granted Kuwaiti citizenship (Crystal 1995, p. 80). Jill Crystal quotes the US consul in Kuwait who, in 1959, described how this system of control benefited the ruling family: "Whenever a temporary labor surplus develops or whenever Kuwaiti authorities become disturbed at the size of the foreign community, the illegal workers are rounded up and shipped to Iran or Iraq" (p. 80). The al-Sabah family later used an identical mechanism of granting differential privileges through citizenship to co-opt and win the allegiance of many Bedouin families.[7]

The Trucial States' longer experience with British colonialism had linked them earlier and more directly to labor flows from India and Pakistan. British companies dominated development contracts in the area and brought labor to work in construction, wholesale trade and retail, and other service sectors. In late 1960s Dubai, for example, the two largest construction companies were the British Costain Construction Company and Taylor Woodrow International, both of which employed this foreign labor extensively. Foreign workers constituted around half of Dubai's population by 1968 (Kazim 2000, p. 247). In Abu Dhabi, where oil exports began in 1962 under the control of British oil companies, migrant workers were an even more important source of labor for the area's development. It is estimated that around 56 percent of Abu Dhabi's population was foreign in 1968 (Kazim 2000, p. 271). With the formation of the UAE in 1971, the privileging of citizenship and reliance on temporary migrant labor was institutionalized in a manner similar to that which had occurred in Saudi Arabia and Kuwait. UAE citizens were allowed to own property (denied to migrant workers) and were given free education, health care, generous marriage dowries and child benefits, cheap land and free housing under the "peoples' houses" scheme (Heard-Bey 1982, pp. 403–6).[8] Nationals further benefited from the ability to rent out property that they had received for free (or very cheaply) from the ruler to the rapidly growing migrant population.

From the 1970s onwards, the temporary migrant worker population grew to a remarkable 50–70 percent of the labor force in Saudi Arabia,

Oman, and Bahrain, and to 80–90 percent in the remaining GCC states (Shamsi 2006, p. 61). In the private sector, the concentration was even greater, with migrant workers constituting close to 100 percent of the workforce in all GCC states except for Saudi Arabia, where they represented over 80 percent[9] Most of these migrants were young males (ranging between 70 and 90 percent), although female migrant labor came to be heavily concentrated in some sectors such as domestic work and the service sector. Of course, this particular class structure showed wide differentiation across the Gulf states. The actual proportion of the population that held citizenship varied from 20–35 percent in the UAE, Kuwait, and Qatar to between 60–80 percent in Bahrain, Saudi Arabia, and Oman (Kapiszewski 2004, p. 117). Poverty did persist within the citizen population—particularly when measured relatively—and was largely refracted through the preexisting religious and geographic divisions (e.g., Shia within Bahrain, Saudi Arabia, and Kuwait; the northern Emirates vis-à-vis Abu Dhabi and Dubai in the UAE, and the poorer industrial town of Sohar relative to the capital Muscat in Oman). Despite these provisos, however, the central point remains: class congealed spatially around temporary migrant labor flows and was demarcated through the institution of citizenship.

Initially this spatial structuring of class depended upon Arab labor such as Palestinian, Lebanese, Egyptian, and Yemeni workers (although, as noted above, South Asian labor was a significant component of the workforce in the UAE). During the 1970s and 1980s, however, many of these workers came to sympathize with Arab and Palestinian nationalism and began to challenge the Gulf regimes and their perceived ties with the Western powers. They also attempted to settle in a more permanent sense, bringing their families and demanding parity with "locals" and rights associated with citizenship (particularly in education and housing). In some cases, these movements connected with Gulf citizens themselves—specifically Shia communities in Bahrain, Kuwait, and the UAE. The 1979 Iranian revolution acted to further radicalize the large Shia populations throughout the Gulf, with demonstrations, bombings, and the formation of various political organizations a frequent occurrence throughout the 1970s and 1980s. In December 1983, for example, a series of bombing attacks occurred against the US and French embassies in Kuwait, as well as other vital infrastructure targets. Shia groups in Iraq and Lebanon claimed the attacks, and 14 men (including two Lebanese residents) were sentenced to death by the Kuwaiti government (Zahlan 1998, p. 172).[10] By the mid-1980s, partially in response to the potential radicalization of Arab noncitizen residents, GCC states had begun to shift migrant labor flows away from Arab countries toward the Indian subcontinent. Laws were instituted that made it more difficult for Arab families to settle for long periods in the GCC countries (in the UAE, for example, it was made illegal for noncitizen children to attend public schools).[11]

The 1990–1991 Gulf War provided an excellent opportunity to hasten the transition toward South Asian labor. Arab residents were expelled en masse under the pretext that the Palestine Liberation Organization and Yemen had supported Iraq's invasion of Kuwait. In Kuwait, the number of Palestinians fell from 400,000 in 1990 to about 50,000 by the mid-1990s (Fergany 2001, p. 7). By 2002, the Arab proportion of migrant workers in the GCC would fall to around 25–29 percent—down from a level of 72 percent in 1975 (Kapiszewski 2004, p. 123).[12] In turn, the shift to South Asian labor meant that many neighboring countries became heavily reliant upon the GCC as a source of labor and remittances. Bangladesh, for example, was sending around 60–70 percent of its overseas workers to the Gulf by the mid-1990s (Bangladesh MEWOE).[13] Pakistan, India, and Sri Lanka were similarly linked to the labor needs of the GCC.

The spatial configuration of class serves as a "fix" for Gulf capitalism in a number of ways. First, the structural reliance on temporary migrant labor acts to increase the rate of exploitation. Temporary migrant workers often face substandard conditions that barely exceed the minimum necessary for physical survival—a situation that is today little changed from the waves of migrant worker flows in the 1970s. In Dubai, for example, construction workers can earn around 50–80 cents an hour and work ten-hour days, six days a week. In the largest labor camp in Dubai, Al Muhaisnah 2, workers are housed in tin-roofed dormitories with up to eight people in a room designed for two. The camp (which residents sarcastically call Sonapur, Hindi for "land of gold") is built around a graveyard and lacks any paved roads. Sewage flows openly in the street.[14] Those workers fortunate enough to live outside of camps such as Sonapur are often forced to cram inside apartments that are partitioned for multiple occupants in unsafe and unsanitary conditions.[15]

Lacking any legal parity with citizen labor, workers send most of their wages back home in the form of remittances. There are no minimum wages in the private sector and the value of migrant labor—reflected in their wage levels—is largely measured relative to the social conditions extant in the worker's home country rather than the country in which they work. This is indicated by the considerable differences in pay between citizen and noncitizen labor for the same jobs—differences that widen even further if nonwage costs were included (housing, education, and health rights for citizens).[16] Sectors where such large wage differentials do not exist, such as banking and finance, came to be populated with migrant labor of a qualitatively different sort—that originating from the Western countries. *Western expat. labor*

One of the reasons for the increased rate of exploitation is related to the size of the Gulf's "reserve army of labor"—the unemployed or those looking for work in the region. In contrast to most capitalist economies, this potential pool of workers is not constituted internal to the state but rather across the new spatial structures that link the Gulf with the surrounding peripheries. Temporary migrant workers find themselves competing with hundreds of millions of compatriots dispersed across the Middle East and South Asia. For these reasons, the spatialization of class—the fact that class is formed through a relationship established between spatially distinct sets of social relations—acts to depress the price of labor power and magnify the exploitation of these workers.

Moreover, as the earlier quote from the US Consul in Kuwait recognizes, this spatialization of class acts as a powerful mechanism of social control. Because the spatial location of temporary labor in the Gulf is constituted through the social relations established in the course of the reproduction of capital—and not through birth or citizenship rights—this labor lacks any permanent *right to space.* As soon as these social relations are severed through the termination of employment, these workers become "illegal" and are forced to return to their country of origin. The fluidity of status is codified through laws that link residency visas with possession of employment. Collective organization, strikes, and other forms of class solidarity are made very difficult because labor can be simply (and legally) threatened with deportation at the slightest evidence of discontent. GCC government spokespeople have explicitly described migrant workers as "a strategic threat" and "national security issue," making it easier to justify these repressive laws.[17] Not only is the ability to discipline labor greatly increased through this process, but, for the worker to struggle against a spatial identity that is solely constituted through their relationship with capital means, in a very real sense, to struggle against oneself. It thus represents an acute form of alienated labor. Overall, the temporary and spatially dispersed nature of working-class identity hinders the development of class-consciousness. Each individual has only a temporary existence within the social relations that constitute class. These social relations are continually being dissolved as workers return home or shift countries to look for new employment. Moreover, this process of spatialization inevitably striates the class with ethnic, national, and religious differences. Particular national or ethnic groups drawn from different geographical spaces tend to concentrate in certain occupations or layers within the class. In practice, this reinforces segregation or partitioning of the class—there is little internal class mobility, often almost insurmountable barriers in communication between workers and, in some cases, long-standing ethnic or religious tensions between different layers. In the case of women domestic workers, mostly drawn from Sri Lanka and the Philippines, these barriers are even more accentuated. Many of these workers suffer physical and mental abuse at the hands of their employers. One researcher has reported, for example, that nearly half of the domestic workers she interviewed in the UAE never left the houses of their employees alone in the two years in which they worked in the country (Gambard 2009, p. 65). In the UAE, labor laws do not apply to work that takes place in private homes and therefore the majority of domestic workers are not covered by the (limited) labor rights of the country.

In many GCC states, these internal divisions in the working class came to be reflected in the highly segregated distribution of communities throughout urban areas. In this manner, the process of spatialization—overlaid with and consolidating other differences in identity—acts to impede possibilities of class solidarity. The class itself is constantly being remade anew, foreclosing possibilities of developing generational continuity, any working-class culture and collective memory of struggle, or stable political organizations. This insight helps to explain the relative political quiescence of the GCC states in contrast to other oil-rich states such as Iraq and Iran—two countries that were unable to adopt the GCC's spatial fix and in which mass struggles have continued to develop with an anti-Western or nationalist hue.[18]

The Formation of the Gulf Capitalist Classes

Concurrent with this spatial structuring of labor, capitalist classes began to form through a series of mechanisms that were remarkably similar across each of the Gulf states. This process was fundamentally based on the redirection of state revenues that began to accumulate as oil-producing countries across the world gained greater control over their oil supplies from the early 1970s onwards. As these nationalizations proceeded, the enormous revenues from oil became the key fiscal basis of the state and the ruler's authority. The private sector was excluded from any involvement in upstream oil production, yet some of the oil revenues were redirected from the state to family-based groups who were drawn, most frequently, from merchant classes or were allied (often related by blood or marriage) to the ruler.

Some of the mechanisms by which this initial "primitive accumulation" occurred were essentially "gifts" from the ruler to sections of the older merchant class and new social elites that had emerged with the development of the state apparatus. A particularly important example of this was the granting of land by the ruling monarch to favored groups or individuals. In the case of Saudi Arabia, for example, traditional collective rights over grazing land had been abolished in 1925 and passed into the hands of the Saudi king, Ibn Saud. Ibn Saud used this power to control access to grazing rights and the movement of tribes (Hajrah 1982; Chaudhry 1997, p. 173). Through the 1960s, Ibn Saud granted land and agricultural inputs such as machinery, seeds, and fertilizers to tribes from the Najd region, which formed the backbone of the Saudi army and were thus a major element to the social base of the regime. Following the oil boom of the 1970s, however, this land policy was transformed. Kiren Chaudhry has documented this process thoroughly, showing how in the latter half of the 1970s, large tracts of land were granted to individuals and private corporations thus encouraging the growth of Saudi agribusiness. Chaudhry argues that this policy was specifically designed to benefit "prominent Nejdi [sic] families with close ties to bureaucrats and political elites" (1997, p. 177). She notes that by 1981, "82 percent of private land was held by only 16.2 percent of the land-owning population, making Saudi Arabia's one of the most inequitable land tenure systems in the world. By the end of the 1980s, the government owned virtually no land" (p. 176).

In other regions of the Gulf where agricultural land use was less prevalent, rulers granted urban land to members of the ruling family and key merchant families who profited handsomely from the rise in land prices as development proceeded. In Kuwait, for example, the al-Sabah family purchased extensive areas of urban land from merchants at artificially high prices and then resold them at low prices to the wealthiest merchants. By the early 1960s, land prices had become the largest element of the state budget although the government only recovered around 5 percent of its outlay on this land (Crystal 1995, p. 76). The World Bank noted in 1965 that this process made "public land transactions a rather indiscriminate and inequitable way of redistributing the oil revenues" (cited in Crystal 1995, p. 76). Similar patterns of land grants by the ruling monarch were displayed in the other Gulf states.

Another important mechanism by which oil-wealth was distributed to the wider society was the expansion of the state apparatus. Jobs in the public sector were seen as a social right that helped to further bind citizenry to the emerging order. As many citizens gained privileged access to employment in the state, an influx of highly exploited noncitizen labor filled the positions outside of the state. The core of the state apparatus (e.g., ministerial portfolios) went to members of the ruling family, while the concentric circles surrounding this core went to prominent merchant families and tribal allies of the ruler (e.g., positions in "consultative assemblies" and other high-ranking state bodies). For the emerging bourgeoisie, higher-level jobs in the state apparatus became an important mechanism of accumulation as they facilitated access to contracts as well as providing large salaries. In Saudi Arabia, for example, the Gosaibi family has long been a close ally of the al-Saud monarchy and during the 1920s and 1930s held diplomatic posts in Bahrain and India. In the 1970s and 1980s, members of the family served in leadership positions in the Saudi Railways, Ministry of Industry and Electricity, and the Saudi Arabian Monetary Agency (Field 1984, p. 109). The Ali Reza and Zamil families have also held several high-ranking posts in the Saudi state. In the UAE, the Al Gurg and Ghurair families are similarly notable. These examples confirm the contemporaneous and intertwined evolution of class and state in the Gulf states.

It is important, however, to emphasize that the development of capitalism in this initial period was not simply a matter of the redistribution of oil revenues to prominent individuals or families. While this process is of course critical to understanding class formation, it needs to be situated in the broader consolidation of capitalism as the dominant mode of production within the Gulf. The accumulation of capital does not automatically reproduce itself through contingent choices of state officials or the ruling monarch, but is systematized and institutionalized through the elaboration and development of the circuit of capital. Capitalism is a system of generalized commodity production in which the pursuit of profit becomes a necessary activity of the capitalist class. It is the development of this system as a whole—in other words, the form taken by the circuit of capital—that needs to be understood. Over time, the individuals and family-based companies that were the initial recipients of state largesse were to develop into massive conglomerates with economic activities stretching across all moments of the circuit of capital: production, the sale of commodities, and financial accumulation. Their activities were buttressed by—and interpenetrated with—accumulation structures of state and large foreign capital (see Appendix A for a sampling of these groups). The challenge in the remainder of this chapter is thus to trace both the ways in which the capitalist class itself was enriched as it formed in the postindependence period, as well as the specific characteristics of the circuit of capital that emerged to underpin this accumulation.

The Productive Circuit

The global importance of Gulf hydrocarbons in the postwar period pushed the production of oil and gas to the core of the region's productive circuit.

Throughout the Gulf, control over this sector has been held by the state (and thus, in large measure, the ruling family) since the process of nationalization began in the 1970s. This state control became most complete in Saudi Arabia and Kuwait. In Saudi Arabia, the state took full control of Aramco in 1980 and changed its name to Saudi Aramco in 1988.[19] It has been the largest oil company in the world since that time. In Kuwait, the state-run Kuwait Oil Company (KOC) took responsibility for the upstream sector in 1975, and a constitutional provision mandated that foreign companies could not control the country's oil resources. In the other Gulf countries, foreign oil multinationals continued to play a role in the production of crude oil (albeit a lesser one relative to the period of direct colonialism).[20]

The embryonic Gulf capitalist class that emerged around the productive circuit was thus excluded from any direct ownership or control of oil and gas. Instead, it pursued accumulation opportunities in other industries that were either derivative to the oil sector or were initiated with state assistance from accrued oil revenues. Initially, the most important of these opportunities were service and construction contracts granted to local companies by governments and foreign multinationals, either in the oil sector or for broader industrialization and infrastructure development. As the groups listed in Appendix A illustrate, many of these are characterized by their continued involvement in these types of service and basic contracting activities: construction, food and transportation, simple manufacturing (pipes, wires etc.), security, and so forth. Through these contracting activities, a portion of the revenues from the upstream hydrocarbon sector was appropriated by an emerging Gulf capitalist class.

With state control over the distribution of contracts overlapping with the enrichment of an incipient capitalist class, processes of state and class formation were closely linked. This has been particularly well documented in the case of Saudi Arabia, where the ubiquitous presence of "brokers" and "gatekeepers"—individuals who control access to decision makers in the state apparatus—confirms the importance of state contracts for capital accumulation. In many cases, members of the royal family who held high-level positions would use the distribution of construction and other contracts to privately enrich themselves or close family members. But the royal family was not the only beneficiary, by the 1970s, a variety of state institutions had been established by the Saudi government to provide emerging business groups with interest-free loans and subsidies for construction projects. From 1970 to 1975, the period of the first Saudi Five Year Economic Development Plan, construction was easily the fastest growing private sector activity (21.4 percent growth) and, by the late

1970s, made up around 30 percent of private sector output (Niblock 2007, p. 84). In 1977 and 1978, laws were passed that required foreign contractors to subcontract 30 percent of their work to local firms, and to employ a Saudi agent through which to channel all their bids for government contracts (who subsequently received a commission). Moreover, Saudi firms profited from the lucrative import of migrant labor for construction activities—garnering fees paid by workers for entry, visa applications, and subcontracting these workers to other firms (Hertog 2010, p. 198). The private sector share in Saudi GDP rose from 12.9 percent in 1970 to over 50 percent by 1983, a strong indication of the benefits that flowed from the construction and contracting work that occurred following the oil boom.

A good example of the importance of these early construction and service-related activities to domestic capital accumulation is shown by the massive Saudi conglomerate, the Dallah Al Baraka Group, controlled by Saleh Abdullah Kamel. The origins of the group go back to 1969, when Kamel founded the Dallah Works and Maintenance Company, in Riyadh. The company won a series of contracts from the Saudi government for the construction of roads, pipelines, and sewage networks, as well as the cleaning and maintenance of the Mecca and Medina holy sites. In 1975, the company became Dallah Avco Trans Arabia Company, which specialized in the construction and maintenance of Saudi airports. It was also involved in the provision of food, maintenance, and operation services at military bases and hospitals. Through these state contracts, Al Baraka developed into one of the largest Saudi companies, eventually owning a network of banks across the Middle East, one of the largest media conglomerates (the Arab Media Corporation), an advertising company, and the largest juice manufacturer in the region. Saleh Kamel was worth an estimated US$4.9 billion in 2009 and was the fourteenth richest Arab in the world (White 2009, p. 30).

Each of the Gulf states shows similar patterns of development, with domestic capital establishing itself through contracting and construction work. In Kuwait, prominent examples include the Al Kharafi, Al Ghanim, Al Sagar, Boodai, and Fulaij groups; in the UAE, Al Jaber, Mazroui, Lootah, Habtoor, and Al Majid groups; in Qatar, the Nasser Bin Khaled Group (NBK), Al Fakhroo (Darwish), and Al Mana groups; in Bahrain, the Mohammed Jamal and Al Moayyed groups; and in Oman, the Zubair and Bahwan groups. Although these conglomerates have extensive activities in other sectors including retail and finance, construction and other contracting work remains an important feature of their accumulation into the current period.

Downstream Industrialization

Beginning in the 1970s, the Gulf states began to augment the upstream hydrocarbon sector with a more thoroughgoing industrialization focused on energy-intensive and oil-related downstream products. This industrialization took place through state-owned industrial companies closely affiliated with (and often subsidiaries of) the national oil companies, which established joint ventures with foreign capital. Each of the GCC countries has one or more of these companies that acted to direct oil revenue into joint ventures in downstream industrial projects. In this first phase, foreign capital was the primary beneficiary of joint ownership and fees from engineering and project management, while domestic private capital profited from the less complex contracting and construction work associated with these projects. It was not until the post-2000 phase of industrialization that the Gulf capitalist class became involved in the direct production of downstream commodities in a significant manner (see Chapter 5).

The preeminent example of this process is the Saudi Basic Industries Corporation (SABIC). SABIC was founded in 1976 when the Saudi Arabian Government decided to capture the natural gas associated with the production of crude oil and use it to make chemicals, polymers, fertilizers, and metals in the new industrial cities of Jubail and Yanbu. Since that time SABIC has grown to become the ninth-largest petrochemical company in the world and now dominates the production of many key petrochemical products at a global level (see Chapter 5 for more discussion of this). The company operates a large network of affiliates, subsidiaries, and joint ventures, mostly held in partnership with foreign multinationals. Many of these subsidiaries were connected to the general increase in the wealth of Saudi citizens through royal decrees that gave employees a share in ownership. The official company history of the Saudi Arabian Fertilizer Company (SAFCO), for example, describes itself as a "joint venture between the Government and the citizens of Saudi Arabia," which was established to "encourage national industries and to recognize the hard work and dedication of the employees."

Although SABIC is easily the largest and most important of these industrial companies in the GCC, other states followed a similar model of utilizing a state-owned company to establish downstream joint ventures. In Qatar, the region's second-largest petrochemical producer, petrochemicals are dominated by Industries Qatar (IQ), which was established as a subsidiary of the national oil company, Qatar Petroleum (in 2003 it was listed on the stock market). IQ holds shares in companies operating in petrochemicals (Qatar Petrochemical Company and Qatar Fuel Additives Company), fertilizers (Qatar Fertilizers Company), and steel (Qatar Steel Company).

These companies are jointly held with foreign capital (except for Qatar Steel, which is 100 percent owned by IQ). In a similar fashion, all other GCC states set up companies that resemble SABIC and IQ: the Kuwaiti Petrochemical Industries Company (PIC), the Bahrain Petroleum Co. (BAPCO), the Oman Oil Co. (OOC), and the Abu Dhabi National Oil Co. (ADNOC). In later periods (see Chapter 5), ownership of the various joint ventures and subsidiaries of these companies was expanded through listing on the stock exchange.

Energy-Intensive Industries

Access to large and relatively cheap energy sources in the GCC affected the character and development of other secondary industries, most notably the production of basic metals (e.g., aluminum and steel) where electricity is a major component of overall cost. In the aluminum industry, for example, energy represents around 30 percent of total costs, with analysts often equating the export of aluminum with the export of electricity (Ford 2006, p. 50). For steel, energy constitutes from 20–40 percent of total costs. Much like downstream petrochemical production, although these energy-intensive industries were established in this earlier phase their expansion and full integration with domestic conglomerates was consolidated in the post-2000 period (see Chapter 5).

Likewise similar to the petrochemical companies, the initial establishment of energy-intensive metal industries during the 1970s occurred through state-owned companies often linked to the oil sector. In the case of aluminum, for example, the largest smelter in the Middle East is Aluminium Bahrain (ALBA), located in Bahrain and established in 1971. It is jointly owned by the Bahraini government (77 percent), SABIC (20 percent), and a German investment firm, Breton Investments (3 percent). The equity owners take their share in aluminum production, and it is considered the most valuable of SABIC's sister companies. Aluminum production also became an important feature of the UAE economy where the aluminum plant, Dubal, was established in 1979.[21]

These basic metal commodities continue to circulate downstream through other industries such as rolled steel, wires, aluminum extrusions, and so on, and it is in this sector that domestic capital has established itself (see Appendix A). The raw aluminum produced by ALBA, for example, is utilized by a number of smaller companies that involve major Bahraini capital groups. One of these companies is Midal Cables, established in 1977, which purchases raw aluminum from ALBA to produce cables and rods. It grew to become the world's largest producer of aluminum conductors with its entire produce exported to over 60 countries. Midal is jointly owned by the Bahraini conglomerate, Al Zayani Investments (AZI), and the Saudi conglomerate, Ali Reza (Xenel Group)—its ownership patterns thus perfectly illustrate the connection between GCC domestic capital in the secondary circuits of production flowing from the basic metals industry.[22]

The importance of these basic metal-related activities as an accumulation base for domestic capital is replicated in other GCC countries. In Dubai, the Dubai Cable Company (Ducab) was formed in 1979 to utilize aluminum production. In Qatar, the Qatar Steel Company (QASCO) was founded in 1974 as the first integrated steel producing company in the GCC and Qatar's only steel producer. QASCO holds 50 percent of the Qatar Metals Coating Company (formed 1990), which it shares with the Qatar Industrial Manufacturing Co. (QIMCO), a large Qatari conglomerate that brings together the major domestic capital groups in Qatar. Major shareholders and board members of QIMCO include the Al Mana Group, the Abdulghani Group, as well as the ruling al-Thani family. QASCO also holds 25 percent of the Bahrain-based United Stainless Steel Company, which it shares with other GCC capital including the Al Rashid Group (Saudi Arabia), the Al Kharafi Group (Kuwait), and the National Industries Group (Kuwait). Another example of this process is Saudi Arabia's largest manufacturer of steel wire and other wire products, National Metal Manufacturing & Casting Company (Maadaniyah). Maadaniyah is owned by the National Industrialization Co., which is owned by the large Saudi conglomerate Kingdom Holding.

The interlock between domestic and state capital is also clear in the case of another energy-intensive sector, cement production, in which energy constitutes around 30–40 percent of total costs. The initial growth of this sector is clearly related to the development of service and construction activities discussed above (such as the early state-sponsored infrastructure projects). All Gulf states with the exception of Oman had established national cement companies by the late 1960s.[23] Ownership of these companies was dominated by the large domestic capital conglomerates in alliance with state investment funds and government authorities (see Appendix A).[24]

Agriculture

Construction and downstream energy-intensive industry were generally the dominant productive activities in this first period. One exception to this was the Saudi agricultural sector, where the land grant policies discussed above were expanded through the 1980s to include massive agricultural schemes that depended upon extensive irrigation, subsidies, and loans from the Saudi state. Chaudhry notes that loans and subsidies from the Saudi

Agricultural Bank jumped from an annual average of 654.6 million Saudi Riyal (SR) from 1975 to 1980, to 3090 million SR from 1980 to 1985 (1997, p. 152). Much of this expansion in agriculture went to the Najd region, which saw its share of total cultivated land in Saudi Arabia grow from 10 percent in 1960 to 57 percent in 1984 (p. 179). These state-led policies were often little more than a direct transfer of wealth through subsidy programs. The much-vaunted "Wheat Program" in the early 1980s, for example, saw the government purchase domestically produced wheat at $1050/ton (compared with the international price of $120/ton) thus providing wheat producers with a massive subsidy (p. 183).

As a result of policies such as these, agriculture became an important source of accumulation for many of the leading Saudi conglomerates. One of these, the Al Rajhi Group, came to own the largest poultry farm in the Middle East and a significant stake in one of the largest shrimp farms in the region. Al Rajhi is represented on the boards of the Tabuk Agriculture and Development Co. (which produces wheat, potatoes, onions, alfalfa, fruits, and olive oil) and the National Agricultural Development Co. (producing wheat, dairy, fruits, and dates)—two companies that were established during the initial period of this agricultural growth. Another significant food and agricultural company is Savola, in which a number of the leading representatives of Saudi capital are involved. It was established in 1979 by 25 founding shareholders drawn from state capital and the largest private groups (see Appendix A) and has grown to control between 70 percent and 95 percent of the Saudi edible oils and sugar refinery markets. It is also a major producer of dairy products, plastics, and packaging and controls one of the largest supermarket networks across the Middle East (see Chapter 5 for more detail on the retail activities of Savola).

Commodity Circuit

The commodity circuit played a critical role in the development of Gulf capitalism and the formation of the leading conglomerates. The overall weight of oil in the Gulf economies has meant a relative underdevelopment of non-hydrocarbon sectors and a heavy reliance on imports. As is to be expected, the scale of GCC imports closely tracks the movement of the price of oil and accelerated significantly following the initial oil price rises of the early 1970s. From 1972 to 1980, the value of world merchandise imports to the Gulf states in current dollars grew by more than 20 percent each year. Although imports dropped in the wake of the world recession that began in 1982, they resumed their upward trend by 1987, growing at an average of 10 percent annually until 1993.[25]

Because of the centrality of oil and derivative industries to the GCC productive circuit, a large proportion of overall exports to the region consist of the machinery and transport equipment that form the fixed capital necessary for these sectors. In the early-1990s, for example, machinery and transport equipment constituted around 40 percent of the value of all exports to the GCC from the leading capitalist countries.[26] In addition to these fixed capital imports, consumer, food, and luxury items grew to be an increasingly prominent feature of the region's markets as wealth levels of nationals increased from the 1970s onwards.

Historically, the ruling families of the Gulf states have generally stayed out of the import trade and other retail activities (with the notable exceptions of Qatar's al-Thani and Dubai's al-Maktoum families). A tacit agreement existed between the ruler and the leading merchants that trade could continue without the ruling family's involvement, provided that the merchants provided the requisite support to the ruler through taxes, loans, and political allegiance. As such, one of the fundamental means that rulers had to win the support of leading merchants was the granting of sole agency rights for foreign imports. In the postcolonial period, this pattern was codified through laws that prevented imports without the representation of a local agent. As the interlocutor with foreign producers, major capital groups have thus arisen around this moment of the commodity circuit.

In Saudi Arabia, large trading houses predated the formation of the Saudi state and had played an important role in facilitating the rise to power of al-Saud, through the provision of loans and other support. After the formation of the state, they were able to obtain agency rights for the import of many foreign-produced goods. Important examples of these family-based trading establishments include the Ali Reza, Zahid, Al Gosaibi, Al Rajhi, Al Rashid, and Al Turki groups (see Appendix A). In 1962, a royal decree was issued that prohibited non-Saudis from operating as commercial agents in the Kingdom. Through the 1970s, agency rights continued to be a lucrative business as laws were passed that required foreign importers to partner with a local company as their agent and distributor. Although many of the largest importers were from new social layers that emerged in the central and eastern areas of the country following the oil boom, the Hijaz region in the west of the country continued to provide a slim majority of the largest trading houses (Niblock 1997, p. 135).[27] In the early 1980s, a commentator on Saudi socioeconomic development was to describe this social layer—agents for everything from cars to migrant workers—as "lumpen capitalists" because of their nonproductive role as intermediaries between the international and national scales (Ibrahim 1982, p. 12). In Kuwait, laws passed through the 1960s gave the Chamber of Commerce the right to regulate permits for foreigners, restricted imports to Kuwaiti-owned companies (thereby forcing foreign importers to seek a Kuwaiti agent), and limited the rights to establish businesses to Kuwaitis (Crystal 1995, p. 90). This process helped to strengthen older merchant families (such as the Al Ghanim, Al Kharafi, and Al Shaya Groups) who were to develop into key conglomerates in the contemporary period. Throughout the entire Gulf, similar laws meant agency rights extended to every conceivable commodity—automobiles, machinery and transport equipment, electrical items, food and beverages, and household consumer items. In most cases, a conglomerate's agency and franchise rights encompassed a variety of different commodities and sectors.[28]

Many examples can be found that confirm these patterns. In Kuwait, the massive Al Ghanim Group holds agencies for General Motors (the first in the Gulf), Toshiba, Philips, Daewoo, Hitachi air conditioners, Kraft Foods, Palmolive, Nabisco, British Airways, Cathay Pacific, and Qantas. In the UAE, the Al Gurg Group, founded in 1960, holds agency rights for over 200 international brands from the consumer and retail sector (e.g., Benetton, Unilever, ID Design, 3M, Better Life, Electrolux, Samsung, Fisher and Paykel), tobacco (Benson and Hedges, British American Tobacco, Dunhill, Lucky Strike, Rothmans, Silk Cut, Viceroy), and industrial goods (Dulux, Siemens, ICI, Leigh Paints, Osram). In Qatar, the Al Mana Group represents Konica Minolta, Océ, 3M, Apple, Hewlett-Packard, Philips, Whirlpool, Daewoo, Frigidaire, Unilever Arabia, Gillette Middle East, Qatar Airways, Emirate Airlines, and KLM.

Import trade is not the only part of the commodity circuit. Retail activities—the establishment of shops, shopping centers, and malls—are another important moment of accumulation in this circuit. In some cases, an agent will bring in certain goods and then sell these goods at wholesale to different retail companies who own the shops in which they are sold. The Al Gurg Group, for example, may sell their foreign-label tobacco products to local supermarkets and other retail outlets that then sell them to the public. In other cases, however, the same Gulf capitalist that holds agency rights for certain import commodities frequently comes to own the store in which these goods are sold. Chapter 5 discusses more recent trends in this sector, specifically the growth of hypermarkets and malls, and their geographical clustering in Saudi Arabia and the UAE.

Military Imports

A further important element of the commodity circuit—which lies far outside everyday retail and industrial goods—is the purchase of military hardware from the leading capitalist countries. This was a strong feature of economic development in the Middle East during the 1980s and 1990s—corresponding to the close alliance between the United States and the GCC countries described in the previous chapter. Saudi Arabia, Kuwait, and the UAE were particularly distinguished by extremely high levels of military expenditure. In 1985, for example, Saudi Arabia spent 22.7 percent of its gross national product on the military. By 1990, 60 percent of Saudi government expenditure was military-related, with a large proportion of that devoted to buying weapons from overseas producers (WMEAT 1996, p. 89). Indeed, the country's military imports represented a remarkable 28–39 percent of all imports for each year between 1985 and 1990. Likewise, the UAE was spending over 40 percent of its state expenditure on the military for each year between 1985 and 1989, increasing to 65 percent in 1990 (WMEAT 1996, p. 95). It should be noted that the Middle East was the largest spender on military imports of any region in the world for each year from 1985 to 1990, with Saudi Arabia, Kuwait, and the UAE the prominent GCC purchasers (matched by Israel and Egypt on the western flank of the Middle East).

As with other components of the commodity circuit, the military trade provided an opportunity for individuals and companies in the GCC to capture part of the import value. Reflecting the character of their strategic alliances, US and UK weapons producers supplied the overwhelming proportion of weapons to the GCC in this period. In order to make these sales, Western military corporations would recruit well-connected Gulf representatives as their mediator for the sale of military hardware—a practice known as "commission harvesting." Huge amounts of money were involved in these contracts, particularly in the case of Saudi Arabia where go-betweens were reported to have received up to 30 percent of the value of contracts (Champion 2003). Moreover, Saudi princes often took large cuts from these military deals and were thus privately enriched by their positions in the state bureaucracy (Hertog 2010, p. 88).

In other cases, foreign military exporters were required to help start new businesses or transfer their technology to local companies as part of winning contracts with GCC states. This requirement—called an "offset"—was codified in laws passed in most GCC states through the 1980s and early 1990s. In Saudi Arabia, offsets were set at 35 percent of the project value through an unofficial arrangement in place since the mid-1980s. In 1992, Kuwait began requiring offsets for all defense purchases over $3 million and set these at 30 percent of the contract value. In the UAE, a 60 percent offset was required on all contracts valued at $10 million or more according to laws passed in the early 1990s (GAO 1996). Offsets became an important feature of accumulation for many domestic conglomerates as they participated as partners in joint ventures that received technology and capital investments from foreign military exporters. The UAE's Nowais Group, for example, was a key partner in Waha Capital—an investment firm established under the country's offset program in 1996 by British Aerospace as it was bidding to sell fighter jets to the UAE government. The group's head, Hussain Nowais, came to chair the board of Waha, helping to arrange financing for military and commercial aircraft sales in the UAE, and Waha remains a major financial partner of the UAE armed forces in the contemporary period.

The Finance Circuit

In the pre-oil period, finance in the Gulf was dominated by the activities of foreign banks tied to the development of colonialism in three countries—Iran, Iraq, and India. The first banks that opened in the Gulf region were branches of colonial banks that existed in one or another of these three countries. Of particular note is the British Bank of the Middle East (BBME), which was later absorbed into the HSBC group. BBME, first known as the Imperial Bank of Persia, was established in 1889 through a royal charter from Queen Victoria and a concession from the Iranian government. The bank was set up by Baron Julius De Reuter as compensation for a concession he was initially granted by the Iranian government to build railways in Iran but which was cancelled under pressure from the Russian Tsar (he later went on to establish Reuters News Agency) (Jones 1987, p. 16).

BBME served as the state bank of Iran until 1928, with the power to issue money and almost completely controlled the Iranian banking sector. Drawing upon the considerable profits it made during World War Two, as well as responding to the nationalist pressures on the bank in Iran, BBME expanded to other Gulf countries. It was the first bank in Kuwait (est. 1941), Dubai (1946), Sharjah (1953), Abu Dhabi (1959), and Oman (1948). Benefiting from its close relationship with British officials who held sway over the financial affairs of these countries, BBME extracted a series of monopoly concessions from local rulers. This included a 15-year monopoly in Kuwait and a 20-year monopoly in both Dubai and Oman. Branches were also established in Bahrain (1944), Saudi Arabia (1950), and Qatar (1954).

British policy toward banking in the region was aimed at undercutting French influence and tying the Gulf to colonial interests in India. A Foreign Office official noted, for example, that the BBME acted as "a counterweight to the [French] Banque de'Indochine" (Jones 1986, p. 12). A historian of banking in the region, Geoffrey Jones, has recorded how British officials blocked the opening of the Ottoman Bank in Bahrain because of its Turkish and French shareholders and the possible competition it presented to the monopoly held by another British Bank, the Eastern Bank (which later became part of the Standard and Chartered Group) (Jones, 1986). A British official reportedly stated: "The existence of British Banks, to the exclusion of all others in the Persian Gulf has . . . made it possible to maintain a sort of exchange control in an area where no statutory control is in force" (Jones 1986, p. 11). With the exception of Saudi Arabia, which had its own currency since Ottoman times, all of the Gulf states used the Sterling-pegged Indian Rupee up until 1959.[29]

The discovery and export of oil from the 1930s to 1950s shifted the way in which Gulf financial circuits were integrated into the global economy. Oil revenues precipitated increased linkages with global financial circuits, with flows directed into foreign banks headquartered in financial centers such as London through rapidly proliferating branches in the Gulf. The General Manager of BBME noted that the bank was "based on oil production" and that "we should remain on our toes to open up a Branch at any centre where oil has been found"—throughout the 1950s, about one-half of BBME's total profits came from Kuwait (Jones 1986, p. 13). With only the embryonic features of a modern state apparatus in many countries throughout the Gulf, foreign banks often played the role of the central or government bank and made enormous profits in the process.[30] In 1959, for example, Kuwaiti deposits along with the deposits of Kuwaiti residents in London represented 47 percent of total BBME deposits (Sherbiny 1985, p. 6).

By the 1960s, however, the growing oil revenues that accompanied the global postwar economic expansion began to stimulate the development of a local banking system. Sentiment for national independence was reflected in the attempt by Gulf monarchies of the two most important oil producers, Saudi Arabia and Kuwait, to establish central banks and monetary authorities in order to issue currency and act autonomously within the market. Concurrently, locally controlled Gulf banks began to emerge under the ownership of large merchant families who were backed by the growing state structures. The appearance of these banks was largely based on the desire of local merchants and rulers to benefit from the lucrative banking business dominated until then by foreign banks and, as such, they followed the same pattern as British banks in investing local deposits in foreign centers such as London (Jones 1986, p. 22).

The first locally controlled bank, the National Bank of Kuwait, was established in 1952 by a group of influential local merchants who—according to official NBK lore—were angered when required to provide a guarantor for a loan from the BBME. In the same year, the Saudi Arabian Monetary Authority (SAMA) was created under the tutelage of the IMF and US advisors to handle the government's oil revenues and issue national currency. The establishment of SAMA paved the way for the opening of the first local Saudi bank, the National Commercial Bank (NCB) in 1953, which had its origins in a local money changing company run by the Bin Mahfouz family.[31] NCB was soon followed by the Riyad Bank (1957) and the Al Watani Bank (1958).[32] Elsewhere in the Gulf other locally controlled banks were also founded at this time, notably the National Bank of Bahrain in 1956 and the National Bank of Dubai in 1963.

The growth of local banks across the region coincided with a series of policies to restrict the entry of the powerful foreign banks. These measures began in Kuwait in 1961 following independence. After formal separation from Britain, no new foreign banks were allowed to operate in the country. Three local banks, all with local merchant interest, were opened during the early 1960s: Commercial Bank of Kuwait (1960), Gulf Bank (1960), and Al Ahli Bank (1967). Independence was also marked by the establishment of the Kuwaiti Currency Board in 1961 and the circulation of a new national currency, the Kuwaiti dinar, which replaced the British-linked currency. When the BBME concession ended in 1971, the local branch was taken over by a Kuwaiti company and relaunched as the Bank of Kuwait and the Middle East. By 1978, there were seven commercial banks—all locally owned—operating in the country.

In Saudi Arabia in 1966, a new Banking Control Law was passed that granted SAMA broad supervisory powers including the granting of licenses and the issuing of rules and regulations. As part of this law, foreign banks were prevented from further expanding their branch networks and the NCB and Riyad Bank consequently ran the vast majority of bank branches in the country until 1975.[33] With the Second Five-Year Development Plan in 1976, the Saudi government introduced a policy that required all foreign-owned banks wishing to expand their branches in Saudi Arabia to incorporate as a local company in which Saudi nationals had majority ownership (SAMA 1999, p. 185). Foreigners were not permitted to own more than 40 percent of the newly incorporated banks but they were given significant management control and interest. By 1979, there were only three non-Saudi banks in operation out of a total of twelve. The total number of bank branches had almost doubled to 140 (SAMA 1999, p. 186).

Reflecting their more dependent character and closer ties to British colonialism, the smaller markets of the Gulf—Qatar, Oman, and the UAE—remained relatively open to foreign banking capital following independence (Bahrain is a slightly different case discussed in Chapter 5). The law establishing the Central Bank of Oman in 1974 contained provisions to facilitate the entry of foreign-owned banks into the Sultanate. In Qatar, the first foreign banks opened following the onset of the oil trade—Standard Bank in 1950, BBME in 1954, and the Ottoman Bank in 1956—and foreign banks continue to play a major role in the country's banking sector. In the UAE, the number of foreign banks has exceeded that of domestic banks since the country's establishment in 1971.

Many of the same conglomerates that benefited from accumulation opportunities in the productive and commodity circuits were also linked to the financial circuit. As can be seen from the list of the top GCC banks in Appendix B, all of these groups are represented on the boards of the large banks and hold significant shareholdings in them, alongside state capital. Indeed, it is striking how well represented these conglomerates are on bank boards—one indication of the importance of the finance circuit to their accumulation. With the exception of the Saudi market and two Omani banks, foreign financial capital has not been heavily involved in the direct ownership of GCC banks, which has tended to remain dominated by capital from the same national origins. This should not be taken to mean, however, that foreign banks did not come to penetrate the GCC financial circuit. As Chapter 5 discusses, this took place through the opening of foreign bank branches in GCC states and activities in offshore markets that hold few restrictions on foreign activities such as exists in Bahrain and, later, the UAE.

Another clear feature of the GCC financial circuit—again paralleling the productive circuit—was the strong involvement of state capital in the banking sector. This was particularly true for the very large banks in each country. The NCB, for example, was for many years the largest bank in the Middle East and came to be 80 percent owned by the Saudi government. The Kuwait Finance House, the second-largest bank in Kuwait and the eighth-largest in the Arab world (by capital) is 43 percent owned by the government.[34] The Kuwaiti government owns one-fifth of Al Ahli United Bank (the third-largest bank in Bahrain) and a share of the Bank of Bahrain and Kuwait, which holds a fifth of all deposits in Bahrain. Likewise, in Qatar and Oman, the state owns significant shares of the two countries' largest banks.[35] Each GCC country has numerous pension funds, state insurance companies, and government institutions through which this state ownership is manifested (see Appendix B).

Caution needs to be taken, however, in drawing an overly sharp distinction between private capital and state funds in the finance circuit. Illustrating once more the fundamental point that ruling families should properly be considered as a component of the capitalist class, banks were often established with initial outlays from the state as a means of assisting private capital that was closely related to those same state structures—with the ruling family controlling both state funds and holding a private interest in the financial circuit. The ruling family of Abu Dhabi, the Nahyan family, provides a particularly clear example. The family dominates economic decision-making in the UAE while simultaneously holding significant private investments in UAE banks including the First Gulf Bank and the Abu Dhabi Commercial Bank. The hazy line distinguishing state and private interests is well captured by the presence of a government department, named the "Department of Private Affairs," which manages the private wealth of the family. Qatar and Kuwait similarly possess many bank boards where members of the ruling family serve in a "private" capacity.

Conclusion

The second half of the 1980s saw a period of "bust" follow the oil boom of the 1970s. From 1980 to 1986 regional crude oil prices fell by nearly 60 percent with merchandise imports dropping by an average of 13.4 percent each year from 1983 to 1986. Consequently, Gulf GDP contracted by 1.3 percent from 1980 to 1989. The subsequent economic crash, however, did not halt the growth of Gulf capital. While all GCC states suffered from fiscal deficits, Gulf citizenry were relatively protected from the downturn and large businesses continued to receive significant subsidies from the state. Indeed, in many cases, this was a period that saw important changes in economic policies that would lay the basis for the growth of Khaleeji Capital in the decades to come. In the UAE, for example, the first of the country's "free zones" was opened in 1985 (Jebel Ali Free Zone) and Bahrain consolidated its offshore banking market by further liberalizing its financial markets. In Saudi Arabia, laws were instituted that protected large conglomerates from foreign competitors and an export-subsidization program was established to assist Saudi businesses in overseas competition (Chaudhry 1994, p. 11).[36]

By the end of the 1980s, large domestic conglomerates had coalesced across the three circuits of capital in each of the GCC states. The development of these circuits was ultimately structured by the nature of internationalization and financialization in the global economy. These two tendencies imbued a major importance to the production of oil as a commodity, with the GCC becoming the key supplier of raw materials and energy to the world market and a central element in the constitution of global financial circuits. Because this took place in the context of sharp rivalries within the world system—all the more significant because of the nature of internationalization—the domination of the Gulf was definitive to the emergence and consolidation of US power.

The development of global capitalism was thus materialized in the formation of each of the Gulf circuits. At a general level, the nature of class in these societies came to be spatially structured around temporary migrant labor flows from surrounding peripheries, overlaid by a relatively privileged layer of citizens. The low levels of population, and the precapitalist social relations that dominated these societies, made this developmental path *possible*—but these factors did not cause or explain the spatial structuring of class. To understand the nature of this spatial structuring (and its link with construction of citizenship) the Gulf must be situated within the broader development of the global economy and the hierarchies that were emerging in the postwar era.

Likewise, in a very real sense, the productive circuit did not arise *within* the local Gulf economies (although it was physically located there), but was constituted as a highly internationalized element of broader global productive circuits. The extended and interlocked branches of the Gulf productive circuit were subsequently structured around energy-rich productive activities, and the immediate needs (such as infrastructure and construction) of societies that were emerging rapidly from the distorted developmental patterns of colonialism. Precisely because of this context, the Gulf commodity circuit was also formed through its relationship with the global economy, characterized by a heavy bias toward foreign imports. And finally, much like the productive circuit, the Gulf financial circuit materialized as a reflection of global capitalism's internationalization and financialization, with a heavy emphasis on constructing links with international financial circuits.

The Gulf state, emerging from the structures established under colonialism, played a key role in enabling and facilitating the development of these new social relations. But, once again, the actions of the state do not explain the *existence* of these social relations or the general form that they took as they materialized within the global economy. The state should be seen as a reflection of these developing capitalist social relations—a mediating link between the Gulf and the international sphere—that emerged alongside the development of class itself. This argument should not be interpreted as minimizing the role of contingency or the actions of individual state (or class) actors, but rather to see the outcome of these contingencies as constrained, shaped, and ultimately reflecting the overall trajectory of world capitalism.

These interrelated processes of the spatial structuring of class and the elaboration of the circuit of capital led to a highly concentrated accumulation of capital in the hands of a narrow social layer across the Gulf states.

The tight linkage between the Gulf circuits of capital and the world economy has profoundly shaped the subsequent development of the region. With the deepening of internationalization and financialization processes in the latest phase of the global capitalist economy, these same capital conglomerates internationalized in step with the internationalization of the Gulf circuits of capital. A new set of social relations is beginning to form around these circuits, Khaleeji Capital, closely tied to the development of US power and the transformation in the global political economy that followed the definitive opening up of China to the world market by the close of the 1990s. The story of this process is told in the following section.

CHAPTER 4

Toward a Single Global Economy:
1991 to 2008

— definitive

The end of the first Gulf War was an important signpost of the major transformation in the global economy that was to ensue over the next decade. George H. W. Bush's proclamation of a New World Order was an initial acknowledgment of this shift, and although it took a number of years to fully develop, by the beginning of the twenty-first century the United States would have achieved the position of global "hyperpower." The collapse of the state socialist bloc and China's opening to the world market during the 1990s meant that a single global capitalist economy was brought into existence. The key feature of this new phase of internationalization was a further qualitative leap in the importance of finance to the functioning of capitalism and, simultaneously, the construction of a world market based upon fully global manufacturing and distribution chains. Both tendencies had enormous implications for the GCC and helped to underpin the rise of Khaleeji Capital at the onset of the twenty-first century.

The economic origins of the new phase of internationalization were found in neoliberalism's triumphant spread across the world during the previous two decades. As Chapter 2 explained, neoliberalism laid the basis for a substantial increase in financial flows and the emergence of complicated production chains interlocked through cross-border ownership structures. A major role in this was played by Third Word debt, which—facilitated by the oil price rises of the 1970s and the concomitant flows of Gulf petrodollars through newly created financial markets—firmly linked poorer countries into the global financial circuits. Neoliberalism's anointment as the accepted economic wisdom throughout the 1980s and 1990s compelled all national economies to open their borders to these financial flows, tying their accumulation patterns to the broader reproduction of the global economy.

A significant step in this process occurred during the late 1980s, when several major debtor countries (notably Chile and Mexico) adopted debt-for-equity plans as part of restructuring debt repayment schedules with commercial banks. These debt-for-equity plans allowed lenders to swap the money they were owed by the debtor country for a stake in a privatized company or asset. At the same time, a World Bank affiliate, The International Finance Corporation (IFC), was developing a theoretical argument that the massive problems faced by the South could be solved if these countries "deepened" their financial markets. The IFC argued that countries in the South should set up stock markets, open up domestic companies to foreign ownership, and offer corporate bonds to private investors in order to mobilize domestic savings and attract surplus capital from around the world. In 1987, the IFC launched an "Emerging Markets Index" and began investing in these markets through a fund of large institutional investors. This change in nomenclature confirmed how the South had been transformed from debt-ridden "problem" into a new investment opportunity.

Under the banner of "financial deepening," countries in the South began to sell sovereign debt on global financial markets to private investors rather than relying on direct loans from governments, commercial banks, or multilateral institutions as had occurred in the past.[1] However, in order for a country to attractively market its debt in this way to foreign investors, it needed to tout its achievements in implementing Structural Adjustment Programs and other neoliberal measures. Forced to attract foreign flows, poorer countries competed among themselves to offer prospective investors enticements such as 100 percent ownership rights and tax-free repatriation of profits. Foreign private capital snapped up privatized assets, bought up shares, and speculated in newly securitized Third World debt. Ever more reliant upon these external capital flows, the deepening of financial markets provoked a self-reinforcing cycle in which greater amounts were needed to cover ballooning private and public debt levels.

Although it took a couple of decades to fully develop, these new financial markets were a pivotal element in the new phase of internationalization. Trillions of dollars of private capital flows moved across the globe, taking ownership shares in assets across every country. One illustration of this shift is shown by the growth in "emerging market" funds: in 1970, according to the World Bank, foreign investment in "emerging country" stock markets was zero. In 1985 it reached US$100 million. By 1994, over US$39.5 billion was invested in "emerging markets" (Henderson 1998, p. 16). By 1999, over 1,000 "emerging markets" funds were operating in the United States alone (Sidaway and Pryke 2000, p. 194).

New Hierarchies of Internationalization

This explosion in global private capital flows was reinforced by the structural transformation of the postwar international state system. As the Soviet Bloc countries collapsed and rapidly opened themselves to foreign investment from 1989–1992, a series of economic policy changes in China also began to reintegrate that country into the capitalist world market. Both these developments extended the reach of capitalist social relations across the vast majority of the globe and consolidated neoliberalism as the dominant economic framework.

As part of the neoliberal drive to reduce wage costs for large firms headquartered in the advanced core, much of global manufacturing was relocated to low-wage and poorly regulated zones in the South. This internationalization of capitalist production, facilitated by the success of neoliberalism in opening up all zones to foreign investment, meant a dramatic cheapening in the cost of production and a large increase in the quantity of commodities entering the world market. The major location of this productive activity was China. Changes in Chinese labor laws and the removal of social protection measures in the countryside during the 1990s encouraged migration from rural to urban areas. This unprecedented wave of proletarianization coincided with measures enacted in 1997 during the Chinese Communist Party Fifteenth Congress that allowed the privatization of state-owned enterprises and the subsequent increase in the proportion of workers engaged in the private sector. Foreign investors flocked to China to take advantage of the seemingly limitless pool of cheap labor. From 1994 to mid-2003, China's exports tripled from $121 billion to $365 billion with foreign investors accounting for 65 percent of the increased exports over that period (Hart-Landsberg and Burkett 2004, p. 83). By 2002, over 40 percent of China's GDP was accounted for by foreign direct investment (FDI) and the country had become the largest recipient of FDI in the developing world (Harvey 2005, p. 135). That year, China became the world's largest exporter of shoes (with a 50 percent market share), produced 70 percent of the world's toys, and was the third-largest exporter of motorcycles. In 2006, China held the largest number of employees of international companies operating overseas in the world, with these foreign affiliates accounting for the vast majority of the country's exports (81 percent in 2002) (UNCTAD 2007, p. 10). By 2009, China would become the world's largest overall exporter.

Other areas such as India, Mexico, Eastern Europe, and some countries in Latin America were also integrated into the global economy as low-wage zones, often dominated by their nearest advanced neighbor. In Mexico, following the 1994 NAFTA agreement, US firms began to shift their most environmentally polluting and labor-intensive production south of the border. Similar processes happened in Eastern Europe, as the former Soviet bloc countries became a cheap labor zone for West European capital. These hierarchical flows were reproduced at a regional level. Thus, within Asia, several countries established Export Processing Zones (EPZs) designed to attract US, Japanese, and European Union (EU) FDI through low wages and minimum regulatory environment. These EPZs were linked into intra-regional trade as producers of intermediate parts and components that were shipped to China for final assembly, and then exported to the US, Japanese, and EU markets.[2]

Finance, Risk, and Debt

At the other end of this hierarchical structure of the world market was the sale of commodities. This became increasingly structured around the consumption of the US (and, to a lesser extent, European and Japanese) consumer. By 2005, the wealthiest 10 percent of the globe accounted for 59 percent of world consumption (World Bank 2008, p. 4). This concentration of consumption in the advanced capitalist countries was starkly illustrated by the fact that, in 2006, private consumption in the United States accounted for 70 percent of US GDP compared to a world average of 59.2 percent and a figure of 38 percent for China.[3] With the United States representing just under 30 percent of global GDP, US consumption was thus the major single source of demand in the global economy. Goods produced in low-wage production zones—using raw materials and labor sourced from other countries in the South—were exported to the United States where they ended up in the ever-expanding homes of an overly indebted consumer. The role of the US market in the global economy was captured in the ubiquitous rise of Walmart as an image of American business success (with its mostly Chinese-produced goods sold in hundreds of stores across the United States, staffed by low-paid workers living close to the poverty line). Most importantly, control of this global chain of production and consumption rested firmly in the hands of large US, European, and Japanese conglomerates.

As this hierarchical structure took form during the late 1990s and 2000s it acted to further reinforce the dialectic of financialization and internationalization. The fully interconnected nature of all zones in the world market meant that companies faced escalating risks due to fluctuations in exchange rates, interest rates, and inflation across the globe. The risks that accompanied the internationalization of capital thus led to the expansion of financial instruments such as derivatives, which allowed investors to "hedge" risk by locking in particular prices into the future.[4] A US company that borrowed money from a Japanese bank denominated in Yen, for example, could purchase a derivative to protect itself against any large fluctuations in the US-Yen exchange rate. Or a US bank that lent money to a company in Brazil could—for a small premium—purchase a derivative (called a Credit Default Swap) to protect itself against the company's default and inability to repay the loan.

Not only did these forms of finance play an essential role in enabling internationalization, they quickly presented an enormous profit-making opportunity for those willing to speculate on changes in future conditions of financial markets (i.e., risk). By betting on movements in currencies, market and commodity prices, interest rates, and so forth, investors could make enormous profits that exceeded those that were to be had by traditional investments. The potential returns could be magnified many times over by increased leverage—borrowing money in order to increase the amount of money available for speculation. Hedge funds and other investment vehicles proliferated to take advantage of these profit-making opportunities by pooling the capital of select groups of "high net-worth individuals" or the pensions of millions of ordinary people.[5]

The development of these financial instruments was instrumental in temporarily overcoming a central contradiction of neoliberalism (later to resurface in the 2007–2008 period): the unprecedented growth in inequality in the advanced capitalist countries caused by the internationalization of capital and neoliberal attacks on employment and wage levels. In the United States, the real annual growth in income of the top 1 percent of earners was 11 percent from 2002 to 2006 while the remaining 99 percent saw their incomes rise by less than 1 percent (Saez 2008, p. 8). Most of the US population had seen a drop in real incomes. An expansion in credit levels helped to ameliorate the problems of global demand that arose from these declining wage levels, with the US consumer able to maintain an ever-expanding consumption through a massive rise in indebtedness. Vast levels of debt taken on through credit cards, mortgages, "zero-down" financing and so forth, helped to maintain the consumption levels that underpinned global demand. US consumer debt levels not only provided real effective demand, but the possibility of seemingly unending consumption played an ideological role that tied the broader population to the support of US financial markets and the political processes that sustained them.

The capital flows that fed this pyramid of debt came from those countries that had accumulated dollars due to their export surpluses. Asian central banks, wealthy private investors, and oil exporting countries purchased US financial instruments, and in effect, lent dollars back to the United States. They were encouraged to do so by the rising prices of various speculative bubbles (stock markets in the 1990s followed by housing prices in the 2000s). These bubbles were fed by low interest rates and speculative flows into new financial instruments called asset-backed securities that combined thousands of different interest payments from mortgages, car and student loans et cetera, in securities that could be bought and sold on the market (a process known as securitization). Banks, US government mortgage agencies (such as Fannie Mae and Freddie Mac), and other firms could then generate more debt for US consumers. In this manner, the recycling of surpluses from the major exporting countries allowed US consumers to take on more debt, which, in turn, they used to purchase the commodities produced in those same exporting countries.

The Gulf Region into the Twenty-First Century

As with the earlier phases of internationalization and financialization, these shifts had critical implications for the Gulf. There were three major elements to this that paralleled the earlier developments in the productive, commodity, and financial circuits. First, Middle East oil and gas exports began an epochal shift eastwards, underpinning the rise of Asia-based production. Second, GCC petrodollars helped to sustain the precarious global imbalances that maintained US dollar hegemony and the US economy's central role in world consumption. Third, the GCC's rapid industrial development meant that the region became an increasingly important market for world exports and services. Each of these trends sharpened the GCC's pivotal position in the reproduction of the global economy and the rivalries that emerged around it.

GCC Oil, World Energy, and International Rivalries

From 2000 to 2006, world energy consumption increased by close to 20 percent, with China alone responsible for 45 percent of the increase in the world's global energy use during this period (IEA 2007, p. 54). Despite the fact that China was the sixth-largest oil producer during this period—and had been a net fossil fuel exporter until 1993—by the mid-2000s the country had become the world's second-largest consumer of oil (behind the United States). By 2006, China was the world's third-largest oil importer, surpassed only by the United States and Japan, with more than 50 percent of its oil needs supplied by imports (IEA 2007, p. 265). China's rapid industrial transformation into the "workshop of the world" was confirmed by the remarkable fact that the country's increase in oil consumption from 1990 to 2006 was the equivalent of a "second Japan" entering the world market during that period.

Throughout this shift, China (along with the rest of Asia) became heavily reliant upon the Gulf as its chief supplier of oil and gas. By 2006, 44 percent of China's crude oil imports came from the Middle East, with Saudi Arabia the largest source of imports (around 16 percent) and Oman and the UAE also figuring prominently (IEA 2007, p. 325). In its annual report for 2007, the International Energy Agency (IEA) projected Chinese oil imports to reach the level of the EU by 2030, with over 80 percent of the country's energy demand eventually met by imports. By 2025, Chinese imports of Gulf oil were expected to reach three times that of the United States—a graphic indication of how the Gulf's commodity exports were shifting eastwards. The growing significance of the Gulf-China relationship was confirmed in 2006 with a visit to China by King Abdullah bin Abdul-Aziz Al-Saud—his first trip outside the Middle East since becoming leader of Saudi Arabia in 2005. The trip resulted in five agreements covering economic and energy issues.

One vital result of this eastward shift in demand for the Gulf's energy resources was a growing struggle between East and West to secure long-term supplies from the area. In 2007 around 40 percent of proven world oil reserves and over 20 percent of proven world gas reserves were located in the GCC (BP 2007). Remarkably, 20 percent of the world's oil production came from just ten oil fields of which four were located in the GCC. The world's largest oil field, Saudi Arabia's Ghawar, was alone responsible for around 7 percent world conventional oil production in 2008 (IEA 2008, p. 225). The GCC was also critical to the world's natural gas markets, with Qatar holding about 14 percent of the world's gas reserves—the third-largest on the global scale following Russia and Iran.

Michael Klare described the implications of this succinctly: "[B]ecause *domestic* [U.S] oil output was expected to experience long-term decline, continued reliance on petroleum would mean ever-increasing dependence on *imported* oil—much of it derived from chronically unstable areas such as the Middle East, Africa, and South America" (Klare 2004, p. 396). The US accounts for around one-quarter of world oil consumption yet holds less than 3 percent of the world's oil reserves (BP 2007). The consequences of this dependency, according to Klare, were clear: "In its pursuit of ever-growing supplies of imported petroleum, the United States is intruding ever more assertively into the internal affairs of oil-supplying nations . . . growing American dependence on these countries is likely to be accompanied by the expanded presence of US military forces in their midst" (2004, p. 420).

Klare's argument receives considerable support from official US government sources. Particularly significant in this regard was the 2001 *Report of the National Energy Policy Development Group*, chaired by US Vice President Dick Cheney. The report clearly linked control of the Gulf region to US "energy security," stating that the Gulf "will remain vital to US interests" and that Saudi Arabia, in particular, would be the "linchpin of supply reliability" (NEPD 2001, p. 4). More than half of all the oil and gas consumed in the United States is imported—close to one-fifth (19 percent) of this consumption comes from the Middle East, mostly from Saudi Arabia (11 percent of total imports) (USEIA).[6] The Cheney report recommended that the US government make "energy security a priority of our trade and foreign policy," a position that has consistently been endorsed by high-ranking officials in the US administration (NEPD 2001, p. 4).

The US and China are not alone in their dependency on Gulf oil supplies. For the EU, it is estimated that 90 percent of oil needs and 70 percent of gas needs would be supplied by imports by 2020 (EC 2000, p. 18). In 2000, a commission of the EU tasked with investigating Europe's future energy security noted the extreme reliance on Middle East—the source of 45 percent of total European oil imports. It concluded that there was an "acute case of . . . dependence" and that "geographic diversification will not be as easily achieved as for natural gas, since the world's remaining oil reserves will increasingly be concentrated in the Middle East" (EC 2000, p. 22). Another major growing economy, India, is also deeply reliant on Middle East oil, with the country predicted to overtake Japan to become the third-largest importer of oil in the world by 2024, behind the United States and China (IEA 2007, pp. 495–96).[7] Most of India's imports come from the Middle East (67 percent), with the largest supplier, Saudi Arabia, accounting for 25 percent of its crude oil imports. Two other GCC countries, the UAE and Kuwait, are also major exporters of crude oil to India.

In this context, the ability to dominate the Middle East formed, in the words of British writer Alex Callinicos, a "potential chokehold on other leading powers in the world" (2005, p. 599). This had been a clearly articulated strategy of the US government since the first Gulf War. Callinicos notes that a Pentagon report, the Defence Planning Guidance, leaked to the *New York Times* in 1992 stated: "Our first objective is to prevent the re-emergence of a new rival . . . this requires that we endeavour to prevent any hostile power from dominating a region whose resources would, under consolidated control, be sufficient to generate global power . . . we must maintain the mechanisms for deterring competitors from even aspiring to a larger regional or global role" (cited in Callinicos 2005).

...se global rivalries, however, in the latest ... to be carefully differentiated. Although ...d the United States was ever-present ...owers continued to share a common per-/global capitalism and the strategic signifi-/Middle East region. In contrast, the rivalry ...ifferent form. As Gilbert Achcar has particu-...ng powers each possessed formidable military strength as a holdover of ... earlier conflict between the state socialist bloc and the capitalist world. China's growing economic weight on the global stage (symbolized by the large quantity of US debt it came to hold) and Russia's ongoing control of significant oil and gas resources, generated a qualitatively different and more pronounced antagonism with US power than that existing between the United States and Europe. Both China and Russia, although not advanced capitalist economies in the sense of the EU and the United States, were the "only two declared opponents of American hegemony whose behaviour [was] unpredictable in the middle and long term and whose physical scale places them on comparable footing with the US" (Achcar 1998, p. 102). Although this rivalry did not precipitate a military conflict with the United States, it was a vital element in the recalibration of US interests and the nature of its projection of power in the Gulf region.

One of the notable features of this shift in US power was the strategic linkage made between Central Asia and the Gulf region. The collapse of the USSR created a number of newly independent states in the Caucasus and Central Asia—Uzbekistan, Kyrgyzstan, Tajikistan, Kazakhstan, Turkmenistan, Georgia, and Azerbaijan. Strategically located at the meeting point of Russia, Europe, Asia, and the Middle East—and possessing extremely large quantities of energy resources (particularly natural gas)—these states were immutably linked in US strategic vision with the GCC countries, Iraq, Iran, Afghanistan, and Pakistan.[8] This single arc of countries lay at the heart of what former Carter administration National Security Advisor, Zbigniew Brzezinski, called "Eurasia." As the new phase of internationalization emerged, Brzezinski, the key architect of Saudi support for the *mujahideen* in Afghanistan during the 1980s (and later an advisor to US President Obama), described the region's significance with startling prescience: "For America, the chief geopolitical prize is Eurasia ... Now a non-Eurasian power is preeminent in Eurasia and America's global primacy is directly dependent on how long and how effectively its preponderance on the Eurasian continent is sustained" (Brzezinski 1997, p. 30). This perspective was confirmed in 1999, when US Central Command

(CENTCOM)—one of the most important US military institutions responsible for all military engagement, planning, and operations across 27 countries—was extended to include five Central Asian countries: Turkmenistan, Uzbekistan, Kazakhstan, Kyrgyzstan, and Tajikistan.

The 2001 attacks on the World Trade Center and the Pentagon provided a sharp ideological justification for the projection of US power across this new zone. The attacks were a clear illustration of "blowback"—the unintended consequences of earlier US foreign policy alliances. In this case, the cultivation of Saudi-Pakistani support for Islamic movements in Afghanistan had helped to nurture a militant, Islamic fundamentalism (Achcar 2002). The September 11 attacks were initially deployed by the US government to legitimate the US-NATO invasion of Afghanistan in 2001, followed by the 2003 invasion of Iraq. Gulf states provided extensive basing, training, and port facilities for the US military during these invasions. In the north of Kuwait, one-third of the country was closed off in order to host US troops during the 2003 US-led invasion of Iraq (Katzman 2006, p. 9). Also in 2003, the US military announced that it was moving CENTCOM forward command headquarters from Florida to Qatar. By 2005, according to a US congressional report, over 100,000 US military personnel were located in Gulf states (in addition to the approximately 130,000 in Iraq or security personnel operating under civilian firms) (Katzman 2006, p. 10).

Petrodollar Redux: Global Imbalances and GCC Surplus Capital

The Gulf's energy supplies were not the only reason for the region's pivotal position within the new hierarchies that emerged in the post-2000 period. With the massive increase in demand for energy that followed in the wake of China's manufacturing growth, the price of oil rose from $9.76/barrel in January 1999 to $90.32/barrel in November 2007—a nearly tenfold increase (USEIA). A second spike occurred in the first half of 2008, as prices jumped from $94/barrel at the beginning of the year and peaked at over $145 in July. As the price increased so did the volume being sold. As a result, revenues in the oil exporting countries rose at a remarkable annual rate of 27 percent from 2002 through 2007, and then by a further 50 percent in 2008 (McKinsey 2009, p. 2). As oil and gas from the Gulf flowed eastwards, a new wave of petrodollars accumulated in the region—much of which was to flow westwards into US financial markets where it was recycled as credit for US consumers and businesses. These flows were thus a critical feature of the particular form that financialization of the global economy took in the post-2000 period.

, ... , percent domestically, by 2006, the split was 56–44 percent (McKinsey 2009, p. 5).[11] For all oil exporting countries, new foreign investments rose at a rate of 53 percent each year between 2002 and 2007. By 2008, investors from oil exporting countries were spending the equivalent of $3.6 billion per day on purchasing foreign assets (McKinsey 2009, p. 2, figures for 2008). It was estimated that every $10 increase in the price of oil sustained for one year added around $90–100 billion to the asset accumulation of oil exporting governments (Tolui 2007, p. 4).

As the key oil exporting zone, the GCC was the single-largest component of these windfall revenues. The foreign assets of GCC central banks and government-related funds increased from $0.5 trillion at end-2002 to an estimated $1.6 trillion at the oil price peak in July 2008, according to the Institute for International Finance (IIF 2007, p. 2) If the considerable amount of foreign-based assets held by GCC private companies, individuals, and the ruling families were included, estimates reached in excess of $2.2 trillion at end-2007 (McKinsey 2009, p. 7). An appreciation of the enormous scale of these assets can be seen in the fact that they exceeded those held by China's central bank in the same year and were more than the combined GDPs of Australia and India for 2008.

Much of these investments were made by Sovereign Wealth Funds (SWFs), large quasi-government agencies established by many countries to manage natural resource revenues. The amount of money controlled by SWFs is huge—in 2007, the world's top 20 funds were estimated to control USD$2.1 trillion, bigger than the amount invested in both hedge funds and private equity funds (Wolf 2007). The GCC is the most important location for these funds at a global scale, with the world's largest SWF, the Abu Dhabi Investment Authority (ADIA), found in the region.[12] ADIA does not reveal its size or investment strategy, but estimates for ADIA's wealth ranged from $457 billion to almost $900 billion at end-2007 (the latter figure was equivalent to 461 percent of UAE GDP or US$207,000 per UAE citizen) (Solh 2008, p. 9; Setser and Ziemba 2009).[13]

Despite general agreement on these broad magnitudes, it is difficult to reliably identify where GCC surpluses have been invested.[14] SWFs generally do not disclose the size or distribution of their holdings and the many individuals and private companies in the GCC with significant foreign assets often do not reveal them publically.[15] Moreover, in some cases, different accounting methods are used by GCC government agencies to measure the value of foreign assets held.[16] With these caveats in mind, however, some estimates are available of the general size and patterns of GCC foreign asset holdings in the first decade of the twenty-first century. According to the McKinsey Global Institute, four GCC countries held most of the GCC's foreign assets during the post-2000 wave of accumulation—Saudi Arabia ($780 million), UAE ($870 million), Kuwait ($300 million), and Qatar ($140 million) (McKinsey 2009, p. 4). This ownership was distributed between three main investor types—SWFs, government central banks, and private bodies (both high-wealth individuals and private companies). At an aggregate level, SWFs held around 67 percent of foreign holdings of the four Gulf countries ($1.39 trillion), with 28 percent ($594 million) and 6 percent ($130 million) held by private bodies and central banks, respectively. These aggregate figures, however, obscure significant differences between each of these four countries. In Saudi Arabia and Qatar, for example, private investors hold very large proportions of the total assets held outside the country (40–44 percent).[17] In the UAE and Kuwait, SWFs predominate (78 percent and 67 percent, respectively).

Although there is no detailed accounting of the types of assets held by these investment bodies, two major sources of information help to piece together some patterns in petrodollar investment. First, as with the earlier phases of internationalization discussed in Chapter 2, some of these flows went to international banks that then recycled them through the international financial system as loans and other forms of credit. These flows can be determined with some accuracy from the Bank of International Settlements (BIS), which presents data on the international position of BIS reporting banks. Second, petrodollars were invested in the global equity and bond markets. Figures for these flows are difficult to determine, as most markets do not break down investments by national origin. Nevertheless, there have been several attempts to measure these flows for the US market, where Treasury International Capital (TIC) statistics give data on foreign purchases of US equities and bonds. It is important to note, however, that TIC data does not reveal purchases made through a third-country broker or custodian. It is generally assumed that Middle East buyers constitute a high proportion of these third-party purchases (through UK brokers in particular) due to a desire to keep purchases anonymous.[18] Furthermore, TIC data does not differentiate between GCC and Middle East oil exporters as a whole.

Middle East oil exporters ended up in banks from 2002–2006—a proportion significantly lower than earlier periods (p. 5).[19] This can be contrasted with a non-Middle East oil exporter such as Russia, which placed 57 percent of its oil revenues in BIS reporting banks over the same period.

Rather than placing petrodollars in the banking system, GCC countries showed a much higher propensity to place these funds in the US markets (equities, bonds, and other asset purchases). TIC data shows that Middle East oil exporters placed from 50–70 percent of their identifiable petrodollars in US equities and bonds from 2002–2007.[20] From June 2005 to June 2006, GCC countries showed the fastest growth of any country in the world in their holdings of US securities—increasing by over 50 percent over the one-year period (Sturm, Strasky, Adolf, and Peschel 2008, p. 43). These figures confirm that GCC capital flows were a major element in sustaining the high levels of US debt that characterized the structure of the global economy in the post-2000 period.

The third major type of foreign asset purchase by GCC countries in this period was cross-border mergers and acquisitions. These need to be tracked on an individual basis, but there is considerable evidence that GCC investors directed a large proportion of their asset purchases to this type of activity.[21] Indications of this became clear in the summer of 2007 as Gulf companies and SWFs made over US$20 billion worth of investments in teetering US and UK banks and other companies. Some of the world's largest firms—Credit Suisse, Barclays Bank, Daimler AG, Volkswagen, Porsche, J Sainsbury, the New York Stock Exchange, the London Stock Exchange, Citigroup, and many others—came to count Gulf investors among their largest shareholders.[22]

Regardless of the exact breakdown of investments, all evidence indicates that GCC petrodollar flows were heavily concentrated in dollar-denominated assets and US capital markets (Chapter 6 discusses flows to Middle East in more detail). Data on mergers and acquisitions—combined with information gleaned from TIC and the rare disclosure of asset distribution by SWF managers—has led to a broad consensus that around 50–55 percent of all GCC investments have been located in the US markets in the post-2000 period (EIU 2008, p. 6). In comparison, around 20 percent has gone to Europe, 10–15 percent to Asia and 10–15 percent to Middle East and North Africa (KCIC 2009, p. 29). Of particular note in this regard is Saudi Arabia, which has continued to direct its oil revenues into the purchase of US-based assets. Two leading analysts of petrodollar flows, Brad Setser and Rachel Ziemba, estimated that 80 percent of the Saudi Arabia Monetary Agency's (SAMA) foreign holdings were dollar-dominated in 2008. The huge size of SAMA's holdings, $390 billion in 2008, coupled with an estimated US$420 billion held by private Saudi investors in the United States, means that Saudi Arabia alone accounted for nearly three-quarters of a trillion dollars investment in the United States (SABB 2008, p. 5).[23] SAMA's dollar-denominated proportion was higher than other GCC SWFs (which were estimated to hold around 50 percent in US dollar assets) but less than some other GCC central banks (the UAE, for example, held 95 percent of its central bank assets in US dollars) (Setser and Ziemba 2009, p. 10). In this regard, it should be noted that media hype around a withdrawal of Gulf-investments from the United States following the September 11 attacks was highly exaggerated.[24]

Whether commanded by SWFs, private capital, or central banks, these new Gulf petrodollar flows thus played a critical role in enabling the hierarchical world market that took shape during the post-2000 phase of internationalization. Along with similar capital flows from Asian countries, they enabled the United States to continue running a growing current account deficit—which deteriorated by about $400bn between 2002 and 2006—and absorb the ever-increasing mass of commodities produced in China and other low-wage zones across the globe. In 2001, the combined surpluses of oil exporting countries were equivalent to around one-fifth of the US current account deficit. By 2006, this had risen to about two-thirds of the deficit (Tolui, 2007, p. 2). From 1998, petrodollar flows essentially switched places with Western Europe as the second major origin of global savings—complementing those from East Asia. In early 2007 oil exporting countries were the biggest source of global savings, having surpassed East Asia in 2005 and adding half a trillion dollars in assets in 2006—close to 40 percent of the total from the world's surplus countries.[25] In recognition of the centrality of the Gulf to the global financial structure, the investment bank Morgan Stanley was to argue that capital from the Gulf was "playing a crucial role in propping up global markets [and] in the adjustment of global economic imbalances" and noted that the Gulf was more important than China in supporting demand for international bonds (2006, p. 6). Another investment firm, McKinsey & Company, described these petrodollar flows as the largest of the world's "four new powerbrokers"—alongside Asian central banks, hedge funds, and private equity firms.

generally accounted for around 50 percent of the value of total North America, European, and Asian merchandise exports to the GCC. Asia ranked second (with around 30 percent of export value) and North America last with 20 percent. From 2000 to 2005, however, the North American share of exports decreased from 20 to 15 percent of total export value from the three blocs, as market share was lost to Asian exporters.[26]

In an attempt to address this falling market share, US economic policy took an aggressive turn during the 2000s aimed at tightening trade and financial links at the expense of rival powers. The United States announced in mid-2003 a plan to achieve a Middle East Free Trade Area (MEFTA) from North Africa to the Gulf by 2013. The US strategy was to negotiate individually with "friendly" countries in the region using a graduated 6-step process eventually leading to a full-fledged free trade agreement (FTA) between the United States and the country in question. These individual FTAs would then be linked over time until the entire Middle East came under US trading influence.

The US government explicitly conceived these FTAs as a means to promote the interests of US capital vis-à-vis rival capitals in alternate blocs. World Bank President and former US trade representative, Robert Zoellick, captured these intentions in an editorial for the *Wall Street Journal* in 2003 when he stated: "The Bush administration's reinvigoration of America's drive for free trade—globally, regionally, and with individual countries—has created a momentum that strengthens US influence . . . [they] level the playing field for US businesses because others—especially the EU—negotiated a host of agreements in the '90s while the US stood on the sidelines" (Zoellick 2003a). The Washington-based CATO Institute further noted in a widely-cited article at the time of MEFTA's announcement, that although winning Middle East export share was "one good reason for the United States to pursue additional FTAs in the region, it [was] not the most important reason" (Lindsey 2003, p. 8). Rather, what MEFTA and the FTA strategy facilitated was "market opening in the Muslim world"—in other words, the penetration of the GCC region (and the remainder of the Middle East) by US capital. Of particular importance—described by CATO as "the biggest prize . . . but the hardest to attain"—was access to the market in services

(Lindsey 2003, p. 8). This blunt assessment by a leading US think tank was indicative of the important changes foreseen in the Gulf region and the potentially lucrative opportunities that would open up for US capital.

Immediately after announcing the MEFTA initiative, US representatives began a rapid succession of FTA negotiations with countries in the Middle East, focusing particularly on the GCC as a central pivot of the overall strategy. The GCC was a gateway region that could be used to generalize links with other countries—an intention explicitly acknowledged by US government officials, who designed FTAs so that countries could "moor" with neighboring states and thereby expand agreements into subregional agreements.[27] The United States signed an FTA with Bahrain on September 14, 2004, and legislation to approve and implement the agreement was passed by Congress in January 2006. In September 2005, the United States and Oman also agreed on the basic principles of an FTA and signed an agreement on January 19, 2006. In 2005, the United States began negotiations with its largest export market in the Middle East, the UAE, although these stumbled toward the end of the decade. In the same year Kuwait and Qatar also expressed interest in obtaining an FTA with the United States (Katzman 2006, p. 28). All of these negotiations complemented other regional agreements between the United States and Egypt, Israel, Jordan, and Morocco. Simultaneously, other countries and blocs began FTA negotiations with the GCC: China in 2004, Japan in 2005, Singapore in 2006, Australia and New Zealand in 2007. The EU had earlier signed an Economic Cooperation Agreement with the GCC in 1988, opening the way to negotiations for a bilateral FTA that began in 1990, but the talks were to be mired in disputes for the next two decades.[28]

Despite the successful agreements with Bahrain and Oman, FTA negotiations tended to move slowly as Gulf states feared the potential implications of opening major economic sectors to international capital. MEFTA and the bilateral US FTAs were not successful in halting the Gulf's eastward trade orientation—trade between the GCC and Asia increased fourfold between 1995 and 2005 and, by 2007, more than half of the GCC's total trade of US$758 billion was with Asia. These rivalries confirmed the signal importance of the Gulf region to the latest phase of internationalization, and the accompanying sharpening of competitive struggles to dominate the region's import markets.

Conclusion: The Foundations of Khaleeji Capital

The fundamental trends of internationalization and financialization—long-standing themes of postwar capitalism—experienced their fullest

... providing the energy and raw materials that girded the expansion of internationalization, its financial flows balancing the global deficits that emerged as a necessary result of the unevenness of the world market. At a political level, domination of this space became a central determinant of the ability to shape and influence the contours of this world system.

The process of class formation that underpinned the emergence of Khaleeji Capital materialized within and through these developments of the global political economy. Khaleeji Capital was a particular, unique, and concrete expression of the tendencies that came to shape the broader global economy. As the Gulf region crystallized as the key energy and financial pivot of the world market, it acted to enable and catalyze the broader tendencies of the most recent phase of internationalization. At the same time, the Gulf region expressed those tendencies internally through a profound shift in its own set of capitalist social relations. A qualitative transformation of the GCC economy ensued, encompassing the large conglomerates across the productive, financial, and commodity circuits. For the capitalist class formed in the earlier phases of internationalization, accumulation came to be more and more conceived at the pan-GCC scale rather than through a nationally bound perspective, while simultaneously tightly linked to global patterns of accumulation.

The Formation of Khaleeji Capital

A new capitalist class is developing in the Middle East. This new class, Khaleeji Capital, expresses the tendencies of internationalization through all moments of the circuits of capital and operates at a pan-GCC scale. Its internationalization is occurring at the regional scale—i.e., it is a process of internationalization through regionalization. To emphasize once again, however, internationalization should not be understood as delineating a "thing" (e.g., quantities of money, investment flows, or a form of company structure) but rather, conveys the manner in which the circuits of capital are themselves elaborated at the regional scale. The notion of Khaleeji Capital is not meant to imply that the Gulf capital groups no longer identify as "Saudi," "Kuwaiti," and so forth. Indeed, these national identities may even become more pronounced as internationalization proceeds. Rather "capital," as Marx emphasized repeatedly, is a social relation, and the concept of internationalization speaks to the nature of social relations as they form around the circuits of capital within the GCC space. Khaleeji Capital represents a new set of social relations that are developing around pan-GCC accumulation opportunities; they are cotemporaneous with—and are overlaid upon—ongoing structures of national accumulation. These social relations more and more crystallize, articulate, and interpenetrate in a pan-GCC space. Consequently, accumulation is increasingly conceived at the regional scale rather than through a nationally bound perspective.

The institutional underpinnings of this pan-Gulf accumulation structure can be traced back to changes that occurred within the GCC in the late 1990s and early 2000s. In this period, the regional integration project embodied by the GCC took major steps forward, facilitating the internationalization of the Gulf conglomerates identified in Chapter 3. A significant legislative market in this process was the Economic Agreement between the States of the Cooperation Council (EASCC), signed at the 2001 GCC Muscat Summit.[1] Its orientation toward GCC capital was made clear in the preamble, where "enhancing market mechanisms and fostering the role of the private sector" was explicitly laid out as a central goal of the agreement. The EASCC also linked the achievement of "advanced stages of economic integration . . . lead[ing] to a Common Market and an Economic and Monetary Union among Member States" as a specific response to "recent global economic developments." Deepening integration was partly conceived as a defensive response to these shifts in the global economy, in order to enable GCC states to "strengthen their negotiating position and competitive capacity in international markets" (SG 2001).

The EASCC helped to begin an institutional restructuring that displaced power upwards to the regional scale, weakening the ability of individual member states to control the movement of capital and goods within the intra-GCC space. These institutional shifts included the establishment of a customs union that promised national treatment throughout the GCC for any good produced by a member state (Article 1), further updated in 2003 with the adoption of the *Common Customs Law for the Arab States of the Gulf (GCC States)*.[2] Article 2 of the EASCC established a common external tariff for the entire GCC region, which was eventually set at 5 percent.[3] The regulations of the customs union and the common external tariff aimed at allowing all goods to move freely across intra-GCC borders (apart from health and quarantine inspections). Article 3 established a common market that permitted GCC citizens to move freely across member states and work without discrimination in all professions. The common market also called for standardized treatment in tax, pensions, and social services, and the ability for citizens to own real estate in other Gulf states. Articles 4, 5, and 6 extended the integration process to the financial circuit by committing member states to fully integrating capital markets, harmonizing all financial laws and regulations, and removing any discriminatory ownership provisions for shares and other investments in the GCC. Requirements for majority national ownership of strategic industrial and financial companies were dropped completely or replaced with majority GCC provisions (Sturm and Siegfried 2005, p. 31).

While these measures have begun to transform the ways in which the circuits of capital are articulated across the Gulf region they should not be read in a teleological fashion, with progress toward regional unity assumed to be an unbroken and inherently linear process. In many cases, these EASCC articles expressed hoped-for goals that have not been completely fulfilled. While many of the GCC agreements have been "enthusiastically embraced by intellectual and business elites" who see the GCC as a "vehicle for 'top down' liberalization," Gulf leaders have sometimes shown themselves reticent to relinquish decision-making ability to the supranational scale

...........impact—an agreement to establish a monetary union and single currency by 2010.[5] A timetable was established for this goal: by 2002 all national currencies would be pegged to the US dollar (fulfilled in 2003);[6] by the end of 2005 a series of convergence criteria would be established that member states would strive to reach by 2010;[7] and in January 2010 a single currency would be introduced. The key element of monetary union (and one of the reasons why some Gulf states have shown reluctance to join) is that it forcibly circumscribes policy choices within a framework established at the supranational, regional scale. The supranational scale becomes the determining sphere for national economic policy. This is a point made clear by the European Central Bank in a report on the GCC, which notes that a "single monetary and exchange rate policy has to be geared to economic, monetary and financial conditions in the single monetary area as whole." In order to achieve this, each member state has to be "deprived of monetary and exchange rate policy as an adjustment tool to cope with divergent economic developments, for example, in the event of an asymmetric shock" (Sturm and Siegfried 2005, p. 45). While the US-dollar peg already restricts "monetary and exchange rate policy" the basic point remains—a single currency means that states will need to relinquish control over important areas of economic decision-making. It is for these reasons that progress toward the monetary union was to encounter difficulties in 2010 (see Chapter 7).

A further pressure propelling the institutional restructuring that underlies the internationalization of capital in the GCC was the proliferation of bilateral and multilateral free trade agreements. All GCC countries joined the World Trade Organization (WTO)[8] and, as noted in the previous chapter, a number of free trade agreements were signed with the United States and several other countries. These agreements acted as disciplinary mechanisms that pushed individual countries to increasingly open their economies to capital flows.[9] This is well illustrated in the case of Saudi Arabia, which, in 2005, became the last GCC country to join the WTO. Its admission to WTO membership was a protracted and complicated process that began in 1996 and took just under a decade to complete. It was predicated on a series of sweeping institutional reforms that reshaped the decision-making structure of the state—setting up institutions that were closely tied to "reform-minded" individuals in the state and leading business elites—and enhancing a series of laws around privatization, opening up of the Saudi economy to foreign investment, and the reduction of tariffs and other obstacles to the inflow of capital. Indeed, some analysts have argued that WTO accession was the main driving force behind economic changes in the Kingdom (Niblock 2007, pp. 185–91; Hertog 2010, pp. 223–45).[10]

These institutional shifts in the trade and financial regimes of the GCC coincided with the massive run-up in the price of oil discussed in the last chapter. From 2002 to 2006, the extra liquidity for countries producing more than 1 million barrels/day of oil amounted to US$1.02 trillion. For the Gulf alone, over US$510 billion of extra liquidity was generated in the 2002–2006 period (Lubin 2007, p. 29).[11] This liquidity was reflected in the rapid increase in the current account surpluses of the Gulf countries, which the IMF estimated to be 22 percent of GDP in 2007, the highest of any region in the world. Table 5.1 shows the differences between the GCC current account surpluses in the 1990s and the first half of the 2000s that resulted from this rise in the oil price. The impact of these unprecedented surpluses on the Gulf circuits of capital was profound. In addition to the wave of foreign asset purchases described in the previous chapter, GCC states used these accumulated funds domestically—pouring money into huge infrastructure and industrial plans.

By 2008, the GCC's average per capita nominal GDP reached $28,000—nearly triple that of the wealthiest non-GCC Arab state, Libya, where GDP per capita stood at $10,519.[12] Table 5.1 summarizes the main changes in GDP and the relative weighting of different economic sectors in the GCC states in the post-2000 period. It confirms that all states saw sustained and rapid growth in GDP throughout this period. From 2003 to 2007, the Compounded Annual Growth Rate (CAGR) of nominal GDP ranged from 15.47 percent in Saudi Arabia to 31.84 percent in Qatar. Across the whole GCC, nominal annual GDP growth reached 19.3 percent over the five-year period, one of the highest in the world. Oil and gas continued to be the main economic component of GDP—averaging more than half of GDP in Kuwait and Qatar, just under one-half in Saudi Arabia and Oman, and fluctuating around one-third in the UAE.[13] Only Bahrain saw a consistent downward trend in oil and gas as a component of GDP over the 2003–2007 period. Saudi Arabia and the UAE represented the largest shares of the GCC economy, constituting between 70–80 percent of regional GDP over the 2003–2007 period.

Coupled with the institutional and economic policy changes at the level of the GCC and within each GCC state, these surpluses helped to enable a rapid internationalization of the leading Gulf conglomerates throughout

Table 5.1 Current account surpluses and GDP growth rates in the GCC

Current Account Surpluses

Country	Current account surplus (US$ billion) 1992–2001	Current account surplus (US$ billion) 2002–2006	Difference between 1992–2001 period and 2002–2006 period (US$ billion)	1999 ca account (percent GDP)
Bahrain	-0.7	5.5	6.2	-0.3
Kuwait	55.5	112.1	56.5	16.8
Oman	-2.2	14.5	16.7	-2.9
Qatar	-4.9	46.2	51.1	12.5
Saudi Arabia	-38.9	302.6	341.5	0.3
UAE	39.1	77.1	38.1	1.6

GDP/ Oil and Gas Growth Rates

	2003	2004	2005	2006
Bahrain				
Nominal GDP (US$)	9.4	11.21	13.42	15.81
Nominal GDP Growth	15.3	19.8	17.8	16.4
Crude Oil and Gas (US$)	2.09	2.07	2.09	2.29
Crude Oil and Gas as % of GDP	22.2	18.5	15.6	14.5
Kuwait				
Nominal GDP (US$)	53	65.2	87.8	109.7

Table 5.1 Continued

	2003	2004	2005	2006	2007 (CAGR 2003–2007)
Nominal GDP Growth	23	22.9	34.7	25	8
Crude Oil and Gas (US$)	21.73	29.1	45.5	61.1	64.6 (31.30)
Crude Oil and Gas as % of GDP	41	44.6	51.8	55.7	54.5
UAE					
Nominal GDP (US$)	87.7	105.3	139.8	170.2	199 (22.7)
Nominal GDP Growth	17.9	20.1	33	22	16.8
Crude Oil and Gas (US$)	25.08	33.59	50.47	61.10	71.44 (29.91)
Crude Oil and Gas as % of GDP	28.6	31.9	36.1	35.9	35.9
Qatar					
Nominal GDP (US$)	23.5	31.7	42.5	56.8	71 (31.84)
Nominal GDP Growth	21.5	34.8	33.8	33.7	25.1
Crude Oil and Gas (US$)	13.87	17.28	25.33	32.55	40.19 (30.45)
Crude Oil and Gas as % of GDP	59	54.5	59.6	57.3	56.6
KSA					
Nominal GDP (US$)	214.6	250.3	315.3	348.7	381.5 (15.47)
Nominal GDP Growth	13.8	16.7	26	10.6	9.4
Crude Oil and Gas (US$)	85.63	104.88	143.15	188.65	183.12 (20.93)
Crude Oil and Gas as % of GDP	39.9	41.9	45.4	54.1	48

Oman			
Nominal GDP (US$)	21.5	24.6	30.8	36.8
Nominal GDP Growth		14.5	25.3	19.1
Crude Oil and Gas (US$)	9.03	10.58	15.22	17.52
Crude Oil and Gas as % of GDP	42	43	49.4	47.6
GCC Total GDP	409.7	488.31	629.62	738.01
Crude Oil and Gas as Share of GCC GDP	38.42	40.44	44.75	49.21
Bahrain as share of GCC GDP	2.29	2.30	2.13	2.14
Kuwait as share of GCC GDP	12.94	13.35	13.94	14.86
UAE as share of GCC GDP	21.41	21.56	22.20	23.06
Qatar as share of GCC GDP	5.74	6.49	6.75	7.70
KSA as share of GCC GDP	52.38	51.26	50.08	47.25
Oman as share of GCC GDP	5.25	5.04	4.89	4.99

Source: GDP figures calculated by author from Central Bank reports. Current account surpluses from Lubin, 2007, p. 3; IMF 2007, p. 236.

*ambitious development
schemes post 1999*

the GCC region. Accumulation patterns began to shift in each of the three moments of the circuit of capital, evincing both a deepening internationalization as well as the growing size and influence of the Gulf capital groups. A closer examination of each of the circuits confirms these patterns.

The Productive Circuit

With the rise in state revenues from 1999 onwards, all the GCC countries embraced ambitious development schemes. These included a vast array of large-scale infrastructure projects—new cities, airports, universities, road and rail facilities, power and water provision, bridges and buildings—as well as industrial development (focused on energy, petrochemicals, and metals). Growth in these sectors had a mutually reinforcing effect. As industrial development proceeded, for example, so did the demand for energy.[14] The development of new cities required construction of rail and road networks to link new population centers and workplaces. The GCC conglomerates identified in Chapter 3 were closely linked to these development projects.

Confirming the scale of this rapid development, the value of Middle East projects reached US$1 trillion in 2006, making it the world's largest project finance market and claiming one-third of global project financing (Scott 2007, p. 9). In July 2007, the total size of projects under way or announced had increased by another 50 percent to US$1.5 trillion—and the importance of the region's expanding project market was graphically symbolized by the decision that year of the US contracting giant Halliburton to move its CEO from the United States to the UAE in order to improve its chances in the region (Standard and Chartered 2007, p. 2). By November 2008, the value of projects reached US$1.9 trillion, the equivalent of 170 percent of the 2008 GCC GDP, with Saudi Arabia and the UAE accounting for almost 70 percent of total value (IIF 2008, p. 1).

One indication of the prodigious scale of this development is shown in Table 5.2, which gives the annual rate of change of Gross Fixed Capital Formation (GFCF)—a measure of the net new investment in fixed capital assets by enterprises, government, and households within the domestic economy. From 2002 to 2007, most GCC states had annual double-digit growth in GFCF, with Qatar and Bahrain showing the most rapid growth. While GFCF should not be interpreted as an exact measurement of the value of fixed capital, it does give a general indication of the remarkable rate at which GCC economies invested their surpluses in development schemes over the post-2000 period.

The scale of these investments is further reflected in the significant expansion in construction and manufacturing activities across all GCC

				ง.๐	11.1
2005	13.6	31.53	49.1	25.1	15.4
2006	26.6	36.1	36.3	19.1	29.0
2007	n.a.	29.7	10.4	25.4	22.7
Average 2002–2007	30.66	27	32	15.4	16.5

Source: Author calculated from national statistics, IMF Database. Data for Oman unavailable.

states in the post-2000 period. By 2007, these two sectors made up just under one-third of GCC non-oil GDP—up from around one-quarter in 2000.[15] There was rapid double-digit annual growth in these productive activities over the post-2000 period—most notably in Saudi Arabia and the UAE, which together contributed around 75–80 percent of regional GDP for these sectors over each year from 2003 to 2007.

The growth in construction and manufacturing was strikingly confirmed in the breakdown of GCC labor forces. In Saudi Arabia, these two sectors constituted nearly 50 percent of all private sector labor in 2005 (SABB 2007, p. 9). Likewise in Qatar, 46 percent of total employment was found in the construction and manufacturing sectors in 2007—virtually all of these workers were migrant labor (GIH 2008a, p. 29). For the UAE, employment in construction and manufacturing accounted for 37 percent of employed labor in 2005, up from 30 percent in 1995 (UAE MoE). The number of these workers meant a pronounced bias in the demographic profile of the UAE—according to the 2005 UAE census more than two-thirds of the population was male, a result of the fact that most migrant construction and manufacturing workers did not earn the minimum amount required to bring their families into the country.[16]

The weight of construction and manufacturing in the GCC economies was particularly significant for the development of domestic capital. Excluded from the upstream oil and gas sector, these two activities were the key moments around which capitalist class formation proceeded in the productive circuit over the post-2000 period. They presented lucrative and numerous possibilities for accumulation, strengthening the development of the large conglomerates and encouraging the centralization and concentration of capital in their hands. Moreover, as a closer examination of each of these activities indicates, the patterns of class development display a growing tendency to interpenetrate across GCC member-state borders, concomitant with the deepening of regional integration.

Construction and Contracting

As Table 5.1 shows, from 2003 to 2007, Saudi Arabia and the UAE were the primary regional centers for GCC construction and contracting work, annually constituting around 50 percent and 30 percent, respectively, of total GCC construction sector GDP over this period. In both these states, the value of construction rose more than 20 percent each year in the 2003–2007 period.[17] Much of this construction was in the real estate sector, but other "mega-project" contracts were also significant. One industry breakdown of GCC projects in 2006 showed real estate construction to be worth $525 billion; oil, gas, and petrochemical projects accounting for the second-largest share ($328 billion), followed by power and water ($70 billion) and other industry ($44 billion) (MEED 2006a).

One of the institutional factors enabling the expansion of construction was the liberalization of property laws that occurred in each GCC state in the late 1990s and early 2000s. In Saudi Arabia, for example, the Investment & Real Estate Law of 2000 allowed non-Saudi residents to own real estate for their private residence with the permission of the Interior Ministry and also enabled foreign investors to own business properties and the accommodation needed for their employees.[18] In the UAE, ownership laws were liberalized in each emirate throughout the post-2000 period. A significant step in this process was the Registration Law (Law No. 7), issued by the UAE government on March 13, 2006, which legalized free-hold ownership of land and property to UAE and GCC nationals (and gave similar rights to non-GCC expatriates in designated areas). The Qatari government also issued a decree in June 2004 that allowed non-Qataris to hold 99-year renewable leases for property in a few selected projects that were to become major investment schemes in the country (Pearl Island, West Bay Lagoon, and Al Khor Resort). In 2006, this scheme was extended to another 18 selected areas and also opened the market for GCC nationals to own and trade property freely. Similarly in Bahrain, Oman, and Kuwait the real estate market was opened to allow some limited foreign ownership in selected projects and areas.

Much of the GCC's construction activity in the post-2000 period focused on the UAE (particularly the emirate of Dubai), which, at the end of 2007, had $121 billion worth of construction projects under way and US$468 billion planned (compared to second-ranked Saudi Arabia's US$21 billion and $150 billion, respectively) (Foreman 2008). Utilizing those striking—11 out of the 15 are from those two countries—indicative of the size of the project market in those two countries and the importance that it plays in capital accumulation for the leading capital groups (see Appendix A). In the overall rankings (i.e., including foreign companies), six out of the top ten companies are Saudi or Emirati, including the top three.[20] Accumulation is heavily concentrated in the hands of the largest companies—66 percent of the project value listed in Table 5.3 was held by the top five companies.

Much like the earlier phases of construction, this activity is generally structured through tiered levels of subcontracting. A development company, usually controlled by a Gulf conglomerates or a state-backed firm, owns the overall project. In many cases, particularly for complex projects, the architectural design and engineering is contracted to a foreign company. The owner will contract another large company (typically from the list in Table 5.3) to construct the project. In turn, this company will subcontract manual labor and specific tasks (such as piling) to smaller companies in order to complete the work. While there are thousands of small-scale construction companies, the large companies listed in Table 5.3 dominate building activities for the major real estate projects.

A closer analysis of these companies indicates their growing pan-GCC orientation. Four out of the ten largest contractors in Qatar in 2007 were UAE and Kuwaiti companies (Redfern 2008a). In the same year, the largest contractor in Bahrain was a UAE company (Redfern 2008b). Table 5.4 also shows that there is an increasing emphasis, particularly by the largest companies, to expand to other GCC construction markets. This is a recent phenomenon, with most of the subsidiaries launched in the early 2000s. The UAE has been a target location for these subsidiaries, which have subsequently won many of the largest projects in the country (such as Bahraini Cebarco's work on infrastructure for the Abu Dhabi Grand Prix), but internationalization is also evident in other GCC markets.

This increasingly pan-GCC character of the GCC construction sector is further confirmed in Table 5.4, which provides an analysis of 87 of the largest construction projects occurring across the GCC at end-2009.[21] The data focuses upon construction of buildings, towers, and residential areas for which information on ownership and contracting status is available

Table 5.3 Top 15 GCC construction companies, 2007

MEED top 50 ranking	Company name	Country of origin	Other GCC subsidiaries	Value of GCC projects 2007 US$mn
1	Saudi Oger	Saudi Arabia	Established Oger Abu Dhabi and Oger Dubai in 2003 and 2005, respectively.	5,340
2	Saudi Binladin Group	Saudi Arabia	Has one UAE-based subsidiary, responsible for many large projects in the country.	4,500
3	Al-Jaber Group	UAE	Launched a Qatari subsidiary in 2002.	3,450
5	Al-Habtoor Leighton Group	UAE/Australian	Joint venture in Saudi Arabia in 2009.	3,030
6	Arabtec Construction	UAE	Subsidiary in Qatar in 2006 and a joint venture in Saudi Arabia in 2009 with the Binladin Group (Arabtec Saudi Arabia).	2,730
10	Al-Hamad Contracting	UAE	Subsidiaries in Bahrain and Oman. Won the contract in 2004 for Bahrain Financial Harbour, which includes the tallest building in the country.	1,500
12	Al-Arrab Contracting	Saudi Arabia	Subsidiaries in Dubai and Qatar.	1,359
16	Al-Shafar General	UAE	UAE-focused	1,100
17	Mushrif Trading	Kuwait	Subsidiaries in UAE and Qatar. In 2007, more than 50% of Mushrif's employees were based in the UAE. Around 45% of the companies turn-over was outside of Kuwait in 2007 (Sell 2008, p.51).	1,045
20	ETA Ascon	UAE	UAE-focused	953
21	Cebarco	Bahrain	Has a UAE subsidiary and was heavily involved in construction work for the Abu Dhabi Grand Prix.	895
24	Dutco Balfour Beatry	UAE/UK	UAE-focused	808
25	Combined Group	Kuwait	Subsidiaries in Qatar (2005), Oman (2008) and plans to launch in UAE and Saudi Arabia.	775
27	Midmac	Qatar	Qatar-focused	730
28	Dubai Contracting Company	UAE	UAE-focused	681

Source: Company Annual Reports; MEED 2006b.

No. of projects involving pan-GCC groups	13	7	9	3	6	2	40
Pan-GCC projects as % of total no. of projects	34%	39%	53%	60%	100%	66%	46%
Pan-GCC projects as % of total project value	53%	87%	67%	56%	100%	92%	75%

Source: Author analysis of project contracting data. Projects are building contracts for towers, buildings, and residential areas with a minimum value of $150 million. Only projects that are ongoing and for which either ownership or contracting information is available are shown (that is, projects under tender are not included unless they are directly owned by a nondomestic, GCC entity). The "involvement of pan-GCC groups" is defined as a major stake in ownership or development, the leading contractor position, or the leading construction role in the project. Project information has been drawn from *Construction Week* database.

(not infrastructure, petrochemical, or oil and gas projects that tend to be dominated by large foreign companies). Each of these 87 projects has been examined to determine the extent of involvement by GCC capital from outside of the project's home country—defined through either ownership, or holding the lead contractor or construction role in the project.

Table 5.4 is a good indication of the manner in which the GCC construction sector has developed in the recent period. As is to be expected, the largest numbers of projects are found in the UAE and Saudi Arabia. These two countries are the location of the largest construction companies and thus have a lower share of involvement in their construction sectors originating from neighboring GCC states. Nonetheless, the pan-GCC proportion remains markedly high (34 percent and 39 percent, respectively) in these two states. Moreover, pan-GCC projects tend to be concentrated in the largest and most expensive projects, as is shown by the proportion of project value that they constitute (53 and 87 percent). In Qatar, Kuwait, Bahrain, and Oman, a strong majority of projects have a pan-GCC character. This confirms that the internationalization process in the construction sector is hierarchical in nature, and has taken place through the penetration of the smaller markets by larger GCC capital (mostly from the UAE and Saudi Arabia)

Manufacturing

One of the drivers of increased construction activity was the expansion of GCC manufacturing in the post-2000 period. Manufacturing grew at double-digit annual rates in all Gulf states during the 2003–2007 period, and although its growth rate was slower than construction, it represented a higher share of non-oil GDP. By 2007, 20 percent of GCC non-oil GDP was being produced through manufacturing activities (as opposed to 11.56 percent by construction).[22] As with the earlier developmental phases of the Gulf, much of this manufacturing involved the production of energy-rich commodities such as aluminum and steel, which—in addition to forming a significant component of the region's non-oil exports—were also vital inputs for building and construction.[23] However, the most important trend in manufacturing over this period was the expansion of downstream petrochemical production. Throughout the 2000s, all Gulf states utilized fiscal surpluses to finance the construction of refineries and plants for chemicals, plastics, and fertilizers.

Each of these manufacturing sectors was closely linked to the development of the domestic capitalist class, with the large capital groups discussed in Chapter 3 major beneficiaries of growth. The expansion of these conglomerates in the manufacturing sector was further characterized by the pronounced degree of internationalization across GCC borders. Ownership cross-penetration was marked in all manufacturing activities, and involved both state capital as well as private domestic capital. This cross-penetration confirmed the growing scale of GCC manufacturing and hence the centralization and concentration of capital within the region. In some cases it also catalyzed the cross-border enmeshing of other industries—notably the supply of raw energy sources to feed the expansion of commodity manufacture. An examination of the aluminum, steel, and petrochemical sectors illustrates these trends.

Aluminum

The Gulf's share of global aluminum production increased from 1 percent in 1980 to 6 percent in 2006 and is predicted to reach 10 percent by 2020 (GIH 2007, p. 9).[24] The two primary smelters mentioned in Chapter 3—Bahrain's ALBA and Dubai's Dubal—continued to dominate regional production of raw aluminum. Other GCC states, however, announced plans to construct smelters in the post-2000 period, including Qatar (Qatalum), Oman (Sohar Aluminium), the UAE (Emal), and two smelters in Saudi Arabia. Sohar Aluminium and Qatalum began producing aluminum in 2008 and 2009, and Emal in 2010. By the end of the decade, Saudi Arabian plans had yet to see fruition. If implemented, however, they would make Saudi Arabia the largest producer of primary aluminum in the GCC.

This upstream component of the aluminum industry generally remained dominated by state capital with a significant level of involvement by foreign

...y ...unority, and the global giant Alcan. Emal is a joint project between the emirates of Dubai and Abu Dhabi.

In addition to the production of raw aluminum, around 20 major firms across the GCC were involved in the further processing of aluminum into wires, cables, sheets, and molded products by the late 2000s. Construction growth was a large driver of demand for these activities—in 2007, for example, it was estimated that 90 percent of the aluminum used in the Middle East was used in architectural applications in the real estate sector (GIH 2007, p. 23). Bahrain, Saudi Arabia, and the UAE were the key geographical locations of this manufacturing activity—holding more than three-quarters of the major downstream aluminum firms (GCG 2008, p. 10). Unlike the upstream sector, these firms were generally controlled by private GCC capital, and involved the expansion of companies established in the earlier phases of industrialization. Important examples of groups with a connection to this sector included the Olayan, Ali Reza, Gosaibi, Aujan, and Aggad Groups in Saudi Arabia; Al Ghurair, Owais, and Mazrui Groups in the UAE; the Al Shaya and Kharafi Groups in Kuwait; and the Zayani Group in Bahrain.

The aluminum market is particularly significant to Bahrain, where ALBA and other aluminum manufacturing companies contribute around 10 to 12 percent of the country's GDP—far in excess of any other GCC country. Downstream Bahraini companies utilize over 40 percent of ALBA's production. Like ALBA itself, these companies show a highly pronounced tendency toward joint Gulf ownership structures. The largest downstream aluminum company in both Bahrain and the Gulf, the Gulf Aluminium Rolling Company (Garmco), is jointly owned by governments and financial institutions from every GCC country (along with a small share held by the Iraqi government). The other two major Bahraini downstream companies Balexco and Midal Cables are also pan-GCC owned, each with heavy involvement of some of the conglomerates listed in Appendix A.[25]

Steel

The GCC steel industry is more developed and dispersed throughout each GCC state than the aluminum sector. Once again, construction has been a major driver of the industry, with per capita Gulf consumption of steel reaching more than double the world average by the mid-2000s (GOIC

2006). In 2005, the UAE was the world's fourth-largest net importer of steel with much of these imports reexported to neighboring GCC countries (IISI 2005). As with aluminum, the region's steel industry is predicted to expand over the next decade as planned steel projects come on line.

Table 5.5 shows the 15 major GCC steel companies and the level of primary steel produced by each country in 2007. Saudi Arabia was the largest producer in the region, contributing around 45 percent of the total steel produced in the GCC. Bahrain was the second-largest producer, with one primary steel company and a stainless steel factory. Oman, the UAE, and Qatar produced similar amounts of steel (around 7–8 percent of the GCC total). Kuwait was the region's smallest producer.

Table 5.5 demonstrates the high level of internationalization in the region's steel industry and its control by GCC private capital. The Bahraini and Omani markets are completely controlled by companies that have pan-GCC ownership structures. The UAE and Saudi Arabia also have significant investment from other GCC capital (although they remain dominated by companies owned by national capital). Steel companies in the two smallest markets, Qatar and Kuwait, are virtually entirely nationally owned—but capital from both these countries has significant levels of investment in other GCC steel markets.

Petrochemicals
The production of refined petroleum products such as plastics, fertilizers, and chemicals became the most important manufacturing sector in the GCC during the post-2000 period. The reasons for this were related to the shifts in the global economy described in the previous chapter. Most significantly, the global demand for petrochemicals expanded as a response to China's growing import needs. In the GCC, the availability of cheaper feedstocks for petrochemical production meant that the region became a major global source through joint ventures involving state, foreign, and domestic capital groups.[26] This hastened the Gulf's transition toward downstream refining and petrochemical production rather than a primary focus on upstream supply of crude hydrocarbons.

The focus of this petrochemical production was ethylene, which constitutes 40 percent of the total volume of worldwide petrochemical production and is a basic building block for more advanced plastics such as polyethylene, polystyrene, and PVC, and fibers such as PET and polyester. Industry analysts predicted that the Gulf would account for 20 percent of global ethylene capacity by 2011, an increase from around 5 percent in 1993. During the same time period, US-based capacity will have dropped from close to 70 percent of world capacity to around 40 percent (HSBC 2007,

(7.8)

	Hadeed	SABIC subsidiary
	Al-Ittefaq steel mills	Al Tuwairqi Group (Saudi Arabia, majority owner) and Gulf International Bank (Bahrain)
	Al-Rajhi steel	Al Rajhi Group (Saudi Arabia)
	United Gulf Steel	Manso Group (Saudi) and Mazrui Group (UAE)
	Attieh Steel	Attieh Group (Saudi Arabia)
	Al Azizia Steel	n.a.

Bahrain (5)

	Gulf Industrial Investment Company	Gulf Investment Corporation (GCC governments), Qatar Iron and Steel (Qatar), Kharafi Group (Kuwait), National Industries Group (Kuwait), Kuwait Foundry (Kuwait)
	United Stainless Steel Company	QASCO (Qatar), Al Rashid Group (Saudi Arabia), the Al Kharafi Group (Kuwait) and the National Industries Group (Kuwait)

Oman (1.5)

	Shadeed Iron and Steel Company	Al Ghaith Holdings (UAE)
	Al-Jazeera Steel Products Company	Global Investment House (Kuwait) and Omani investors

UAE (1.4)

	Al-Ghurair Iron and Steel Co.	Al Ghurair Group (UAE)
	Qatar Steel Company	QASCO (Qatar)
	Emirates Steel Industries	Abu Dhabi government
	Al-Nasser Industrial Enterprises	Al Nasser Holdings (UAE)

Qatar (1.2)

	QASCO—Qatar Steel Company	Industries Qatar (Qatar)

Kuwait (0.6)

	United Steel Company	Kuwaiti and German investors

Source: Steel production numbers from Global Investment House 2008c. Company information from company reports and regional stock market databases.

p. 8).[27] The average ethylene capacity per production site in the Middle East nearly doubled from 1993 to 2005, surpassing the average for Western Europe by the mid-2000s.[28]

Much like the trends for crude oil discussed in the previous chapter, this increased supply of petrochemicals from the Gulf was accompanied by an eastward shift in exports—particularly to China. In 2004, China imported about 42 percent of globally traded polyethylene, 44 percent of polypropylene, 45 percent of PVC, and 48 percent of polystyrene (Nexant 2004, p. 31). By 2005, almost half of SABIC's petrochemical sales were going to Asia (compared to only 10 percent to the United States and 14 percent to Europe) (Kharboush 2006, p. 11). One of the consequences of this increased eastern demand for petrochemicals was an expansion of Chinese investments in both GCC upstream and downstream sectors.[29] At the same time, GCC companies made several significant investments in Chinese petrochemical and refinery industries. In 2007, for example, Saudi Aramco, in partnership with Sinopec and Exxon-Mobil, launched an integrated refinery and petrochemical facility in the Quanzhou province in Fujian, China. The project, completed in 2009, received the largest ever project financing for a Sino-Foreign joint venture in China (around US$4 billion) (Winning 2007). It also included a long-term crude supply agreement with Aramco, which meant that the company's logo would be displayed on 750 retail locations throughout the country. Aramco is not alone in these Chinese investments—two other Saudi petrochemical companies, SABIC and Sipchem; the UAE's Borouge; Qatar Petroleum International; and the Kuwait Petroleum Corporation (KPC)—all announced major investments in the Chinese petrochemical sector in the late 2000s.

Not surprisingly, Saudi Arabia dominated the expansion of the GCC petrochemical sector in the post-2000 period, accounting for 76 percent of the total regional petrochemical production in 2007, followed by Qatar with 11 percent. Some estimates put the share of the global petrochemical industry of Saudi Arabia as almost doubling from 7 percent in 2005 to 13 percent by 2010 (GIH 2007, p. 37). In 2006, Saudi oil, gas, and petrochemicals "megaprojects" were valued at US$115 billion and constituted around 40 percent of the total projects under way in the country (SAMBA 2006, p. 17).[30]

Like the construction and manufacturing sectors, the expansion of the downstream Gulf hydrocarbon industry has been structured through tiered levels of subcontracting and ownership. In this sector, however, the demands of complex technical and design work strengthened the weight of large international engineering, procurement, and construction (EPC) firms that are active on the global scale. The largest EPC contracts in the

...mentation of the GCC economies and affirming the logic behind US trade policy in the region (see Chapter 7).

In 2006, around two-thirds of all project value in the Saudi petrochemical sector originated in state or state/foreign joint ventures—mostly related to investments made by SABIC. Nevertheless, there were significant indications of the pan-GCC nature of accumulation in this sector. In 2005, the UAE overtook Japan to become the largest source of Foreign Direct Investment (FDI) into Saudi Arabia, much of it in the petrochemical sector. One-third of the largest petrochemical projects in the country were being carried out exclusively by pan-Gulf groups (7 out of 21 projects) in 2006, constituting around 18 percent of the total project value (SAGIA 2007, p. 49). Table 5.6 shows the ownership patterns for the largest non-state, non-foreign owned petrochemical companies in Saudi Arabia by ownership of the eight publicly listed petrochemical companies (Saudi Arabia Industrial Investment Co., Tasnee, SIPCHEM, Alujain, NAMA, Sahara, APPC, and Saudi Kayan) and one limited liability company (Chemanol). These nine companies are the largest non-SABIC petrochemical companies in the country. It confirms the extensive interlocking of Saudi and non-Saudi GCC capital in the petrochemical sector, seven out of these nine petrochemical companies have significant levels of GCC cross-ownership. This interlocking has mostly taken place through hierarchical joint ventures, in which one or more Saudi conglomerates dominate ownership and other large GCC capital are inserted as junior partners.

These trends for the Saudi petrochemical sector confirm the importance of cross-border investments to the Gulf productive circuit. Alongside the growing pan-GCC activity in the construction and other manufacturing sectors, they are an indication of how capital groups from across the Gulf conceive their accumulation from the perspective of the Gulf as a whole, rather than just within their individual countries.

Other Sectors of the Productive Circuit

The productive circuit is not restricted to the production of physical goods but also includes the development of new technological industries such as media and telecommunications. As industrialization proceeded in the Gulf region, these have emerged as key accumulation points for the leading

Table 5.6 Largest non-state, non-foreign petrochemical companies in Saudi Arabia

	Largest shareholders and board representation	GCC ownership
Saudi Arabia Industrial Investment Group	Rajhi, Gosaibi, Juffali, and Bin Zagr groups; Saudi government	Saudi Arabia
Tasnee	Al Shaer Corporation 12.8%	Saudi Arabia
	Gulf Investment Corporation 7.9%	Owned by all six GCC governments
	Kingdom Holding 6.1%	Saudi Arabia
	National Industries Group 5.2%	Kuwait
	Saudi Pharmaceutical Industries and Medical Appliances Corporation 5.2%	Saudi Arabia
SIPCHEM (The Saudi International Petrochemical Co)	Zamil Group 10%	Saudi Arabia
	National Industries Group 8%	Kuwait
	Olayan 7%	Saudi Arabia
	Al Ghurair 5%	UAE
	Al Rajhi 3.3%	Saudi Arabia
Sahara	Zamil Group 10%	Saudi Arabia
	Al Jazeera Petrochemicals 5%	UAE
	Bin Mahfouz Group 3%	Saudi Arabia
	Frimex 3%	UAE
Alujain Corporation	Prince Mohammed Bin Nayef Al Saud	Saudi Arabia
	Binladen Group	Saudi Arabia
	Ali Reza	Saudi Arabia
	Rajhi	Saudi Arabia
	Mohammed Ali Naki	Kuwait
	Yusef Kanoo	Bahrain
Nama Chemicals Company	Zamil	Saudi Arabia
	Gosaibi	Saudi Arabia
	Al Moajil	Saudi Arabia
	Dubai Investments	UAE
	Al Bahar	Kuwait
Chemanol	Zamil 22.5%	Saudi
	Kanoo 22.5%	Bahrain
	Mazrui 10%	UAE
	Nafisi 10%	Kuwait
	Mohammed Jalal and Sons 10%	Bahrain
	Al Mana Group 10%	Qatar
APPC Advanced Polypropylene Co. (also has Belgian and US ownership)	Dar Chemicals 15.92%	Saudi Arabia
	IDB Infrastructure Fund 9.02%	Bahrain
	National Polypropylene Company [NPPC] 7.96%	Saudi Arabia
	Mada Industrial Investment Company 2.65%	Saudi Arabia
	Abdul Rahman Saad Al Rashid and Sons 2.55%	Saudi Arabia
	Al Ghurair Group 1.45%	UAE
	Khaled Abdulrahman Saleh Al Rajhi 1.24%	Saudi Arabia
Saudi Kayan	Saudi Investors	Saudi Arabia

Source: Various company reports (share ownership shown where known).

...........istics. In the case of television, for example, the number of channels across the Middle East grew from 18 in 1993 to 150 in 2005 (BAH 2005, p. 16). By 2009, a spokesperson for MBC Group, one of the largest media conglomerates, claimed that there were over 450 channels in operation, but with control highly concentrated—the top 10 channels claiming more than 70 percent of advertising revenue (EB 2009). Five major media conglomerates came to dominate free-to-air and satellite TV throughout the 2000s (major ownership in parentheses): ART (Saudi Arabia's Dallah Al Baraka Group); Middle East Broadcasting Corporation, MBC (Sheikh Walid bin Ibrahim al-Ibrahim the brother-in-law of Saudi Arabia's King Fahd); LBC-Rotana (Saudi Arabia's Kingdom Holding Group); Orbit (Saudi Arabia's Mawarid Group); Showtime Arabia (Kuwait's KIPCO [79 percent] and the US' CBS [21 per cent]).

For each of these groups, the Middle East region (and particularly the GCC) is seen as a single market. One-third of the free-to-air TV market share in Saudi Arabia, Kuwait, and the UAE is held by the two Saudi companies MBC (26 percent) and LBC-Rotana (7 percent) (BA 2005, p. 20).[31] Virtually all of the Pay TV audience in each GCC country is divided between ART, Showtime, and Orbit, with close to 150 channels between them. In 2009, the internationalization of capital in this sector was further confirmed by the merger of Showtime and Orbit, with ownership divided equally between the Kuwaiti KIPCO and the Saudi Mawarid Group. The headquarters of the new company, Orbit-Showtime, as well as those of MBC, are located in Dubai's Media City, a media-focused economic free zone. The merger is a strong illustration of internationalization in the GCC—a joint Saudi/Kuwaiti company, headquartered in the UAE, holding a major share of the market in all GCC countries.[32]

The telecommunications sector in the Middle East shows similar trends of ownership concentration and internationalization. It is considered an important target of the global telecommunications industry, with the highest worldwide growth rate in cellular subscribers from 2002 to 2007 (GIH 2008b). As with media, it is highly concentrated, with a few large GCC-based companies dominating the provision of mobile, fixed-line, and Internet services for the entire region. All GCC countries underwent liberalization during the 2000s, as they opened up their markets to telecoms from neighboring countries. Kuwait was the first to offer a second telecom license (1998–1999), followed by Saudi Arabia, Bahrain, and Oman (2002–2003) and the UAE and Qatar (2006–2007) (Halaoui, Hasbani, Mourad, and Sabbagh 2008, p. 3). By the end of the decade, five GCC telecoms dominated the region (see Table 5.7). The internationalization of these companies has moved in step with liberalization, so that three pan-GCC companies came to control cellular market share in Saudi Arabia (Saudi STC, Kuwait's Zain, and UAE's Etisalat), Kuwait (Zain, STC, and Qatar's Q-Tel), and Bahrain (Batelco, STC, and Zain). The later liberalizers, Qatar and the UAE, remain dominated by local companies (Q-tel and Etisalat, respectively) although this is likely to change as their markets open.[33] It should be emphasized that each of the five companies in Table 5.7 have extensive operations in other regional markets across Africa, the rest

Table 5.7 Telecommunications companies in the GCC

Company	Country of origin (date of establishment)	GCC operations
Zain	Kuwait (1983)	Holds the third mobile license in Saudi Arabia. Holds the second mobile license for Bahrain through its subsidiary MTC Vodafone, with 40% market share in 2007.
Saudi Telecom (STC)	Saudi Arabia (1998)	Holds the third Kuwait mobile license, through its ownership of Viva. Viva held 10% share of the Kuwaiti cellular market after one year of operation. Awarded the third mobile license in Bahrain in 2009.
Etisalat	UAE (1976)	Holds the second mobile license in Saudi Arabia through its subsidiary Mobily. Mobily held 41% of the Saudi mobile market by end-2007.
Q-Tel	Qatar (1987)	Holds second mobile license in Kuwait through its 51% share in Wataniya. In 2007, Wataniya held 43% of Kuwait's mobile market. Wataniya also operates in Saudi Arabia, through its subsidiary Bravo. QTel's Omani subsidiary, Nawras Telecom, held 41% share of the Omani market.
Batelco	Bahrain (1981)	Holds a 15% stake in Atheeb Telecommunications, which holds Saudi Arabia's second license for operating fixed-line services. Owns a subsidiary, Qualitynet, which holds the largest market share of internet service in Kuwait.

Sources: Company websites.

...panies have also been listed on regional stock exchanges and through this mechanism are closely linked to the large GCC conglomerates. These linkages are frequently reflected by the representation of the major conglomerates as board members of the telecom companies.

The Commodity Circuit

The enormous pool of surplus capital accompanying the post-2000 phase of internationalization has been the central factor shaping the development of the GCC commodity circuit. These flows have meant that the region has become a significant market for imported commodities; a tendency reinforced by the characteristics of the productive circuit outlined above. Industrial production of capital goods such as machinery and heavy equipment is largely undeveloped. Instead, industrial manufacturing is dependent upon imports from the advanced capitalist countries. Likewise, the production of basic consumer goods (e.g., food products, automobiles, household items, etc.) has been small scale and the sector is import-dominated. This dependence on imports is reflected in the large proportion of retail sales generated by international brands: in 2006, more than 50 percent of GCC retail sales were international products with the ratio as much as 80:20 (international brands versus homegrown) in the leading malls (Furey 2007).

For each year from 1980 to 2000, the Gulf's import trade grew slower on average, than the rest of the world.[35] From the early 2000s, however, this relative weight shifted. In the 2003–2006 period, imports to the GCC grew by more than 20 percent annually, more than double the world average. During this period, GCC import growth even exceeded the levels of China, a country frequently held up as symbolizing the new era of globalized trade. These rapid increases in the value and size of imports were commensurate with growing oil revenues, urbanization processes, and the development of the downstream sectors noted above.

At the level of consumer goods, the growing demand for foreign imports was partly a reflection of the increasing wealth of GCC citizenry, with public sector workers receiving record wage increases through the second-half of the 2000s. The largest such increase was in the UAE, where public sector workers were granted a 15–25 percent raise in 2005 followed only two years later by a remarkable 70 percent salary increase. Likewise, public sector workers in the remaining GCC states received double-digit annual pay rises throughout 2005 to 2007. While these increases were framed as a means of lessening the impact of high inflation rates on Gulf residents, their magnitude far exceeded inflation levels. Their limitation to the public sector—where the overwhelming bulk of citizens are employed—further confirmed the privileging of citizenry that underlies the spatialization of class in the GCC. In addition to demand for consumer goods, however, the pace of construction and industrial development meant that machinery and transport equipment also constituted a large proportion of imports throughout the 2000–2008 period. This was particularly the case in Saudi Arabia, Qatar, and Oman, where imports of this type made up more than 40 percent of total import value in each year from 2002–2007. In Bahrain, the UAE, and Kuwait, the proportion was around 20 percent.[36]

The increasing scale of both consumer and industrial imports in the GCC meant that foreign exporters—from their position as the main supplier of goods—sought ever larger and unified markets. The ability to access neighboring markets was also a major incentive for GCC conglomerates, particularly considering the limited population base of the smaller GCC states (the Saudi market, for example, approaches 24 million potential consumers compared to less than 1 million in Qatar). This provides a strong tendency toward the internationalization of commodity flows through the Gulf region, in which each GCC member state operates in a regionally articulated fashion within a unified commodity circuit. These trends have been further propelled by the establishment of a customs union and free trade area across the Gulf; goods can move relatively freely between different GCC states, and the duty for any item entering the region is largely standardized regardless of the point of entry (see above).

An important implication of this internationalization tendency is that the regional bloc increasingly mediates the import and export patterns for each individual GCC state. Externally sourced imports enter the GCC through two states in particular—the UAE and Saudi Arabia—and, in turn, other GCC states tend to rely upon these two countries for their imports. In 2005, for example, Saudi Arabia and the UAE imported approximately US$10 billion and US$12 billion worth of manufactured goods, respectively, from the rest of the world. These levels were 5–10 times greater than those received by any of the other Gulf states.[37] In the case of the UK, around 80 percent of the country's exports to the GCC in 2006 went to the UAE and Saudi Arabia (GDN 2007).

There is an important difference, however, between the UAE and Saudi Arabia in regard to these GCC imports. This difference relates to the phenomenon of "reexports"—goods that are exported from one country to

...world, and then reexports them to other GCC countries. In 2004, the UAE was responsible for 81 percent of the total US$23 trillion worth of GCC reexports.[38] In 2003 and 2004, reexports constituted around one-third of the value of all UAE exports (this figure is all the more striking in that it includes the export of hydrocarbons to the international sphere) (UAEY 2006, p. 80). At an international level, the UAE is one of the global centers for the reexport trade (along with Singapore and Hong Kong), operating primarily out of the UAE's free zones that provide a tax and regulation-light environment for foreign investors.[39]

As the major interlocutor between the national and international scales, it is unsurprising to find that international capital views the UAE as a "gateway" market to the rest of the region, where the receptivity for goods can be tested before being tried in other GCC countries.[40] Saudi Arabia is also a major entry point for foreign commodity capital but these flows are of a qualitatively different nature than the UAE entrepot trade. Due to Saudi Arabia's central position in the regional productive circuit, foreign commodity imports such as machinery, equipment, or chemicals are utilized within the Saudi productive circuit. Rather than the reexport of internationally produced commodities, Saudi exports to the GCC are concentrated in food and dairy products, cement and other building materials, and basic industrial chemicals such as organic chemicals and plastics in their primary form.

The importance of this regional trade is confirmed by the ratio of non-oil intra-GCC exports to total non-oil exports, rising from 17 percent in the mid-1990s to 23 percent by 2005 (GCC Secretariat General 2010, Table 63). United Nations trade data indicates that by 2004/2005, Saudi Arabia and the UAE were supplying Bahrain, Qatar, and Oman with approximately one-third of all their imports in the key sectors of food, manufactured goods, chemicals, and machinery. This marked a qualitative jump from ten years earlier in which these three countries received around 15–20 percent of their imports in these sectors from Saudi Arabia and the UAE.[41] Indeed, by the mid-2000s, the UAE or Saudi Arabia ranked as one of the top five exporters to Kuwait, Bahrain, Qatar, and Oman for every import sector except for machinery and transport. For Oman, the UAE was the top exporter in every sector except for machinery and transport (in which it ranked second).[42]

These characteristics indicate that the trade relationship between individual GCC states and the international sphere cannot be understood solely through the lens of the national space. Rather, each Gulf state needs to be located within a regional system, which interacts with the global economy as a whole and is then articulated internally through the network of intra-GCC trade. The region as a whole must be conceived in systemic terms, in which the GCC forms an integrated unity rather than a simple agglomeration of component states. This is powerful evidence of the internationalization of the GCC commodity circuit, in which the new regional space mediates the relationship that exists between the national and the global scales.

GCC Logistics and Distribution Sector

One important consequence of this integrated regional commodity circuit is the significance of the logistics, warehousing, shipping, and freight business for the GCC capitalist class. The value of this sector in the GCC was estimated at US$18 billion in 2008, around 4 percent of non-oil GDP (Kogler, Majdalani, and Kuge 2009, p. 3). A handful of large companies dominate this business regionally, most of which operate out of Dubai (further indication of the emirate's role as the primary entrepot center in the GCC). In addition to international companies such as DHL, FedEx, and UPS, several GCC-owned firms are prominent in the industry. These local firms have formed an important site of accumulation for Gulf capital.

Two illustrative examples of these firms are the Kuwaiti-owned Agility and the UAE-Jordanian company Aramex. Agility is the largest GCC logistical firm, and has been controlled by the Essa family since its privatization in 1997 (known at the time as the Public Warehousing Company). Agility provides transport, facility management, and warehousing across the GCC, with its largest Middle East distribution center located in the Jebel Ali Free Zone in Dubai. In addition to these services, Agility has been a prominent contractor for the US military, supplying food to US military troops in Kuwait and Iraq, and providing logistical services and construction work for US bases in Afghanistan.[43] The Essa family is a strong indication of the development of Khaleeji Capital, with involvement in retail and financial activities across the GCC (see Appendix A).

Aramex is a logistics and freight-forwarding company and although headquartered in Amman, Jordan, its main base of activities is in the UAE. It was established privately in Jordan in 1982 and became the first Middle Eastern company to be listed on the Nasdaq in 1997. In April 2002, a majority stake in Aramex was purchased by the GCC private equity group Abraaj, an important example of Khaleeji Capital (see below for further discussion of Abraaj), and the company was delisted. Later that year it was across each of the GCC states, and many of the large Gulf conglomerates have a connection to this industry in some manner (see Appendix A). The industry naturally lends itself to the internationalization of the commodity circuit, with integrated road transport and freight networks established through the GCC. The growth of this industry has thus also strengthened the tendency toward large regionally integrated infrastructure projects such as the GCC rail and highway networks (see Chapter 7 for further discussion).

GCC Retail Capital

The internationalization of the commodity circuit is further reflected in the nature of class formation around retail activities. With the system of agency and distribution rights established in the earlier phases of internationalization remaining largely unchanged, control over the sale of imported goods in the GCC has become concentrated in fewer and fewer hands. This can be seen in the proliferation of supermarkets and, most notably, "hypermarkets"—huge shops that sell a wide range of commodities ranging through fruits and vegetables, meats, clothing, hardware, household, and electronic appliances within a single store. In 2007, the value of hypermarket sales in Saudi Arabia and the UAE constituted 50 percent and 70 percent, respectively, of total retail sales and made up the fastest growing retail sector in both countries (BMI 2007, p. 50).

Large Gulf capital, particularly those originating from Saudi Arabia and the UAE, dominate ownership of these retail chains. In some cases, this capital operates franchises for foreign hypermarkets such as the French-owned Geant and Carrefour, with their rights extending across all Gulf countries. Geant is the fifth-largest retail chain in the world. In the GCC, it operates in Saudi Arabia, Bahrain, the UAE, and Kuwait. The franchise is owned by the UAE-based Ghurair Group in Bahrain, UAE, and Kuwait, and by the Saudi-based Fawaz Al Hoikar Group in Saudi Arabia. Carrefour is the second-largest retail group in the world with GCC stores located in the UAE (first opened in 1995), Qatar (2000), Oman (2001), Saudi Arabia (2004), Kuwait (2007), and Bahrain (2008). It is operated by the UAE-based Majd Al Futtaim Group across the GCC. Both these examples thus confirm the pan-GCC nature of hypermarket activity in the circuit of commodity capital.

In other cases, large retail chains are fully owned by GCC-based conglomerates, which have placed a very noticeable emphasis on expansion throughout the GCC. Indeed, the internationalization of the commodity circuit is perhaps even more pronounced than the productive circuit; ownership and agency rights for the largest retail chains are concentrated in the hands of UAE and Saudi conglomerates, and operate across all GCC states. Three leading UAE and Saudi conglomerates are dominant: (1) the UAE-based Emke Group, which operates 51 supermarkets and hypermarkets in the UAE, Qatar, Oman, Bahrain, and Kuwait with plans to open in Saudi Arabia. Emke is the largest retailer in the UAE, and the twelfth-largest retailer in the Middle East and Africa with US$1.07 billion in sales for 2006. (2) The massive Saudi conglomerate Savola, which owns Aziza Panda and Hyperpanda hypermarkets. Savola is the largest food retailer in Saudi Arabia and the thirteenth-largest retailer in Africa and the Middle East with sales of US$1.06 billion for 2006 (Thomson 2006, p. 49). It operates 65 hypermarket stores in Saudi Arabia and the UAE. (3) The UAE-based Al Maya Group, which operates 13 supermarkets in the UAE, Bahrain, Kuwait, Oman, and Qatar under the names Lal's Supermarkets; Al Maya Supermarkets and Hypermarkets; British Home Stores; Citi Mart Supermarket; Jesco Supermarket; and Shop N Save Supermarket. Two smaller UAE conglomerates also worth noting are the Safeer Group (operating in the UAE, Oman, and Qatar) and Choithrams (UAE, Oman, Bahrain, and Qatar). The preponderance of UAE and Saudi capital in the retail chain, however, is not exclusive—Kuwait's Americana Group, for example, is the largest fast-food operator in the Middle East and runs the KFC, Pizza Hut, and Hardees franchises across the Gulf region. These examples from across the GCC are strong confirmation of the internationalization of the commodity circuit.

Malls and Shopping Centers

The circuit of commodity capital can be extended to include malls and shopping centers, which further reflect these internationalization tendencies. The expansion of this form of commodity capital is a very noticeable feature of recent Gulf development and is linked to the construction boom noted above. In 2006, GCC malls were generating around US$30 billion in sales annually, and represented around 84 percent of the Middle East's Gross Leasable Area (GLA), a measure of total shopping space (Rahman 2006).

The UAE, particularly Dubai, dominates this mall expansion with the second-largest number of recreational shoppers in the world (people who shop for "something to do" or "entertainment purposes"), and a tourism retail space in Dubai was estimated to be 4 times that of the United States and predicted to hold 16 times more per capita sales floor space in malls than the average of the EU 25 by the end of the decade (Harrison 2008). Most of the large shopping malls in the UAE are anchored by a hypermarket or supermarket chain, and then filled with international franchises and entertainment facilities. Examples of these entertainment attractions include an Olympic-size skating rink and the world's largest aquarium in the Dubai Mall (the world's largest mall), a dinosaur theme park in the Mall of Arabia (scheduled to be the world's largest mall on completion), and the world's largest indoor ski slope at the Mall of the Emirates.

The development of malls is an important part of the formation of the Gulf capitalist class around the commodity circuit. Many of these malls are owned by the same large conglomerates that are active in other moments of the commodity circuit (that is, as agents and distributors of foreign imports or as owners of supermarkets and hypermarkets). The largest of these groups tend to originate from Saudi Arabia and the UAE, and generally own malls in more than one GCC country. The UAE-based Majd Al Futtaim Group provides an excellent illustration. As noted above, Futtaim owns the franchise rights for Carrefour, which it operates in every GCC member state. It launched the first GCC mall, Deira City Center, in Dubai in 1995. It now runs four malls in the UAE, two in Oman, one in Bahrain, and is building one in Saudi Arabia through a joint venture with a Saudi firm. Further malls are planned for Saudi Arabia and the UAE, as well as elsewhere in the Middle East. Most of these malls are anchored with a Carrefour. In the UAE, Futtaim holds the franchise rights for Greater Union Cinemas, which are also located in its key malls in the country. Early in 2006, the group established MAF Fashions, which holds the agency for leading international women's fashion brands. It sells these brands through 90 freestanding stores across six countries.[44] Other examples of UAE-based private capital with pan-GCC ownership of malls are the Ghurair Group, which owns four malls in the UAE and Bahrain; the Emke Group, noted above as a main player in the hypermarket sector, which owns one mall each in the UAE, Qatar, Kuwait, Saudi Arabia, and Oman; and the Safeer Group, which owns six malls spread across the UAE, Oman, and Qatar.

In addition to this private Gulf capital, real estate companies closely linked to the state play a very significant role in the ownership and operation of malls, particularly in the UAE. Emaar Properties is one example of this state-linked capital that illustrates well the fuzzy line between the state and the capitalist class. Emaar is the largest real estate company in the GCC and owns—among many other properties in Dubai—Dubai Mall, which was the world's largest shopping space when it opened in 2008 with over 1,200 stores. Emaar was founded in a private capacity by the current Chairman, Mohammed Alabbar. Alabbar, however, is a senior aide to Dubai's ruler, Sheikh Mohammed bin Rashid Al Maktoum, and is a member of the Dubai Executive Council, essentially the "cabinet" of Dubai. Today Emaar is 32 percent owned by the Dubai government with the remaining shares listed on the DFM, thus providing an important mechanism of accumulation for large private investors (see below). Emaar is also internationalizing through the GCC (and elsewhere in the Middle East)—in 2005, the company became the master developer for the largest single private investment in Saudi Arabia, King Abdullah Economic City.

These patterns of ownership and expansion in the retail sector confirm how the process of GCC integration has facilitated the internationalization of the commodity circuit through the new regional space. The development of supermarkets, hypermarkets, malls, and shopping centers show how the Gulf region is increasingly viewed by Gulf commodity capital as a single market rather than an agglomeration of separate national markets. This emerging regionally integrated commodity circuit is structured around a Saudi-UAE axis—through these two countries' entrepot relationship with the global economy and the control of the key moments of the commodity circuit by Saudi and UAE capital groups. The development of Khaleeji Capital in the Gulf commodity circuit is, in other words, characterized by the extension of Saudi and UAE commodity capital through the regional space and their growing domination of other GCC member states.

The Finance Circuit

Many of the "megaprojects" (both industrial and real estate) discussed above required prodigious levels of financing.[45] Accumulated state reserves from oil sales met some of these costs, used to back government-sponsored plans for new cities, airports, tourism schemes, universities, power plants, transport networks, and the like. State-linked companies were established for this purpose (such as Emaar and another UAE real estate developer, Nakheel), which were often listed on the country's stock exchange as a means of enlisting wider capital flows. In addition to the deployment of petrodollars, however, two other major sources of financing were used to support the vast development plans. First, FDI flows underpinned much of the region's

...........banks and other external private debt flows entered the region at a very rapid rate. In 2007, for example, international banks provided an estimated 60 percent of total project financing in the GCC (with local banks providing another 25 percent) (SAMBA 2009, p. 7). The stock of GCC foreign liabilities—a measure of how much the region was borrowing from the rest of the world—more than tripled from end-2005 to end-December 2008 (IIF 2010, p. 2). The UAE accounted for the bulk of this borrowing—holding more than 65 percent of GCC outstanding international securities and 32 percent of cross-border bank loans extended to GCC countries.[46]

These flows met an increased demand for both corporate and consumer credit in the GCC. Annual credit growth across the GCC rose from just 9 percent in 2001 to a remarkable 37 percent in 2008 (Qatar reached 57 percent in 2007). For the region as a whole, credit as a share of GDP increased to 59 percent in 2008 from 40 percent in 2001.[47] Growth in credit was highest in the UAE, which recorded a 93 percent credit to GDP ratio in 2008. This credit reinforced the shift in the commodity circuit noted earlier—malls and shopping centers became an omnipresent feature of the GCC landscape—as well as the feverish pace of real estate construction. In Saudi Arabia, for example, credit for building and construction purposes—which had remained fairly constant over the period 1998–2001—started increasing rapidly in 2002. In 2005, 2006, and 2007, this sector showed the largest growth of all areas of bank lending, increasing 38 percent, 19 percent, and 18 percent in each year, respectively (GIH 2008e, p. 51). Likewise in the UAE, the value of mortgage loans increased by over 70 percent each year from 2005–2007 as both citizens and wealthier expatriates took on loans to purchase property across the country (GIH 2009, p. 50).

Some of these financial flows went through the local banks established in the earlier phases of internationalization and thus provided an important source of accumulation for the leading conglomerates. As Appendix B shows, ownership of these banks remains concentrated in the hands of groups with the same national origins. What is noticeable in the post-2000 period, however, is the considerable expansion in cross-border activity within the GCC banking sector. An important step in facilitating this activity was the eighteenth GCC summit in Kuwait (1997), where an agreement was reached to allow all GCC banks to open branches in member countries. The decision took several years to implement, but in 2004 Kuwait amended its Banking Law (1968) to become the final country in the GCC to open up its market to other GCC banks. Today, many of the large GCC banks have branches or representative offices throughout the Gulf region.

A particularly significant route for this cross-border expansion was the establishment of special financial zones that exempted banks and other financial institutions from tax and ownership restrictions. Bahrain, building upon the financial infrastructure and laws established in the early period, has been the major site for this cross-border expansion. Appendix B shows the very deep cross-border ownership patterns exhibited by the top Bahraini banks. Indeed, with the exception of the National Bank of Bahrain, all of the largest Bahraini banks are dominated by non-Bahraini GCC capital, mostly drawn from Saudi Arabia and Kuwait. In other words, Bahrain has acted as a key spatial zone for the internationalization of the finance circuit within the GCC. Other GCC countries have followed suit, however, with similar offshore structures established in Dubai (the Dubai International Financial Centre) and Qatar (the Qatar Financial Centre) in 2005.

In addition to the existing banking system, the growing importance of finance and the scale of surplus capital precipitated the formation of new mechanisms that could attract and manage capital flows within the region. Three new financial institutions were critical to the developing financial circuit: equity markets, debt markets, and private equity companies. Each of these three institutional forms helped to mediate the financial flows underpinning the mounting costs of industrial, real estate, and other development projects across the GCC. The potential profit-making opportunities that formed around this financial circuit, which was closely linked to the productive and commodity circuits and increasingly elaborated at a pan-GCC scale, became central to the accumulation and development of Khaleeji Capital.

GCC Equity Markets

Stock markets formed in Kuwait (Kuwait Stock Exchange, 1977), Oman (Muscat Stock Exchange, 1988), Bahrain (Bahrain Stock Exchange, 1988), Saudi Arabia (Tadawul, 1989–2001), Qatar (Doha Securities Market, 1997), and the UAE (Abu Dhabi Securities Market, 2000; Dubai Financial Market, 2000) in the earlier phases of development. Nevertheless, while "GCC countries made significant progress in financial deepening and in building a modern financial infrastructure," the IMF would argue in the late 1990s: "Domestic money markets have remained underdeveloped, exchange, and open up stock markets to cross-border investments.

Bolstered by the massive surplus capital flows in the post-2000 period, subsequent policies to increase market capitalization and attract investment in regional stock markets had a marked effect. This was evident, for example, in the largest and most important of the GCC stock markets, Saudi Arabia's Tadawul, whose market capitalization increased more than eightfold, from $145 billion to $1,225 billion, from 1994–2006 (Tadawul 2006). The level of funds flowing into the market can be seen in the volume of shares being traded on Tadawul, which doubled from 1990–1992, increased a further fourfold from 1992 to 1994, and then another four times from 1995 to 2000 (Molyneux 2005, p. 118). A key step in the expansion of Tadawul occurred in 2003, with the passing of the Capital Markets Law (CML) by the Saudi Arabian Council of Ministers. The law inaugurated a significant increase in financialization as it allowed nonbank bodies such as brokerages and investment firms to offer stock market services in the country. The US government noted that "[n]ew financial firms established under the new law will drive an increase in corporate and consumer finance activity. The IPO [initial public offering] market will likely develop slowly as commercial banks and other underwriters gear up to help private Saudi firms go public under the law's streamlined registration procedures" (US Embassy 2004, p. 7). These predictions proved prescient, with the number of shares traded on Tadawul increasing 50-fold from 2002 to 2006 (Tadawul 2006). By 2003, Tadawul comprised nearly 50 percent of the total market capitalization of all stock markets in the Middle East, and 83 percent of total Middle East stock market trading volume (IAIGC 2005, p. 14). The number of Saudi investment funds increased from 52 in 1992 to 199 in 2005, and total assets owned by these funds went from 12.4 billion Saudi Riyals to 136.97 billion Saudi Riyals over the same period. But this increased activity on GCC stock markets was not restricted to Saudi Arabia. From June 2001 to October 2005, the Kuwaiti Stock Exchange rose by roughly 560 percent, and from October 2002 to October 2005, the DFM increased by approximately 1024 percent. Total GCC market capitalization exceeded $1 trillion at end 2005, compared to $543 billion on December 31, 2004, and $119 billion in December 2000.[48]

This growth of GCC equity markets played an important role in the development of Khaleeji Capital, with many conglomerates listing parts of their businesses on the stock exchange as a means to significantly enlarge their capital base. These markets enabled diversification in the activities of the groups, as they took stakes in a range of companies across sectors different from their core business (or across different GCC markets). Although in some cases this has weakened the control of individual companies by single families, it has further increased the interpenetration of ownership among the capitalist class (and across GCC borders). In many cases, companies seeking to establish themselves in neighboring GCC states will do so by listing on the stock exchanges of the target market, thereby encouraging a further cross-border integration of ownership and the development of Khaleeji Capital (examples of this include the listings of Zain (Kuwait) and Etisalat (UAE) on the Saudi stock market prior to operating licenses in the country).

Large GCC capital also benefited considerably from the partial privatization of state-owned firms through initial public offerings (IPOs) on the stock market. IPOs effectively acted to redistribute revenues to the leading capital groups (and the broader citizenry) from state-owned companies that had been established in the first period of industrialization discussed in Chapter 3. There were two mechanisms that facilitated this process. First, share ownership was often limited to citizens or GCC nationals and thus directly privileged the emerging Khaleeji Capital conglomerates. This happened even in those markets that formally permitted 100 percent non-GCC foreign ownership (Kuwait, Dubai, Abu Dhabi, and Oman) through restrictions that were placed at the individual company level. On the DFM, for example, 14 out of 68 companies listed in 2008 permitted 100 percent ownership by GCC nationals but restricted investment from non-GCC investors despite the fact that the market as a whole permitted full foreign ownership. Bahrain permits GCC nationals unrestricted ownership in all companies but non-GCC foreigners are limited to 49 percent. The GCC's largest market, Saudi Arabia, has been closed to foreign investors since its inception—GCC nationals, however, have been allowed to invest directly in Saudi equities since 2007.[49] In this manner, IPOs of state-owned companies generally acted to benefit all Gulf capital regardless of country of origin, and further encouraged the development of a pan-GCC financial circuit.

Second, newly privatized companies continued to be advantaged through their ongoing ties to the state (such as partial state-ownership, government funding, cheap land, or close partnerships with other state institutions). Hence the state acted to directly facilitate the development of Khaleeji Capital, despite the apparent lessening of state-ownership through the IPO process. An important illustration in the UAE is the aforementioned Emaar, of capital formation for many of the leading groups (the Ghurair Group, for example, is represented on the board of directors). Over 90 percent of Emaar's shares on the DFM are owned by UAE and GCC citizens.[50] There are many other examples of IPOs in which companies retained strong ties to the state, thus helping to strengthen the leading capital groups through the financial mediation of the stock market: Q-Tel (listed 2001 in Abu Dhabi, and 2002 in Bahrain), Industries Qatar (2003), Saudi Telecommunications Company (2003), Saudi Kayan (2006), and Kuwait National Airlines (2006).

The growing scale of equity markets and the development of Khaleeji Capital is further reflected in attempts to establish an integrated pan-GCC stock exchange—a course of action that leading economic analysts and influential GCC policy makers have vocally endorsed. Nasser Saidi, the Chief Economist at the Dubai International Financial Center (Dubai's financial free zone) has noted for example, "We need to rapidly move towards an integration of the financial markets and payment systems in KSA and the [UAE], which are the core economies of the GCC." Saidi believes that this integrated market could underpin "the massive investment required in networks (power, transport, telecommunications, oil and gas), by developing the capacity to invest, manage and control region's financial wealth of more than $2 trillion invested abroad, and by enabling and supporting economic and financial reforms." Confirming the central position of Saudi Arabia and the UAE in the formation of Khaleeji Capital, Saidi characterizes these two countries as "natural allies and partners in moving to greater financial market integration to support regional economic integration, the GCC Common Market and Gulf Monetary Union" (Saidi 2009). Saidi's comments echo those made by the IMF over a decade earlier: "[T]he integration of the national [GCC] markets into a larger regional market through opening them up to regional trading . . . would greatly enhance their growth; [and] may include cross-listing of shares, coordination of primary issues, common secondary trading arrangements, and coordination of regulatory and supervisory functions" (IMF 1997, p. 22).

Although Saudi Arabia is lagging in this respect, other GCC states have taken significant steps toward stock market integration. In 1985, only 25 percent of companies listed on GCC stock markets were open to investments from other GCC nationals (42 out of 170 companies). By 2005, the figure had risen to 98 percent (522 out of 532 companies) (Rutledge 2009, p. 48). All markets now allow the cross-listing of shares from other GCC exchanges, and cross-border shareholding makes up a growing proportion of market values. Most notable in this respect is the Bahrain Stock Exchange, in which non-Bahraini GCC investors accounted for 40.35 percent of the value of all traded shares in 2008. In the investment sector, ownership of shares by GCC nationals on the Bahraini Stock Exchange actually surpassed Bahraini ownership (48.1 to 41.4 percent) (BSE 2008a). In Oman, 16.32 percent of shares of companies listed on the Muscat Security Market in 2008 were owned by non-Omani GCC investors, with a particularly high share in the banking and investment sector (22.42 percent) (MSM 2008, p. 18). For the DFM, nearly one-third of listed companies are from other GCC countries (20 out of 68 companies). Share ownership on the DFM also shows a high degree of pan-GCC ownership, with 19 companies having at least 10 percent of their shares held by non-UAE, GCC investors in 2008, and 9 of these majority controlled by such investors (DFM 2008, pp. 25–26). An IPO of the UAE energy company Dana Gas in 2005 reportedly saw "plane loads of Saudis" descend on the country in order to purchase shares (cited in Rutledge 2009, p. 47). Cross-border linkages are less pronounced on the Abu Dhabi and Kuwaiti stock markets.

Debt Markets

The market for debt—whether in the form of corporate or state bonds, asset-backed securities, or bond derivatives—was a key feature of the latest phase of internationalization, supplying greater levels of credit and linking different markets globally. In the GCC these debt markets remained embryonic, with companies generally seeking financing through bank loans, or to a lesser extent, equity markets, rather than bonds (in the overall MENA region, equities and bank assets constituted 94.4 percent of total financing compared to just 5.6 percent for debt securities in 2008) (Saidi 2009, p. 6). The one important exception to this is Bahrain, where close to half of the financing needs of Bahraini corporations are met through the debt market (NCBC 2009, p. 3).

There are two broad categories of debt securities offered in the GCC—conventional bonds, which resemble those found in any other financial market, and Islamic financial instruments. Of the latter, the most common are *sukuk*, asset-based securities that do not pay interest but give the investor ownership of an underlying (*Sharia*-compliant) asset through which payments are generated as a share of the profit.[51] Both conventional bonds and reaching around 30 percent of all GCC debt in 2006, 40 percent in 2007, and 45 percent in 2008 (KFC 2009, p. 2).[52]

Despite the greater reliance on equity and bank loans there are strong indications that debt will play an increasingly important role in future financing. For the GCC as a whole, total issuance of debt rose from US$3.5 billion in 2004 to reach around US$36 billion annually in 2006 and 2007, before retreating to an estimated US$23 billion in 2008 (NCBC 2009, p. 9). The growth in these debt markets—both conventional and Islamic—was driven by UAE corporate offerings. Saudi Arabia's National Commercial Bank estimates that UAE corporations accounted for 50–60 percent of all debt securities issued in the GCC from 2005 to 2008, including both conventional bonds and *sukuk* (NCBC 2009, p. 9).[53] Dubai real estate companies, in particular, borrowed heavily to finance the construction boom in the post-2000 period. It is estimated that Dubai's total debt reached US$80 billion over this period, including a $3.52 billion *sukuk* in 2006 issued by the real estate developer Nakheel to fund the artificial island developments, The Palm and The World (at the time the world's largest *sukuk*). Dubai World, Nakheel's parent company, was estimated to have accrued US$ 60 billion in overall liabilities by 2009—the majority of which were owed to European banks (Credit Suisse 2009).

Although most of this debt was issued in European markets rather than in the GCC, a growing number of both conventional bonds and *sukuk* began to be listed on regional exchanges in the post-2000 period. Of particular significance was the development of bond and *sukuk* issuances on stock markets in Dubai and Bahrain, which emerged as the leading financial zones for these instruments in the GCC. In 2005, Nasdaq Dubai, a new stock exchange located in Dubai's financial free zone, was launched with the intention of developing the region's debt markets as well as strengthening the linkages between European markets and East Asia. In December 2006, it became the world's largest *sukuk* market in terms of the value of listed *sukuk* (since that time, it has been overtaken by the Malaysian stock exchange) (Nasdaq Dubai, p. 3).[54] In 2009, the DFM acquired 100 per cent ownership of Nasdaq Dubai, although it announced the two markets would continue to operate as distinct entities. The aim of the acquisition was "[to create] a powerful capital markets hub for the GCC and the wider Middle East" (Borse Dubai 2009).

GCC Private Equity

A third significant shift in the GCC financial circuit was the emergence of the private equity business. Private equity is a relatively new form of finance capital that has developed alongside the deepening international-ization of capital. PE funds provide high-return asset management services by offering a variety of funds that invest in local and international markets, participate in privatization offers, buy out companies, or invest in private businesses that require funds for expansion but are unwilling to fully list on the stock market. They have been widely criticized for purchasing companies with the intention of obtaining a controlling (or major) interest in the target company, and then restructuring it through severe cuts in staff, selling-off of assets, debt refinancing, and splitting the company up into profitable sections such as real estate. Once restructuring is complete, the companies are then offered for sale (typically through a public offering on the stock market) after which the fund exits with a highly profitable return.

Although the GCC private equity sector is relatively new, it underwent a very rapid and recent expansion—raising $20 billion in the post-2000 decade (MEED 2009a, p. 20).[55] The attention shown to the region by global PE firms is indicative of its growing importance—indeed, the cofounder and Managing Director of one of the world's largest PE firms, the Carlyle Group, stated in 2007 that the Middle East "will be the fourth private equity center of the world five to 10 years from now" (Ijtehadi 2007). The majority of Middle East private equity funds are managed out of the UAE with Saudi Arabia and Bahrain other key PE centers (one 2008 survey showed that 78 percent of all PE funds are based in the UAE) (Solh 2008, p. 10).

Much of the PE activity in the Gulf and broader Middle East is directly controlled by GCC investors, with GCC-controlled PE investment consti-tuting around 22 percent of total committed private equity in the region, around the same amount as private equity funds from USA/Canada and exceeding that from Europe (De Saint-Laurent 2009, p. 10). In the early days of PE—from 2000 to 2004—most investments tended to be made outside the MENA region, but from 2005 onwards Gulf PE increasingly turned toward intraregional investments (around $6 billion in private equity investments were made in the MENA region during the 2005–2008 period compared to only $500 million in the 2000–2004 period). These magnitudes confirm the significance of PE in reconstituting regional owner-ship structures.

In contrast to GCC banks, ownership of private equity companies is strongly marked by the interpenetration of capital from different GCC result of the post-2000 growth in PE activity, Table 5.8 reveals the extent of internationalization in the finance circuit.

Table 5.8 is a powerful indication of the extensive cross-GCC ownership characterizing this form of finance. Only a single firm in the list provided—the UAE's The National Investor—does not have pan-GCC representation within its board of directors. Eleven of these companies have boards of directors made up of representatives from three or more GCC countries. As is to be expected, Saudi, Kuwaiti, and UAE groups dominate ownership, but Bahraini, Qatari, and Omani groups also hold stakes in these companies.

Virtually without exception, the major investments of these firms are international in nature—distributed across the GCC and the region. One of the largest private equity groups in the Middle East, Abraaj Capital, provides a textbook example of this cross-GCC integrated finance capital.[56] The company was started by Arif Naqvi, who was a Vice President with the Saudi-based Olayan Group. Prominent GCC business groups invested in Abraaj and represented on the board of directors include al Turki (Saudi Arabia), Qassimi (UAE), Kanoo (Bahrain), NBK Group (Qatar), Nowais (UAE), and al Jaber (UAE). The geographical spread of these component groups indicates that ownership of Abraaj is widely distributed across different capital groups throughout the GCC region. In addition to this private GCC capital, management and ownership of Abraaj involves state bodies such as the Public Institution for Social Security (Kuwait), and the General Retirement and Pension Authority (Qatar).

By 2008, Abraaj had over US$4 billion under management. Its investments clearly indicated the internationalization tendencies at the core of the GCC finance circuit. The firm purchased strategic stakes in some of the largest companies across the GCC and the Middle East: Amwal, the leading investment banking firm in Qatar; Spinneys, the largest supermarket chain in the Middle East; Air Arabia, a low-budget UAE airline; JorAmco, an aircraft maintenance company privatized by the Jordanian government; maktoob.com, the leading Arabic Internet portal; and Aramex, the logistics company discussed earlier. It became the largest shareholder of Jordan Ahli Bank (JAB), the fifth-largest bank in Jordan, and of EFG-Hermes, one of the largest investment banks in Egypt and the number one securities broker on the Cairo and Alexandria Stock Exchange. Outside of the Middle East,

Table 5.8 Leading private equity firms in the GCC, 2007–2008

Name of company	Board of directors
Abraaj Capital (UAE)	Sheikh Abdulrahman Ali Al Turki (Saudi Arabia); Hussein Nowais (UAE); Hamid Dhiya Jafar (UAE); Saud Abdulaziz Kanoo (Bahrain); Sheikh Khaled Bin Zayed Al Nahayan (UAE); Sheikh Sultan Bin Saqr Al Qassimi (UAE); Hamad Abdallah Al Shamsi (UAE); Sheikh Nawaf Nasser Bin Khalid Al Thani (Qatar)
Al Imtiaz Investment Company (Kuwait)	Ghanim Bin Saad Al Saad (Qatar); Khalid Bin Ibrahim Suwaiti (Qatar); Khaled Boodai (Kuwait); Abdullah Dakheel Al Jassar (Kuwait); Mohammed Al Mutair (Kuwait)
Al Mal Capital (UAE)	Abdul Jalil Yousuf Darwish (UAE); Adel Al Hosani (UAE); Khalid Madi (UAE); Naser Nabulsi (UAE); Ahmed Al Darmaki (UAE); Hamed Al Nuaimi (UAE); Abdulmonem Bin Eisa Bin Nasser Al Serkal (UAE); Sheikh Mishal Bin Herhlain (Saudi Arabia)
Amwal Investment Company (Qatar)	Sheikha Al Thani (Qatar); Majid Saif Al Ghurair (UAE); Adel Ali Bin Ali Al Muslimani (Qatar)
Amwal Al Khaleej (Saudi Arabia)	A K Al Muhaidib and Sons (Saudi Arabia); Al Fozan (Saudi Arabia); Amar Al Khudairy (Saudi Arabia); Fahad Al Mubarak (Saudi Arabia); Mohammed Ali Al Abbar (UAE)
Arcapita (Bahrain)	Mohammed Abdulaziz Aljomaih (Saudi Arabia); Sheikh Jassim Bin Hamad Bin Jassim Bin Jabr Al-Thani (Qatar) Khalid Mohammed Boodai (Kuwait); Ghazi Fahad Alnafisi (Kuwait); Abdulla Abdullatif Al-Fozan (Saudi Arabia); Khalifa Mohamed Al Kindi (UAE); Abdulrahman Abdulaziz Al-Muhanna (Saudi Arabia); Atif A. Abdulmalik (Bahrain).
Capivest (Bahrain)	Sheikh Nasser Mohammed Almutawa Alotaibi (Saudi Arabia); Waleed A.Rahman Al-Rowaih (Kuwait); Abdullah Ali Al Sane (Kuwait); Ahmad Ahmad Al-Harmasi Al Hajeri (Bahrain); Alaa Hamad Al Roumi (Kuwait); Ali Mohammed Al-Alimi (Kuwait); Majid Abdullah Al Kasabi (Saudi Arabia); Mishari Zaid Al Khalid (Kuwait).
Capital Management House (Bahrain)	Khalid Abdulla Al Bassam (Bahrain); Abdulhakeem Alkhayrat (Bahrain); Khalid Mohammed Najibi (Bahrain); Jamal Saeed Al-Ojaili (Oman); Khalid bin Mohammed Al Khalifa (Bahrain); Saleh Hasan Al-Afaleq (Saudi Arabia); Hisham Saleh Al-Saie (Bahrain); Abdul Hakim Al-Adhamy (Bahrain)
CORECAP	Sheikh Mohammed Wajih bin Hassan Sharbatly (Saudi Arabia); Abdulla Saeed Al Thani (UAE); Sultan bin Khaled AlTurki (Saudi Arabia); Abdul Hameed Al Sunaid (Saudi Arabia).
Gulf Capital (UAE)	Hareb Al Darmaki (UAE); Waleed Zahid (Saudi Arabia); Sohail Al Mazrui (UAE); Riad Kamal (UAE); Ahmed Belbadi (UAE); Mishal Kanoo (UAE/Oman).

HBG Holdings (UAE)	Abdallah Y. Al-Mouallimi (Saudi Arabia); National Commercial Bank (Saudi Arabia); Imtiaz Hydari (Saudi Ar Almoayed (Bahrain); Ziad Galadari (UAE); Yeshwant Desai (Oman).
Investcorp (Bahrain, London, New York.)	Al-Ateeqi (Kuwait); Kanoo (Saudi Arabia); Alireza (Saudi Arabia); Almoayyed (Bahrain); Boodai (Kuwait); F. (UAE); Al-Turki (Saudi Arabia); Al-Zamil (Saudi Arabia); Al Zayani (Bahrain); Al Otaiba (UAE)
Global Investment House (Kuwait)	Maha K. Al-Ghunaim (Kuwait); Dubai Financial Group (UAE); Public Institution for Social Security (Kuwai (Kuwait); Khalid Al Wazzan (Kuwait)
Saffar Holdings (UAE)	Ali Zaid Al-Quraishi (Saudi Arabia); Shoaibi Group (Saudi Arabia); Al Rashed Group (Kuwait)
Unicorn Investment Bank (Bahrain)	Yousuf Shalash (Saudi Arabia); Bader Sulaiman Al-Jarallah (Kuwait); Bader Abdulaziz Kanoo (Saudi Arabia); M Al-Refai (Bahrain); Ayman Ismail Abudawood (Saudi Arabia); Waleed Al Sharhan (Kuwait); Ayman Abdullah /
Millenium Finance Corporation (Dubai)	BofD unavailable
	Major shareholders Dubai Islamic Bank (UAE), KIPCO (Kuwait)
Growth Gate Capital (Bahrain)	Abdullah Rashid Al Noaimi (UAE); Saleh Habsi (Oman); Badr Jafar (UAE); Fahad Al Khalifa (Qatar); Ali Ma Nerguizian (UAE); Mu'taz Sawwaf (Saudi Arabia)
Addax Bank (Bahrain)	Hussain Nowais (UAE); Jassim Hassan Zainal (Kuwait); Salem Al Noaimi (UAE); Wael Aburida (UAE); Nawa Ghobash (UAE); Omar Abdul Aziz Al Mutawa (Kuwait); Saleh Saleh Al Selmi (Kuwait); Waleed Al Mokarrab
Shuaa Capital (UAE)	Al Ghurair (UAE); Abdulla Al Mulla (UAE); Sameer Ansari (UAE); Fahad Yacoub Al Jouaan (Kuwait); Al Saga Qassim (UAE)
Gulf Finance House (Bahrain)	Esam Yousif Janahi (Bahrain); Hamad Al-Shaya (Kuwait); Abdullah Ali Al Hamli (UAE); Yousif Khayat (Saudi Abdullah Al Meer (Qatar); Abdulaziz Mohamed Al Hinai (Oman); Mohammed Ebrahim Mohammed (Bahrain Ohali (Saudi Arabia); Mosbah Saif Al Mutairy (Oman); Bader Al Subaiee (Kuwait)
The National Investor (UAE)	Abdullah M. Mazrui (UAE); Mohamad Abdulla Alqubaisi (UAE); Abdulmajeed Al Fahim (UAE); Fatima Obei Hamad Abdulla Al Shamsi (UAE); Mohamad Mohamad Fadhel Al Hamli (UAE); Omeir Saoud Al Dhahiri (U. Al Naseri (UAE); Abdulla Nasser Al Mansouri (UAE)
Venture Capital Bank (Bahrain)	Ghassan Ahmed Al Sulaiman (Saudi Arabia); Abdulfatah Mohammad Rafie Marafie (Kuwait); Abdullatif Moha (Bahrain); Ali Mousa Al Mousa (Kuwait); Marwan Ahmad Al Ghurair (UAE); Nedhal Saleh Al Aujan (Bahrain) Abanumay (Saudi Arabia); Ajlan Abdulaziz Al Ajlan (Saudi Arabia); Ibrahim Hamad Al Babtain (Kuwait); Abdu Shahwani (Qatar); Sulaiman Ibrahim Al Hudairi (Saudi Arabia)

Source: Company reports.

Abraaj announced in May 2006 a buyout fund of US$300 million focused on Pakistan. In November 2006, the Fund acquired an 80 percent stake in MS Forgings, Pakistan's leading steel forging house.

Another example of this regionally integrated finance capital is Investcorp. Investcorp was formed in 1982 and by 2008 had around $13 billion in managed assets. The company prides itself on its "flat corporate structure" with management distributed between three offices in Bahrain, London, and New York. Investcorp is involved in private equity, hedge funds, real estate, and venture capital. Most of the private equity investments are located in Western Europe and the United States and often involves the purchase of private companies in trouble that are then floated on the stock market.[57] Investcorp's structure illustrates the complexity of the financial arrangements between different holding companies and banks that comprise the group. The company itself is a limited liability company incorporated in Luxembourg, which is wholly owned by Investcorp Holdings Limited (IHL), incorporated in the Cayman Islands. IHL is owned by Investcorp Bank, incorporated in the Kingdom of Bahrain. In turn, Investcorp Bank is majority owned by Ownership Holdings Limited (OHL), which is also incorporated in the Cayman Islands. The top of this ownership structure leads finally to SIPCO Limited (Cayman Islands), which holds majority ownership of OHL and is controlled by around 150 strategic shareholders. As with Abraaj, the ownership profile of SIPCO and Investcorp indicates a truly internationalized and integrated GCC finance capital, drawn from the largest capital groups across the GCC. They include Al Fardan (Qatar), Turki (Saudi Arabia), Zamil (Saudi Arabia), Ali Reza (Saudi Arabia), Al Gurg (UAE), Boodai (Kuwait), bin Hamoodah (UAE), Mazrui (UAE), Jalal (Bahrain), Kanoo (Bahrain), Zayani (Bahrain), Almoayyed (Bahrain), and Ateeqi (Kuwait).

In addition to their ownership of strategic corporations distributed across the GCC, these firms have a significant impact on economic policy in the GCC through the development of policy proposals, economic analyses, and research studies that are often utilized by state institutions and are very widely cited in the regional financial press.[58] In some cases this influence on economic policy is direct. In Bahrain, for example, economic decision-making power has clearly shifted toward a coterie of state officials and large GCC capital often represented through PE companies. In 2005, the Bahraini monarch passed a royal decree (no. 31 for 2005) that delegated full control over national economic policy to the EDB, a body that had previously been an economic think tank. The EDB's board of directors consists of seven key ministers and seven "leading executives" from the private sector. The companies represented by the latter include the PE firms head of the Bahrain Chamber of Commerce and Industry.[59] In its *Trade Policy Review* (TPR) for 2007, the WTO catalogues this shift in the institutional structures of the Bahraini state that has displaced the development of economic policy into the hands of Khaleeji Capital. The TPR remarks that these structural changes are aimed at "ensur[ing] full integration of the private sector into the economic development process, with the whole process being coordinated with the Bahrain Economic Development Board (EDB)." The state "has been reshaped in order to focus on the private sector as the economic driving force, and consequently has been gradually removing itself from involvement in the productive processes, through the process of privatization and divestiture" (WTO 2007, p. 5).

In all cases, private equity companies act as vehicles for the interpenetration of capital from a variety of GCC member states and thus the development of Khaleeji Capital. The activities of these companies are highly internationalized, spread across a large number of international markets and holding significant stakes across all moments of the circuit of capital. The outlook of these firms is best expressed by a leading GCC private equity fund: "We look at the whole GCC, we believe that there is a customs union, a monetary union almost with a very close peg to the dollar, there is a cultural union and anything that sells in Saudi Arabia would sell in Dubai. So for us, we don't look at these markets as being separate entities we look at them as being one" (cited in Dun and Bradsheet 2008, p. 8).

Conclusion: The Overall Structure and Nature of Khaleeji Capital

The core of Khaleeji Capital is structured around a Saudi-Emirati axis, with other GCC conglomerates congealing as subordinate partners within interlocking hierarchical structures. The formation of these hierarchies occurs through the internationalization of the circuit of capital, with this process of internationalization taking a particular geographical and institutional form within each circuit. The institutional changes prompted by the regional integration project—a customs union, common market, and move toward integrating capital markets—have strengthened these internationalization tendencies by enabling capital, goods, and citizens to move more freely across GCC borders.

Capital accumulation in the productive circuit is structured around the activities of construction and the manufacture of energy-intensive commodities. Saudi Arabia and the UAE are the main spatial zones in which this accumulation has taken place, although all states have witnessed an increase in the pace and scale of these activities. Saudi and UAE capital dominates this circuit, building upon those firms established in earlier phases of capitalist development. The largest private firms have clearly sought to expand their regional activities to neighboring GCC states, and pan-GCC interpenetration of ownership is a marked feature of the construction, aluminum, and steel sectors. In the most important productive activity, petrochemical production, Saudi Arabia is overwhelmingly dominant—with other large GCC capital seeking joint investments in Saudi downstream petrochemical projects. This interpenetration forms hierarchically, with Saudi capital the principal component of the interlocking capital groups. In the newer high-technology industries, a handful of large firms control accumulation across all GCC countries and clearly conceive the region as a single market.

The internationalization of the commodity circuit is expressed through the entrepot roles played by Saudi Arabia and the UAE vis-à-vis international imports, and the subsequent reexport trade throughout the regional space. Other GCC states are tightly linked to UAE and Saudi exports, confirming the importance of trade integration over the past decade. The area is viewed by both international exporters and large GCC capital as a unified and regionally articulated commodity circuit. The system of agencies and distribution rights established in earlier periods remain a key feature of this circuit. In this case, the institutional form taken by Khaleeji Capital is the expansion of supermarkets, hypermarkets, malls, and shopping centers throughout the GCC region. Saudi and UAE conglomerates control this element of the commodity circuit, often holding agency rights for many different GCC states and with a clear orientation toward extending their retail activities at a regional level.

The Saudi-Emirate core likewise dominates the finance circuit. An important element to this is the development of capital markets, which indicate the growing linkages between Khaleeji Capital and the architecture of global finance. These capital markets (both equity and debt) confirm the increasing scale of accumulation in the GCC—the ability to embark on the types of industrial, real estate, and other development projects discussed in this chapter requires tapping the resources of both local and international financial markets. Capital markets pool together the money resources across the GCC. Bahrain, in particular, plays a specific geographical role in this internationalization of the finance circuit with policy makers to prioritize returns aimed at satisfying bond and *sukuk* holders. The influence of these debt holders, which include the most powerful banks and financial institutions in the world, means that the reproduction of Khaleeji Capital becomes increasingly tied to the patterns of accumulation at the global scale. Most strikingly, the full institutional expression of Khaleeji Capital is found in the development of financial forms such as private equity, interlocking the large capital groups within single ownership structures, which then reinvest through all moments of the GCC circuits.

Khaleeji Capital is tightly linked to state capital and the institutions of the Gulf state, with many individuals related to the ruling families involved in these accumulation structures in a private capacity (the examples of the Kingdom Group, NBK Group, and Al Qassimi are illustrative in this respect). Moreover, as the institutional make-up of Bahrain's EDB confirms, Khaleeji Capital has a growing influence on financial and economic policy-making throughout the GCC. These linkages and the consequent realignment of state policies have the potential to generate significant contradictions within the GCC because, to date, the political integration of the GCC has not been as far advanced as in the economic sphere. Despite the important economic agreements noted in this chapter—such as customs and trade integration, and moves toward a monetary union—the political institutions of the GCC remain only weakly integrated. The further development of Khaleeji Capital, however, necessitates a reconstitution of these political institutions with economic and political decision-making much more closely aligned to the accumulation needs at the regional scale. At the same time, political elites within each GCC state continue to hold considerable interest in ensuring control over national policies and thereby appropriation of rents that accrue at the national scale. How this plays out for the future development of the GCC remains an open question—but the contradiction between the autonomy of the GCC state and the internationalization of the circuit of capital is a potentially significant tension within the regional integration project and is one important implication of the development of Khaleeji Capital.[60]

The development of Khaleeji Capital is an indication of the tendencies of internationalization and financialization across the GCC space, structured by the Gulf's location in the global economy. These tendencies are not limited, however, to the GCC. The entire Middle East is increasingly moving to a single beat—inextricably linked to the rhythms of accumulation and class formation in the Gulf. The development of this regional structure of accumulation, and the evolution of Khaleeji Capital following the onset of the global financial crisis, are the subjects of the final section of this book.

CHAPTER 6

Khaleeji Capital and the Middle East

Soon after the US-led invasion and subsequent occupation of Iraq in 2003, a range of authors commented critically on the profound economic changes that followed in the wake of the US presence. Under the tutelage of US diplomat Paul Bremer, the Coalition Provisional Authority (CPA) signed into law one hundred military orders that transformed the nature of Iraq's political economy.[1] These laws included measures to privatize 200 state-owned companies, establish a flat tax of 15 percent with no distinction between individuals and foreign corporations, made it illegal to limit foreign ownership in the economy, and even restricted Iraqi farmers from saving their seeds from one season to the next (thereby compelling them to purchase seeds from large agribusiness conglomerates). Differing from the standard neoliberal prescriptions of the International Monetary Fund (IMF) and World Bank only in the manner in which they were introduced—through military invasion rather than an agreement with the country's elite—it appeared to many that these new laws were designed to open up the Iraqi economy to a wave of US ownership. Many commentators expected that large US corporations would soon take advantage of the end of restrictions on foreign ownership to buy up wide swathes of the Iraqi economy—real estate, telecommunications, retail, finance, and, of course, the world's second-largest supplies of oil and gas (Looney 2003; Juhasz 2004; Whyte 2007).[2]

Reality turned out to be more complex. It was certainly true that Bremer's laws—and those of subsequent Iraqi governments whose economic program differed little from the CPA—opened the country to capital inflows and ownership by foreign investors. Labor, political, and religious groups in Iraq protested widely against these laws, which they saw as handing control over their country's resources to foreign interests.[3] The surprising detail, however, lay in the nationality of these investors. The initial wave of investment did indeed come from US companies that benefited from lucrative contracts provided by the US government. But, particularly following the dissolution of the CPA in June 2004, the investments of US companies were soon surpassed by those from the GCC. From 2003 to end-January 2009 more than half of all investment in Iraq came from the GCC (DFC 2009, p. 4). By mid-2009, for example, four of the six Iraqi banks with majority foreign ownership were controlled by GCC-based banks (NIC 2009, p. 82). In land and housing, two massive projects by Damac Properties (UAE) and Al Maabar (UAE) accounted for 75 percent of all investment in the country's real estate (DFC 2009, p. 8). GCC companies noted in the previous chapter came to own all three of Iraq's mobile phone licenses (the two Kuwaiti companies, Zain and Agility, and the Qatari-based Q-Tel).[4] In the oil and gas sector, the largest private-sector project was a $650 million gas production and pipeline scheme owned by two UAE companies operating in Iraq's Kurdistan region.

Although these figures should be treated with some caution and cannot necessarily be generalized across all sectors of the Iraqi economy, they are indicative of the profound impact that the internationalization tendencies embedded at the core of Khaleeji Capital are having on the Gulf's Middle Eastern periphery. It is estimated that the Middle East region garners around 10–15 percent of GCC capital flows, a substantially higher proportion than the earlier phase of petrodollar flows and with very significant implications for these peripheral areas. Capital flows to the Middle East originating in the Gulf have grown to exceed those from the leading capitalist countries. In 2008, for example, World Bank figures recorded that Gulf countries were responsible for 36 percent of the total foreign investments in the area, surpassing those of North America (31 percent of total investments), Europe (25 percent), Asia (4 percent), and the other MENA countries (3.5 percent) (World Bank 2009, p. 56). These GCC investments have transformed the traditionally laggard nature of FDI in the MENA region. In the early 2000s, for example, the region received less than 1 percent of global FDI flows despite having 3–4 percent of global population. By 2004–2008, primarily as a result of capital flows from the GCC, the region's share of world FDI flows had risen to 3–4 percent—essentially equivalent to its global proportion of population (de Saint-Laurent 2009, p. 1). Indeed, by 2006, FDI originating from GCC countries was equivalent to a remarkable 13 percent of the rest of the Middle East and North Africa's GDP (IIF 2008, p. 18).

A handful of companies linked to Khaleeji Capital—both state-owned and private—dominate these intraregional flows. Reflecting the process of

Kuwait, Ahli United Bank, Gulf Finance House, Global Investment House); media (Dallah al Baraka, Kingdom Holding); and telecommunications (Q-tel, Etisalat, Zain, Batelco). The sectoral focus of these conglomerates differs from non-GCC FDI in the Middle East (such as that originating from Europe), which tends to have a greater concentration in the industrial, manufacturing and energy sectors (de Saint-Laurent 2009, p. 6). Frequently, the large GCC groups have interests that cross several different sectors. In addition to these conglomerates, SWFs and private equity groups are also prominent intraregional investors.

Figures presented by ANIMA, an EU institution that monitors FDI in the Mediterranean region, confirm the pivotal role of the Gulf in Middle East capital flows. Instead of measuring FDI through official central bank data, ANIMA uses publicly available information on project deals in the Mediterranean region (which it defines as Algeria, Egypt, Israel, Jordan, Lebanon, Morocco, Palestinian Authority, Syria, Tunisia, and Turkey). From 2003 to 2009, according to ANIMA, the value of projects announced by Gulf investors in the Mediterranean area exceeded those from any other country or region in the world. GCC investors made up 38 percent of the total value of projects announced in 2003–2006 period (Europe constituted 34 percent, the USA/Canada 13 percent).[5]

The significance of GCC capital flows becomes even more pronounced when this data is differentiated at the subregional level. Most affected have been the Mashreq countries—Jordan, Lebanon, Egypt, Palestine, and Syria—which received more than 60 percent of all GCC investments. These GCC investments vastly exceed those from any other major capital-exporting region to the Mashreq: GCC FDI in the Mashreq was 69.2 billion Euros in the 2003–2009 period compared to 22.9 billion from Europe and 5.2 billion from USA/Canada according to ANIMA.[6] For Syria and Lebanon, GCC FDI constituted more than 70 percent of the country's total FDI in 2008. In Egypt, the country's Minister of Investment reports that the share of GCC capital in Egypt's FDI rose from 4.5 percent in 2005 to over 25 percent in 2007 (Mohieldin, 2008, p. 41). In Jordan, GCC FDI was 35 percent of the country's total FDI in 2007. The Jordanian stock exchange is heavily dependent upon GCC investors—although they make up less than 1 percent of all shareholders they hold approximately 20 percent of market capitalization.[7]

Influence on Class Formation in the Middle East

Standard economic interpretations of these capital flows from the Gulf tend to be grounded in the claims to neutrality and "bias-free" science that typify the positivist approaches of international financial institutions such as the IMF and World Bank. Gulf investment flows are held to be a positive-sum game that matches capital surpluses in one area of the Middle East with investment deficits in the rest of the region. These investments are assumed to be potentially employment-creating, and embraced as evidence of success in the slow march to overcome state-ownership and other *dirigiste* tendencies that allegedly have held back many countries from fully integrating with the new global economy.

This perspective obfuscates the fact that capital is not a sum of money, but rather a social relation grounded in the extraction of value. GCC capital flows to peripheral regions are, in the final analysis, aimed at the maximization of profit. This is not to deny that some GCC investments may be linked to foreign policy objectives, but, in general, and in the overwhelming majority of cases, the dominant force behind the internationalization of capital is the extraction of profits and the transfer of wealth from these peripheral regions to the GCC.[8] This drive has led to a vast increase in the control by GCC capital of banks, telecommunications companies, land, and other assets across MENA—particularly those countries located in the Mashreq subregion.[9]

How does this penetration impact the development of class in the region? Several decades ago, Nicos Poulantzas provocatively suggested that the penetration by US capital of the European states should be understood as an "internal bourgeoisie"—with the European state playing the role of mediating and supporting this component of the European social formation on par with any "national bourgeoisie" (Poulantzas 1978, p. 72). Can Poulantzas' approach be applied to the Middle East? In other words, has Khaleeji Capital become so internalized within the class structures of the Middle East that it needs to be understood as a key (perhaps dominant) component of the distinct national capitalisms across the region? This may not yet be the case, but even as a tendential development it deserves further exploration given the conflicts that it will likely generate within each national social formation.

Two sets of empirical data explored in this chapter—one sectoral and one geographically focused—confirm that the imbrication of Khaleeji Capital (and state-controlled Gulf investments) with capitalism in the Mashreq is having a pronounced impact on the nature of class formation in the region. The first set of data examines the penetration of GCC capital ground for decision makers and exercise an important influence on the shaping of economic policy. For these reasons, the involvement of Khaleeji Capital in the Mashreq banking sector is an important indicator of the direction and trajectory of capitalism in the broader Middle East.

The second set of data examines the involvement of GCC-based capital in the Palestinian West Bank. This case partially captures a further significant role that the GCC plays in the regional political economy—an accumulation zone for regionally displaced diaspora capital. Because the Middle East is an area of prolonged war and conflict—which, it should be noted, is largely a consequence of the region's centrality to global accumulation—it possesses a relatively large population of refugees and displaced peoples. Three national groups stand out in particular: Palestinians dispossessed in 1948; Lebanese displaced as a result of the decades of civil war in that country; and, most recently, Iraqis who fled as a result of the US occupation in 2003. The wealthiest social layers in these diasporas have often found their way to the GCC countries where they have established themselves in profitable businesses and, in some prominent cases, have been absorbed as a component of the Gulf capitalist classes. The analysis below of the Palestinian West Bank confirms that these Palestinian/Gulf capital has become central to the reproduction of the Palestinian economy.

The Jordanian, Egyptian, and Lebanese Banking Sector

The following analysis is based upon the largest banks in Jordan, Lebanon, and Egypt according to an annual ranking of the Top 100 Arab Banks, by *Banker Magazine* (BM) (October 2009 rankings).[10] BM ranks banks by the size of their assets, profitability, and Tier 1 capital (the core capital of a bank, which includes equity capital and disclosed reserves). As has been the case for many decades, GCC banks dominated the top Arab banks in 2009, with 58 of the top 100 banks headquartered in the six states of the GCC. At a monetary level this dominance is even more pronounced. Around 80 percent of both the Tier 1 Capital and the total assets of the Top 100 are held by GCC banks. All of the top 10 banks are from the GCC with the exception of Jordan's Arab Bank (and, as is discussed below, this bank is closely linked to GCC capital).[11]

Table 6.1 shows the banks from Jordan, Lebanon, and Egypt that made the BM Top 100 list, with the addition of other important nationally based banks operating in those countries (those too small to make the Top 100 Arab banks but still prominent at the national scale as indicated by their inclusion in the industry directory of the *Union of Arab Banks*). It should be emphasised that only nationally based banks are listed in Table 1 (that is, banks listed as Jordanian are considered to be based in Jordan or to have Jordanian origins, foreign banks that are operating in the Jordanian market are not listed).

Table 6.1 shows the Tier 1 capital of each bank (which conveys the relative strength of the banks vis-à-vis one another) as well as any ownership relationship the bank may have with GCC-based capital (including being a subsidiary or affiliate of a GCC bank; having equity held by a GCC bank, company, or SWF; or having GCC-based representation on the bank's board). This information is drawn from an individual analysis of each bank's publicly available records such as annual financial statements and the company's board of directors. The definition of "ownership relationship" used here is deliberately looser than that which would be formally considered as FDI by the IMF or other international institutions. The reason for this is that the table aims to show a qualitative appreciation for how GCC capital is internationalizing through the financial sectors of Jordan, Egypt, and Lebanon. What matters is not so much the precise magnitude of equity held by GCC capital but the extent to which GCC capital is itself oriented toward this sector. Furthermore, in many cases, it is necessary to dig below an initial ownership stake that appears on the surface to be based in a non-GCC country in order to find an indirect, but highly significant, relationship with the GCC (e.g., see EFG-Hermes discussed below). The information below should thus be understood in the sense of a snapshot of the social relations emerging throughout the Middle East, rather than a direct quantitative measure of a continually changing institutional reality.

Table 6.1 confirms the remarkable penetration of the Jordanian, Egyptian, and Lebanese banking sectors by a range of GCC-based capital. This is most pronounced in the Jordanian banking sector. Of the top 15 Jordanian banks, 13 are either directly controlled by a GCC-based company or have a GCC investor as a major shareholder. Overall, the country's banking system is dominated by the Arab Bank, whose ownership is distributed between the state-run Jordanian Social Security Corporation (14.3 percent), and the private Saudi-based conglomerate Saudi Oger (8.9 percent; a company discussed in the previous chapter for its important role in the GCC construction sector). Saudi Arabia's Ministry of Finance also holds a significant share (4.5 percent) and is represented on the bank's board

Table 6.1 Banking sectors in Jordan, Lebanon, and Egypt

Bank	Tier 1 capital (US$ million)	Relationship with GCC-based capital groups
JORDANIAN BANKS		
Arab Bank	4,638	Arab Bank is the second largest bank in the Arab world. The largest private sl Oger, a Saudi-based conglomerate with interests in construction, telecomm finance (owned by the family of the late Lebanese Prime Minister Rafik Ha
The Housing Bank for Trade and Finance	1,117	Largest shareholder is Qatar National Bank, which holds 33.93% of shares. Re is concentrated in other GCC-based groups such as the Kuwait Real Estates 18.61%, and the Ministry of Finance, Oman, 2.98%.
Jordan Kuwait Bank	314	Subsidiary of the Kuwaiti-based Burgan Bank (51% ownership).
Union Bank for Savings and Investment	275	Largest shareholding is held by Polaris Investment Company, which is controll Jordanian group of investors (with largest share from UAE).
Capital Bank of Jordan (formally Export and Finance Bank)	228	One of the largest shareholders is Mohammed Musa'ed El-Seif (5.51%) from tl Saudi Arabia.
Jordan Ahli Bank	227	Top two shareholders are the UAE-based private equity company, Abraaj Capita the Kuwait Investment Authority (6.32%).
Jordan Islamic Bank	188	Subsidiary of the Bahrain-based Al Baraka Banking Group. In addition, the Ku investment bank, Global Investment House owns a significant share of the ba
Bank of Jordan	175	The Saudi-based Zahrani Group is represented on the board of directors. Appro the bank's shares listed on the Amman Stock Exchange are controlled by Emi investors.
Cairo Amman Bank	168	Al Masri Group (see below for discussion of this Palestinian-Gulf based conglom
Jordan Commercial Bank	90	Second largest shareholder is Saudi businessman Nasser Saleh (23.32%). The oth is the Al Sayegh Group, of Palestinian origin but with their main headquarter: the UAE through National Paints Company.

Table 6.1 Continued

Bank	Tier 1 capital (US$ million)	Relationship with GCC-based capital groups
* Arab Banking Corporation (Jordan)	n.a.	Subsidiary of the Bahraini-based Arab Banking Corporation (Bahrain). The majority shareholders of the parent company are Kuwait Investment Authority 29.7% and Abu Dhabi Investment Authority 27.6%.
* Arab Jordan Investment Bank	n.a.	Owned by The Arab Investment Company (TAIC), which is a joint fund of 17 Arab states, headquartered in Saudi Arabia with largest shares owned by Saudi Arabia and Kuwait. In addition, the Qatari Sheikh, Hamad Bin Jasser Bin Jaber Al Thani owns around 9% of AJIB.
* Jordan Investment Finance Bank	n.a.	No direct relationship.
* Jordan Dubai Islamic Bank	n.a.	Controlled by a UAE-Jordanian consortium made up of Dubai International Capital (DIC), Dubai Islamic Bank, and Jordan Dubai Financial (JDF).
* Société Générale Bank Jordan (MEIB)	n.a.	Second largest shareholder is the Kuwaiti-based Global Investment House (30% of shares).
EGYPTIAN BANKS		
National Bank of Egypt	1,205	No direct relationship (State-owned bank).
Commercial International Bank	950	A major shareholder is the UAE-based, Dubai Capital Group 5.2%.
Arab African International Bank	472	The Kuwait Investment Authority jointly owns the bank with the Central Bank of Egypt (each with 49.37% share).
Banque du Caire	469	No direct relationship (State-owned bank).
National Bank for Development	191	A UAE-based consortium made up of the Abu Dhabi Islamic Bank and Emirates International Investment Co. own a majority 51.29% share of the bank.
Société Arabe Internationale de Banque	145	46% is owned by the Arab International Bank (a consortium consisting of 25% ownership of the Abu Dhabi Investment Authority; 5% State of Qatar, and 5% Sultanate of Oman among other Arab governments). 4.8% is owned by the Saudi Prince Khaled Ben Turki.
Housing & Development Bank	140	No direct relationship (State-owned bank).
Faisal Islamic Bank of Egypt	122	Major shareholders include the Saudi-based Dallah Al Baraka Holding Co. 3.4%, Dar Al Mal Al Islami Trust (Saudi Arabia) 9.1%, and the Saudi prince Mohamed Al Faysal Al Saud 3%. Bahrain-based Shamil Bank of Bahrain also owns 9%.

Bank		Notes
Egyptian Saudi Finance Bank	96	Subsidiary of Saudi Al Baraka Banking (73.68%).
*Al Watani Bank	n.a.	Owned by National Bank of Kuwait.
*Delta International Bank	n.a.	DIB is 80% owned by Nile Strategic Company, a Kuwaiti consortium.
*Egypt Gulf Bank	n.a.	Largest shareholder is Misr Insurance Company, a subsidiary of the Kuwaiti-t Company. Other Kuwaiti and Saudi investors are major shareholders.
LEBANESE BANKS		
Bank Audi Sal	1,769	Key shareholder is the Egyptian investment bank, EFG Hermes, which holds largest single investor in EFG Hermes, however, is the Dubai Financial Gro 25% of the company. Major stakes in Bank Audi are also owned by the Ku Homaizi (6.5%) and Al Sabah (6%) who are both represented on the board UAE Al Nahyan family are also major shareholders (5%).
BLOM Bank	1,310	The Saudi-based Shaker Group is a significant shareholder (5.39%) and is repr of directors.
Byblos Bank	1,070	No direct relationship.
Bank of Beirut	509	Key shareholders include Emirates Bank International (9.81%), which is repres directors.
Fransabank	499	The Kuwaiti state institution, The Public Institution for Social Security, has 29 represented on the board of directors. The Saudi conglomerate, the Al Fadl g around 3% and is also represented on the board of directors.
Banque Libano Francaise	492	No direct relationship.
Bankmed	476	Bankmed is controlled by the Hariri family, whose core company, Saudi Oger, i Arabia.
Credit Libanais	331	CL is 79% owned by Capital Investments Holding, Bahrain, which in turn is c businessmen.
Bank of Beirut and the Arab Countries	207	Second largest share, 37%, acquired in 2005, is owned by Fransabank (see abov
Societe Generale de Banque au Liban	121	No direct relationship.
Banque Bemo	65	The second largest shareholding, at 10%, is held by the Saudi banking group, Ban

* These banks are too small to be listed in the Top 100 Arab Banks but are prominent at the national scale. Information drawn from publicly available ban

of directors.[12] The second-largest Jordanian bank, the Housing Bank for Trade and Finance, has more than 60 percent of ownership held by GCC-based investors.

In Egypt, GCC penetration is less marked than Jordan mainly because of the larger share of state-ownership in the banking sector—a continuing legacy of nationalization measures in the wake of the 1952 revolution. Nevertheless, GCC firms are major shareholders or directly control 9 out of 12 of the major Egyptian banks. Several of the smaller banks have become direct subsidiaries of Gulf banks following takeovers in recent years. Moreover, the Egyptian government has stated its intention to pursue a policy of privatization in the banking sector and has been openly courting GCC capital for this purpose; if this trajectory continues, it is extremely likely that the GCC share will increase in the coming years.

Lebanese banks have historically played an important role in the regional financial system. From the 1950s to the early 1970s (prior to the onset of civil war in 1975), the country was widely described as the "Switzerland of the Middle East" because of its open resemblance to Europe's banking capitals. The country's prosperity (largely concentrated among an elite in the country's capital Beirut) derived from its specific role as an interlocutor in regional accumulation patterns. Its earlier political and economic links with its former colonial master France followed by US penetration from the 1950s onwards, geographical proximity to Europe, and its relatively advanced infrastructure (ports, airports, roads et cetera) assisted the country in becoming a central link between the advanced capitalist economies and the Middle East. Consequently, for much of the twentieth century Beirut was seen as the banking capital of the Arab world. However, with the onset of the country's civil war in the 1970s and the subsequent Israeli invasion in 1982, the locus of regional banking shifted to Bahrain, which, as discussed in Chapter 3, had introduced a set of offshore banking legislation and had become a key node in the flow of petrodollars from the Gulf to the United States and Europe in the post-1973 period.

For these historical reasons, the largest Lebanese banks continue to have a close link with France, as well as prominent Lebanese business groups that prospered during the 1950s and 1960s. Nevertheless, the presence of GCC capital is once again strongly reflected in the banks listed in Table 6.1. Eight out of the eleven banks listed have some relationship with GCC firms. The largest bank, Bank Audi Sal, counts as its major shareholder the investment and private equity firm EFG-Hermes, which, although based in Egypt, has the Dubai Financial Group and the UAE-SWF, ADIA, as its two largest shareholders. Alongside EFG-Hermes, Kuwaiti and UAE groups also hold significant chunks of Bank Audi Sal. Many of the other Lebanese banks,

..., and Lebanese banking systems. These are all linked in some way to Khaleeji Capital and its internationalization across the GCC space. Indeed, it could be argued—with the possible exception of national state-controlled capital—that Khaleeji Capital is the single most significant factor structuring the ownership of banks in each of these three countries. Around 90 percent of the "national" banks in those countries have high levels of GCC investment reflected in either major share ownership or membership on the board of directors. Moreover, it should be remembered that these figures do not include the cross-border expansion of GCC banks into these markets through the establishment of branches and representative offices. Given that Jordan, Egypt, and Lebanon have each embraced the liberalization of their banking markets over the past decade, this regional expansion is likely to register significant growth and further confirm the dominance of Khaleeji Capital in the regional banking system in the coming years.

Alongside these capital flows, there is significant indication that linkages with the GCC are also affecting the direction of economic policy. Lebanon provides a good example of the GCC's impact on the region's political economy. Gulf capital flows to Lebanon go far beyond the banking sector outlined above. From 2003–2008, nearly 50 percent of all foreign financing for projects in Lebanon came from the GCC—way in excess of those from any other country or region (ANIMA 2009, p. 155). For 2006, almost 90 percent of total FDI in Lebanon came from just four GCC countries: Kuwait, Qatar, Saudi Arabia, and United Arab Emirates (ESCWA 2008, p. 10). Leading Khaleeji Capital groups involved in nonbanking sectors include Al Futtaim and Al Habtoor from the UAE, Al Shaya and Al Kharafi from Kuwait, and the Kingdom Group from Saudi Arabia—alongside Gulf SWFs and state-owned companies.

As Lebanon has become closely tied to the reproduction of capitalism in the Gulf through these capital inflows, the trajectory of its economic policy-making has shifted to include a much more direct and assertive role for the GCC. An indicative example of this can be seen in the so-called Paris III Conference, organized in January 2007, in which foreign donors promised aid to Lebanon (after its 2006 war with Israel) conditional on implementation of a neoliberal economic program involving privatization of core sectors including telecommunications, power and water, and other public utilities. The Gulf states were a key driver of the Paris III process, making up the largest pledges to the country and exceeding funds promised by the United States, the World Bank, the IMF, and the European Commission (LMF 2007, p. 22). Concurrently, the GCC (particularly Saudi Arabia) has forged a very close relationship with Lebanon's political leadership. Most notably, this included Rafik Hariri and—following his assassination in 2005—his son, Saad Hariri who is now Prime Minister of Lebanon. Much like the Palestinian groups that are discussed below, the Hariri family could be considered a subcomponent of Khaleeji Capital—its accumulation is centered in its ownership of the Saudi-based construction company Saudi Oger, and the family holds Saudi citizenship. In this sense, the neoliberal trajectory of the Lebanese government—and the country's economic penetration by Khaleeji Capital—are directly linked to the GCC's political influence.

The Palestinian West Bank

Economic development of the West Bank (and Gaza Strip) is dominated by the Israeli military occupation of these areas and the following analysis is not meant to suggest otherwise. Myriad Israeli military orders regulate Palestinian industrial and agricultural production, have guaranteed Israeli dominance of Palestinian commodity markets, and ensured the supply of cheap Palestinian workers as a reserve army of labor for the Israeli economy. Following the signing of the Oslo Accords in 1993, the Palestinian economy was tightly circumscribed by the system of movement restrictions that gave Israel total control of the flows of commodities and labor power in and out of Palestinian areas. Industrial zones were established at the edges of these areas—most noticeably at the entrance to the Gaza Strip—where Palestinian labor could operate as an adjunct to the Israeli economy while remaining geographically separate (Abed 1988; Roy 1995; Samara 2001; Farsakh 2005; Hanieh 2011).

However, within the truncated areas that came under the control of the Palestinian Authority (PA) following the Oslo Accords, a handful of large Palestinian-owned conglomerates and holding companies have emerged.[13] These companies are closely tied to the Gulf, although the form in which this has taken place needs to be distinguished from the direct investments of the GCC in other areas of the Mashreq. Specifically, the core of Gulf-based investments in the West Bank has occurred through individuals with Palestinian national origins, but whose primary base of accumulation and historical formation are tied to the GCC and the development of Khaleeji Capital. In this sense, they can be considered a Palestinian subcomponent of Khaleeji Capital. This diaspora capital plays a dominant economic role in the PA-controlled parts of the West Bank and is closely involved in steering policy in the area.

A clear example of this Palestinian diaspora capital is the Masri family, who locate their origins in pre-1948 Palestine but were integrated into the emerging Gulf capitalist class in the post-1970 period in a manner that parallels the development of the conglomerates discussed in Chapter 3. The family's wealth is principally divided between two cousins, Munib and Sabih, and their relatives. Sabih Al Masri founded the Arab Supply and Trading Corporation (ASTRA) in 1967 in Saudi Arabia.[14] The company began building its fortune through a series of contracts to supply food and other provisions to Saudi military bases in the northwest of the country. Like many other GCC conglomerates at the time, ASTRA established a construction division in 1976 that successfully won contracts to build two hospitals near the military base of Tabuk. It also carried out construction work for government buildings, air bases, and housing complexes in the area. Through successive government contracts, ASTRA developed into the largest single food supplier for the Saudi military and later diversified into agricultural production and distribution. It is today a major provider of fertilizers, pesticides, and seeds throughout the Middle East and North Africa.

In addition to being one of the most important agricultural companies in Saudi Arabia, subsidiaries of ASTRA are involved in manufacturing industries (prefabricated steel buildings, plastics, irrigation systems, and bedding) and telecommunications. A huge boost to the company's balance sheet was the 1990–1991 war on Iraq, in which ASTRA won the contract from the US military to supply food to all 1.1 million soldiers involved in the invasion. By 2006, ASTRA had become the second-largest private conglomerate in Saudi Arabia and ranked twenty-third on the Top 100 Saudi Companies. Sabih al Masri must also be noted for his ownership of one the most important banks of Jordan and the West Bank, the Cairo Amman Bank (CAB). He owns around 5 percent of CAB directly but through Al Masira Investments (wholly owned by the Al Masri family) and the 10.5 percent of CAB owned by Sabih's wife, Najwa Madi, the Masri total holdings reaches around 34 percent.[15]

Similarly, the growth of Munib Al Masri's business empire was closely related to the development of the Gulf states and their oil industries. In 1956, Munib established EDGO, one of the region's first privately owned engineering companies. Although EDGO continues to be headquartered in Jordan, its principal activities derive from the provision of equipment, maintenance, drilling, and engineering support to companies in the Gulf and the UAE. In addition to its traditional oil and gas activities, the company is participating in the privatization of power and water assets in Oman, Qatar, and the UAE. In 2006, Munib al Masri was worth $1.62 billion and was listed as the thirty-fourth richest Arab in the world by *Arabian Business.*

The Masri family, along with a handful of other Palestinians closely linked to accumulation in the GCC, dominates the economy of the PA-controlled areas in the West Bank.[16] In addition to direct ownership of companies in the West Bank, Masri founded and is the key private investor in the Palestine Development and Investment Company (PADICO), a massive holding company that is the most important economic entity in the Palestinian territories—controlling the major companies in the sectors of real estate, industry, hotels, and telecommunications. PADICO holds 80 percent of the Palestinian Stock Exchange, as well as a large share of the first Palestinian telecommunications company, Paltel. The chair of PADICO is Munib al Masri, with Sabih al Masri also sitting on the company's board. Other significant investors in PADICO include Saudi Arabia's Kingdom Group and the Arab Bank.

Many of the subsidiaries of PADICO are, moreover, closely linked to other GCC capital. The Kuwaiti private equity company, Global Investment House, for example, has two seats on the board (including vice-chair) of the Palestine Real Estate Investment Company (PRICO), the most important real estate company in the West Bank. The Jordan Kuwait Bank (a subsidiary of Kuwait's Burgan Bank) and the Housing Bank for Trade and Finance (see Table 6.1) are both represented on the board of the Palestine Industrial Estate Development Company, a PADICO subsidiary responsible for building industrial zones in the West Bank and Gaza Strip. Saudi Arabia's Kingdom Holding is a major investor in PADICO's Jerusalem Development and Investment Co. (JEDICO), a major real estate developer in Jerusalem. These patterns are replicated throughout most of PADICO's subsidiaries.

But PADICO and the Masri family are more than just investors in the West Bank—they have also played a central role in Palestinian economic development strategy. Maher Masri, a member of the Masri family and former General Manager of one of PADICO's subsidiaries, was the

....y, and is best encapsulated in the *Palestinian Reform and Development Plan for 2008–2010* (PRDP), which became the official PA economic strategy in November 2007 following the extensive efforts of the World Bank and other international financial institutions. The PRDP promotes an aggressive neoliberal policy, aimed at private-sector-driven economic growth and cutting back the social expenditure of the PA (Hanieh 2008). PADICO has played a major role in supporting the plan, with subsidiaries such as the Palestine Industrial Estate Development Company launching industrial zones in line with its development component. In addition, PADICO was a principal organizer of a major international conference convened in Bethlehem in May 2008 to promote the PRDP and attract foreign support and investment.[17]

Khaleeji Capital is heavily involved in the Palestinian economy through another major holding company in the West Bank, The Arab Palestinian Investment Company (APIC). APIC was launched in 1995, with its founding shareholders mostly drawn from Saudi Arabia, including the Aggad, Kingdom, Rashid, Olayan, and Al Jomaih Groups.[18] Although APIC is smaller than PADICO in terms of capitalization, it is an influential holding company due to its role as import agents for major international capital. APIC controls, for example, UNIPAL (75 percent ownership), which is the agent in the West Bank and Gaza Strip for Phillip Morris, Procter and Gamble, and Kraft among other companies. Furthermore, APIC is the sole distributor for major pharmaceutical and cosmetic companies including Abbott International, Aventis, Eli Lilly, and GlaxoSmithKline through its subsidiary Medical Supplies and Services Co. (MSS), and the sole agent for Hyundai vehicles through its Palestine Automobile Company (98 percent ownership). It also owns significant holdings in the telecommunications company Paltel and the Palestine Electricity Company. In comparison to PADICO, APIC is less directly tied to the institutions of the PA, with one important exception—the son of PA President Mahmoud Abbas, Tareq Abbas, is APIC's Vice President as well as General Manager of the largest advertising company in the West Bank (an APIC subsidiary).

These ownership patterns demonstrate the profound influence exerted by Khaleeji Capital on the structure of the Palestinian economy.[19] Virtually without exception, the major companies in the West Bank are controlled by groups that are directly connected to accumulation in the Gulf states—whether Palestinian groups whose main accumulation originates and continues to be based in the Gulf, or direct investments by Saudi, Kuwaiti, or other GCC investors. In addition to their domination of the Palestinian economy, these groups are also closely connected to the structures of the PA and thus play a major role in the development and implementation of economic policy.

Conclusion: Schisms in the Middle East?

An analytical framework that recasts the political economy of the Middle East through the regional lens clarifies the significance of Khaleeji Capital for the Gulf's broader periphery. Increasingly, the development of class and state throughout the Middle East is deeply wrapped up in the formation of Khaleeji Capital and the internationalization processes in the Gulf. This means that accumulation and processes of class formation within the states of the Middle East need to be understood as not simply driven by endogenous factors, but rather structurally defined by the broader trends of the regional economy. The development of Khaleeji Capital, and the penetration of the regional economy by this class, places significant pressure on state elites to restructure the modes of accumulation within each individual nation state accordingly and align themselves with the accumulation patterns of the regional scale.

These developing regional flows should not be understood as signaling the weakening or undermining of the role of the individual state in the Middle East. To the contrary, this process acts to strengthen state institutions and cast a particular form to state building in the region—it does not negate or undermine these institutions. These processes are necessarily complex and contradictory, and need to be interpreted through the ongoing (and sharpening) geopolitical rivalries for regional influence. They also confront the enduring salience of the national scale, and the conflictual interests of different states in the region. Nevertheless, despite these provisos, there is a great need to squarely locate the broader development of the Middle East within the internationalization tendencies of the Gulf.

The full implications of this are yet to be seen. It can be conjectured, however, that the alignment of the Middle East with the profit-oriented expansion of Khaleeji Capital portends a sharpening contradiction between the region's poor and marginalized classes on one side, and the GCC and the elites of other Middle Eastern states on the other. The internationalization of Khaleeji Capital is not socially neutral but transformative—shaping the regional character of state, class, and market in ways that are always

... in Lebanon's ... to this very fact). The types of policies that generally result from these measures—including state restructuring, privatization, and liberalization—threaten to widen even further the socioeconomic gaps between the GCC and the rest of the region.

CHAPTER 7

Future Trajectories

The 2008 Crisis

The mix of financialization and internationalization that characterized the post-2000 global economy always contained within itself the potential to unravel. The tendency of overaccumulation inherent to postwar capitalism—fed by technological innovation and the seemingly limitless production capacities of the world's low-wage zones—could not be sustained despite the accelerating piles of debt. The stability of this system began to erode with the collapse of the US real estate bubble in 2007. Asset price declines placed severe pressure on highly leveraged banks and financial institutions, which in some cases had extended more than 40 times the amount of capital they actually held. Beginning in the summer of 2007 and continuing throughout 2008 a series of dramatic events occurred: the collapse of Bear Stearns, the fifth-largest US investment bank; the bail-out of Fannie Mae and Freddie Mac, which had accounted for 80 percent of new US mortgages; and then the quick succession of financial institution failures—Lehman Brothers, Merrill Lynch, Washington Mutual, and American International Group (the world's largest insurer). By the end of 2008, approximately US$30 trillion of value in world share markets had evaporated and the US government had pledged the remarkable figure of $8.5 trillion, equivalent to 60 percent of the total value of the US GDP in 2007, in order to prop up financial markets (Sterngold 2008).

The export-oriented development strategies imposed by the World Bank and IMF throughout the 1980s and 1990s meant that the crisis unfolded in the context of a highly internationalized global economy. Countries in the South had been fully integrated into global production chains and had opened their borders to vast flows of capital and goods. Because virtually every country was linked into this chain at some level—as low-wage production zones, exporters of migrant labor, or suppliers of raw materials— the crisis rapidly spiraled through the globe with devastating consequences

(Hanieh 2009). One key transmission mechanism was the plunge in overall demand as US credit markets froze, triggering a profound slump in global manufacturing. A measure of this was shown by a relatively obscure economic indicator, the Baltic Dry Index (BDI), which measures the cost of long-distance shipping for commodities such as coal, iron ore, and steel. As such, it provides an excellent indication of the demand of industry for these commodities; higher industrial demand leading to increased shipping costs. From June 2008–January 2009, the BDI fell by a massive 92 percent, with rental rates for large cargo ships dropping from $234,000 a day in June 2008 to a remarkable 1 percent of that figure by early December. This enormous drop reflected both the reduced world demand for raw materials and other commodities and the shippers' inability to have their payments guaranteed by banks because of the credit crisis.

Falling commodity prices confirmed this drop-off in industrial demand. Copper and aluminum prices, for example, fell more than 60 percent from July 2008 to January 2009. Chinese consumption of copper, critical for much industrial production, fell by more than half in 2008. ArcelorMittal, the world's largest steelmaker, stated on November 5, 2008, that its global output would decline by more than 30 percent (Jolly 2008). Most significantly for the GCC, prices of oil, gas, and petrochemicals also plunged—oil fell to a low of around US$30 in December 2008 from a peak of $147.27 in July 2008; natural gas from over $13 per million BTUs in July 2008 to around $6 in January 2009; ethylene from a high of $1670/mt in March 2008 to just over $700/mt by January 2009.

Financial Implications

A collapse in productive activity, and hence exports, was not the only impact the crisis had on the global economy. As Chapter 4 emphasized, increased financial linkages across the world market had underpinned the most recent phase of internationalization. One of the consequences of this was the heavy reliance of many countries on credit and other foreign inflows. With the beginnings of the credit crisis in July 2007, large private banks in the advanced capitalist economies became extremely wary of lending because of the risk of default. Initially, with fears of institutional and stock market collapse in the core economies, large funds directed financial flows into raw material and some stock markets in the South. This was one reason—along with rising oil prices and the increasing diversion of food crops to biofuels—for an 18-month rise in food prices from July 2007–December 2008. While providing large surpluses for some commodity exporters, this increase in food prices (and, until July 2008, oil prices) led and other financial institutions pulled funds from the South in order to cover themselves from the rapidly evolving crisis in the core. By January 2009, "emerging" markets—including those in the GCC—had lost more than half their value from their peaks in mid-2008 as financial institutions shifted money to safer vehicles such as US Treasury bonds (IMF 2010, p. 6). Furthermore, the process of credit contraction and deleveraging meant that many countries were no longer able to sell sovereign or consumer debt in order to attract capital. Those regions that had been recipients of large levels of credit inflows in earlier years (such as Dubai), or had low foreign currency reserves and a high dependence on exports, were particularly susceptible to a sudden contraction in liquidity. In this situation, countries faced a potentially deadly mix of capital flight with a simultaneous plunge in foreign earnings. Crisis hit a range of economies in the South—Pakistan, Indonesia, Argentina, India, South Africa, Brazil, Turkey, South Korea, and Mexico among others—with enormous pressure placed on domestic banking systems and ability to finance social outlays.

Crisis in the Gulf

In the context of its deep integration with international financial and commodity flows, the GCC could not escape this unravelling of the global economy. First, the collapse in oil and other hydrocarbon prices from July–December 2008, as well as a decline in the volume of oil sold, significantly impacted available state funds. Estimates in early 2010 put the value of combined oil exports of GCC states at $302 billion over 2009, a 42 percent drop from the 2008 figure of $522 billion (ADC 2010, p. 8). GDP fell from $1.073 trillion in 2008 to $887 billion in 2009, with GDP per capita dropping nearly 18 percent to $23,000 in 2009. These trends were reflected in a plunge in current account surpluses—record levels during the 2000s were halved and, in the case of the UAE and Oman, became deficits.[1]

The global collapse in equity markets and asset prices also reduced the value of GCC foreign-held investments in the second half of 2008. Particularly hard hit were those Gulf countries that had pursued riskier investment strategies (i.e., targeting equities, hedge funds, private equity). Only Saudi Arabia, which had invested more heavily in safer fixed-income securities such as US Treasury Bonds, experienced a marginal increase in the value of their foreign assets (an estimated 4 percent in the case of SAMA). As a whole, the value of assets held by the Gulf's central banks and SWFs was estimated to have fallen from around $1.3 trillion in 2007 to $1.2 trillion in 2008. This relatively small drop, however, obscures the large losses of the governments of Kuwait, Qatar, and the United Arab Emirates, whose foreign assets were estimated to have fallen in value by around 30 percent over 2008.[2]

The impact of these two trends—the drop in both oil revenues and foreign asset values—was further compounded by the reversal of financial flows into the GCC. Following the collapse of the US banking giant Lehman Brothers in September 2008, loans from international banks and other private sources dried up at a global level. Net private capital flows to the Africa and Middle East region fell precipitously from $105 billion in 2008 to an estimated $43 billion in 2009 (IIF 2010, p. 21). Furthermore, speculative capital flows, which had earlier moved into the GCC in expectation of a currency revaluation, pulled back as it became clear that a repegging to the dollar would not occur.[3] These outflows were reinforced as asset bubbles, notably in the Dubai real estate market, began to deflate and capital owners attempted to move funds to safer and more stable investments outside of the region. The departure of these foreign private capital flows severely impacted the availability of credit in the region, which, as noted earlier, had been a prominent feature of the GCC's recent development. With the drop-off in international lending, credit growth shrank dramatically from around 37 percent in 2008 to a tiny 0.2 percent in the first quarter of 2009. Particularly affected was the real estate sector—in the UAE, for example, credit to the construction sector fell 9 percent in the first quarter of 2009 after recording an astonishing 81 percent annual growth in 2008 (UAECB 2009).

The GCC had become heavily reliant on these flows to finance domestic development and was thus faced with a huge fiscal challenge. GCC states owed around $222 billion worth of debt to international banks in late 2008, 70 percent of the entire debt of the Arab world (Kawach 2010, p. 6). In the first eight months of 2009, the value of loans from international banks to the GCC for project financing was only $22.8 billion, about a third of the $69.6 billion recorded in the same period last year (SAMBA 2009). International banks were responsible for only 25 percent of project financing in 2008, compared to levels of around 60 percent in earlier years. Many of the region's projects were starved of funds—of an estimated $2 trillion of projects (both public and private) in different stages of implementation as of end-2008, around 23 percent were placed on hold or cancelled. In the UAE, the figure reached 39 percent (IIF 2009, p. 3).

worth of debt from the government-linked firm Dubai Holding, for example, rose from a mere $19,000 in March 2008 to over $100,000 in January 2009—indicating that traders felt a debt default was extremely likely. Corporate and government debt issuances became much harder in this environment with the total GCC debt market more than halved in 2008 compared to a year earlier (Ghose 2010, p. 29). The share of GCC countries in the world's *sukuk* market fell to one-third in 2009 from nearly 60 percent in 2006–2008 (Kotilaine 2009, p. 19).

Due to its deep integration with global markets, the emirate of Dubai was particularly hard hit. The value of construction and infrastructure projects in the UAE plunged from $60 billion in 2008 to just over $10 billion in 2009. By early 2010, 92 percent of all real estate projects that had been put on hold in the GCC were located in Dubai, and the US property company Jones Lang LaSalle estimated that more than half of all projects in the emirate had stopped (Redfern 2010, p. 30). By some estimates, property prices in Dubai dropped by as much as 70 percent and commercial rents by 60 percent (*Khaleej Times* 2009). Dubai was perhaps the most extreme example but other Gulf states also felt the effects of the project slowdown. In Saudi Arabia, for example, 54 major projects were put on hold, including delays in the construction of the massive King Abdullah Economic City—a US$27 billion investment planned to house 2 million people by the time of its completion in 2016. In Kuwait, real estate sales dropped by 60 percent to January 2009 according to leaked government data, and major projects in other GCC states were also delayed or cancelled (*Arabian Business* 2009, p. 13).

Furthermore, declining credit levels, a collapse in business activity, and the reduction in external capital flows hit equity markets. Losses ranged from 30 percent (Bahrain and Kuwait) to 68 percent (Dubai) in the period December 31, 2007, to November 28, 2008. As the value of equity and real estate plummeted, many of the region's institutions—banks, state-run companies, and corporate groups—that had built up significant leverage in the earlier period ran into trouble repaying debts. This was particularly the case for those institutions that had issued debt in the form of corporate bonds or *sukuk* and were unable to meet repayment schedules or—as with many of the region's banks—had extended loans on the basis of collateral that was now losing value.[4]

In December 2009 the full extent of these leverage issues became clear with the announcement that one of the UAE's flagship conglomerates, Dubai World, would need to restructure a US$4.1 billion *sukuk* issued by a subsidiary, Nakheel. Although Dubai World was rescued by a $10.1 billion loan from the neighboring emirate Abu Dhabi, Dubai's overall state and quasi-state debt burden was estimated by Morgan Stanley at $108 billion, or 140 percent of the emirate's GDP (Jaber 2009). Most of this was owed to international banks (44 percent), UAE banks (13 percent), and other GCC banks (9 percent). There were also some large, high-profile financial casualties including two of the region's largest private conglomerates, the Saudi holding companies Saad Group and Al Gosaibi Group, which announced in mid-2009 that they would need to restructure US$10bn worth of debts. The news sent panic through neighboring Gulf countries due to the extensive cross-border investments of these two companies.

Support of Khaleeji Capital and the Spatial Displacement of Crisis

The severity of this crisis provoked a series of economic and political responses from all GCC governments throughout 2009. Buoyed by an upturn in oil prices in early 2009, these actions were largely successful in containing the worst impact of the global meltdown. But as these events unfolded one overriding characteristic became apparent: the crisis—and the measures undertaken by GCC governments to address it—acted to deepen the tendencies of internationalization and reinforce the position of Khaleeji Capital within the structures of accumulation. Khaleeji Capital emerged from this crisis fortified, with the internationalization of capital a much clearer feature of accumulation in the region.

The first element to this was the bolstering of credit levels and the provision of state assistance to banks, private companies, and state firms under strain. GCC states were well-placed to provide this aid—flush with accumulated surpluses from a decade of high oil prices. Saudi Arabia injected around $10 billion into the banking system and provided US$2.7 billion in credit to citizens having difficult accessing loans. In the UAE, US$19 billion was placed in local banks in the form of long-term deposits and the Dubai government set up a US$20 billion emergency fund, the Dubai Financial Support Fund (DFSF), to cover any losses from large infrastructure and real estate projects that were overleveraged. In Saudi Arabia, Kuwait, and the UAE, all bank deposits were guaranteed by the government. Interest rates were cut in each country and reserve requirements for banks were lowered in an attempt to encourage lending. In Qatar,

...included a government guarantee of 50 percent for new loans extended by banks to local firms over two years, and a 15-year guarantee against any fall in the value of banks' real estate and other investments. In a clear example of the privileging of citizenship and the large banks in the country, Kuwait's parliament was reported in late 2009 to be discussing a plan to buy all $23 billion worth of bank loans taken by Kuwaiti citizens (*not* all residents) for homes, cars, and other purchases—while simultaneously reducing the amount that needed repayment (MacDonald 2009, p. 5).[5] These measures underscored the first priority of GCC governments—the strengthening and support of Khaleeji Capital. The banks at the core of accumulation in the finance circuit were provided with a massive injection of state support that mitigated any threat of significant fall-out from overleveraging or bad loans.

Despite this support of the banking system, Khaleeji Capital was faced with another major problem as a result of the crisis—the collapse of credit flows that maintained the project market (most notably in Dubai). The shoring up of banks did not necessarily translate into liquidity—banks simply took the money given to them by governments and placed it in Central Banks rather than extending loans for project development. In Saudi Arabia, for example, the amount of commercial bank deposits held by SAMA more than doubled from October 2008–December 2009, while credit growth to the private sector dropped by 0.04 percent (SAMA 2009, Table 10a). This problem was compounded by the lack of lending from foreign institutions, particularly in the wake of Dubai's near-default on its Nakheel *sukuk*.

In response, GCC governments stepped in to support infrastructure and project markets. In Saudi Arabia, the 2010 budget of US$144 billion was the largest ever and earmarked nearly 50 percent to investment in new and existing projects.[6] Dubai—reflecting the severe impact of the crisis in that emirate—was forced to reduce its budget for 2010 with a 6 percent cut in expenditure. However, confirming the priority of the government's response to the crisis, just less than half of the Dubai budget was allocated to infrastructure and transportation projects, of which the major beneficiaries would be the region's construction and contracting companies. In Kuwait, the country's 2010–2014 development plan earmarked around 50 percent of its spending to "private sector development."[7] This was centered on a strategy of Public-Private Partnerships (PPPs) in the country's energy and power sector, and the launching of five new state-backed companies that would be 60 percent listed on the stock exchange—thereby attracting a lion's share of investment from the leading capital groups. It remains to be seen how effective these measures will be given the ongoing global nature of the crisis and the overproduction that characterizes much of the GCC productive circuit, particularly real estate.[8] But the nature of the response by GCC states indicates that the primary goal has been to support the core points of accumulation for the leading Khaleeji Capital groups.

Moreover, although private-sector-initiated projects stalled, GCC governments reversed their initial slowdown of many projects and announced plans for $1.4 trillion worth of projects from 2009 to 2015—more than the combined GDP of the GCC countries in 2008 (McKinsey 2009, p. 6). These included six new cities in Saudi Arabia—four times the area of Hong Kong and with an economic output equal to Singapore—as well as an $80 billion expansion of the country's oil, gas, and petrochemical industry. In Abu Dhabi, plans for constructing a transport system, four sporting stadiums, and the world's first carbon-neutral city were launched. Qatar announced plans for deep-sea ports and gas projects. Saudi Arabia and the UAE remained the two largest project markets in the Gulf—and indeed the region—with around 30 percent of all projects planned for 2010 in the whole of MENA located in those two countries (MEED 2009b, p. 20). As with earlier rounds of development, the primary beneficiaries of these projects were the large GCC construction companies and foreign engineering and technical firms.

Concurrent with this state-led support, there were pressures toward the centralization and concentration of capital in the finance circuit, further acting to support Khaleeji Capital. Local financial press and prominent government spokespeople urged banks to merge in order to maintain adequate capitalization. Early 2009 saw the formation of the region's largest bank—Emirates National Bank of Dubai—born from the merger of Emirates Bank International and the National Bank of Dubai. Consolidation also occurred in other GCC banking markets through share-swaps that merged conventional banks with those that offered Islamic banking services.[9] There were indications that this centralization and concentration could take on a pan-GCC character, with calls to form a regional bank that integrated capital groups from a range of GCC countries.[10] The Oman Central Bank Executive President Hamood Sangour al-Zadjali stated in November 2009 that Gulf central banks should encourage "merg[er] between national banks in the GCC as a first stage [followed by] regional expansion and mergers . . . after the financial crisis and the effect on some present global financial crisis) to change" (Chawdhry 2009, p. 47). Although a fully regional bank raises regulatory issues and would require deeper agreement between GCC states, these comments were indicative of how the trends of internationalization in the finance circuit were accentuated under the pressure of the crisis.[11]

Although not pan-GCC in the strictest sense, Abu Dhabi's announcement on December 14, 2009, that it would provide $10 billion to support its neighbor Dubai, was further indication of the way the crisis reinforced regional economic interpenetration. The threat of financial collapse in Dubai had significant implications for other areas in the Gulf. Abu Dhabi (along with other Gulf states) had invested heavily in Dubai's economy, and a default by a high-profile company such as Nakheel would raise borrowing costs across all GCC states.[12] Abu Dhabi's intervention both reflected the interlocking of the financial circuit over the recent period while simultaneously acting to strengthen this tendency. Indeed, in the wake of the bail-out, the UAE federal government announced it would be issuing a joint-UAE sovereign bond during the following year—the first time that such a funding would be attempted at the federal level rather than through individual emirates. Moreover, like much of the financial interpenetration at the pan-GCC scale, the bail-out was hierarchical in nature, with Abu Dhabi strengthening its position vis-à-vis its neighbor. One indication of this was the surprise name change at the opening of the world's tallest building in Dubai on January 3, 2010. The tower was renamed Burj Khalifa (after Sheikh Khalifa bin Zayed, the ruler of Abu Dhabi) instead of Burj Dubai. The unexpected announcement shocked the region—street signs, the nearby metro station, and even the uniforms of the tower's staff carried the old name—and was a thinly veiled nod to Abu Dhabi's ascendancy.

Likewise, the deepening of internationalization tendencies could be seen in the productive circuit. With the weakening of the Dubai construction market, many of the largest Gulf construction companies adopted internationalization as a strategy for overcoming the crisis, placing their hopes on Saudi Arabia and Abu Dhabi as their next major accumulation zones. A flurry of UAE-Saudi construction joint ventures were announced in order to capitalize on the upturn in project financing in the Saudi kingdom.[13] The CEO of Arabtec, one of the largest construction companies in the UAE, noted in mid-2009, "We're making the necessary arrangements to mobilise for our first project in Saudi Arabia immediately . . . we haven't laid any labour off here in the UAE. They may go home as projects draw to a close, but we will redeploy thousands to Saudi Arabia . . . [Saudi Arabia's construction market] can compensate for a drop in works in the UAE" (Walter 2009, p. 6).[14] The trends of internationalization noted in Chapter 5 were powerfully confirmed in early 2010 with the announcement by Arabtec that most of its work for 2009 was located in Saudi Arabia rather than its home market of the UAE (MEED 2010, p. 18). A similar joint venture was announced by the UAE's Habtoor group, which followed a range of Saudi companies expanding into Abu Dhabi to capitalize on the UAE capital's construction projects. Further afield, the Saudi Bin Ladin Group and Qatari Diar launched a new construction company in March 2010, QD SBG Group, which would give the Bin Ladin Group greater access to projects in Qatar and allow Qatari Diar to utilize the supply chain of their Saudi partner (Gluffrida 2010, p. 2). While arguably optimistic about the prognosis for the global economy, this cross-border response to the economic crisis was indicative of the way in which the Khaleeji Capital conceives accumulation in the productive circuit from the perspective of the regional scale.

Reinforcing these cross-border accumulation trends in the wake of the crisis were a range of institutional projects developed under the auspices of the GCC. In December 2009, the 30th GCC Summit in Kuwait agreed upon a pan-GCC railway that would connect all member states within a single network. Construction on the $60 billion project would begin in 2011 and involve the integration of existing national rail lines into the system. Another pan-GCC project, a regional electricity grid, also moved ahead. The first phase was completed in July 2009 with the linkage of Bahrain, Saudi Arabia, Qatar, and Kuwait, and construction of the second phase—the internal connection of the electricity grids in the UAE and Oman—was scheduled to finish by 2011. Although planning for both the rail and electricity projects predate the crisis, their ongoing development strengthens emerging regional accumulation structures. Indeed, the development of this pan-GCC infrastructure has been explicitly linked to economic integration by leading GCC officials.[15]

Perhaps the GCC project with the most dramatic potential to strengthen internationalization is the formation of a single currency and monetary union. In mid-2009, the initially ambitious plan for launching the *khaleeji* was forced to give way to the reality of ongoing rivalry between member states over the location of the proposed GCC Central Bank and a fear of losing control over domestic economic policy. Saudi Arabia eventually won the CB location over the protests of the UAE, leading the latter to retreat

. . ., and the establishment of a powerful central bank are measures that require monetary and fiscal policy to be centralized at the supranational scale and inevitably generate tensions at the national scale (as the experience of the European Union testifies).

Nevertheless, in the wake of the crisis, Saudi Arabia, Kuwait, Qatar, and Bahrain strongly affirmed their commitment to the single currency and signed a monetary union pact at the thirtieth GCC summit in December 2009. The four states agreed to establish a GCC Monetary Council that would develop into a central bank, and eventually issue the single currency. If successful, the formation of the monetary union will significantly deepen the internationalization tendencies underpinning Khaleeji Capital. The GCC Secretariat has explicitly highlighted this goal, noting that the single currency "deepens the concept of the common market, efficiently contributes to the development and integration of the GCC capital markets, particularly the securities market . . . increase[s] the capability of the GCC corporations to merge into or procure other corporations in the member states . . . and, in the field of the banking and financial services, encourages [mergers] among institutions at the regional level in order to benefit from the economies of scale" (GCC SG).

The Spatial Displacement of Crisis

This book has repeatedly emphasized the strong link between the rise of Khaleeji Capital and the very deep exploitation of noncitizen labor. Over 85 percent of the Bangladeshi, Pakistani, and Sri Lankan overseas workforces could be found in the GCC in the period immediately preceding the crisis. In the Philippines, the figure exceeded 60 percent. For India, 95 percent of all labor outflows were going to the GCC by end-2007 (MOIA 2010, p. 54). This spatial structuring of class is critical to understanding how capitalism in the Gulf region responded to the crisis. As the crisis unfolded—and concurrent with the measures discussed above that aimed at strengthening Khaleeji Capital—large state and private companies stopped hiring migrant workers and repatriated thousands as projects were postponed or cancelled. Layoffs were particularly notable in Dubai as the epicenter of the collapse of the region's project market. The Indian consulate in the emirate reported in March 2009 that UAE construction companies had removed 20,000 workers through block-booking entire planes (*Arabian Business* 2009, p. 30). The Dubai Roads and Transports Authority announced in mid-2009 that it was revising its spending plans to take into account an anticipated one-fifth drop in population levels over 2009–2010 as migrant workers were repatriated (MEED 2009c, p. 19). Workers could be deported legally and with relatively little protest and, in this manner, GCC states could avoid any of the potential social dislocation that unemployment produced in other countries. Indeed, leading GCC economic analysts acknowledged this potential as one that was uniquely available to the Gulf region. An analyst for the Saudi National Commercial Bank, for example, made the oblique observation in 2009 that the ability of the GCC to send workers home in times of crisis and return them when growth resumed was indicative of "a positive externality of labor market flexibility" (Kotilaine 2009, p. 21). Precisely because of the extraordinary dependence of many South Asian countries on the GCC's labor markets, and the accompanying lack of citizenship rights held by these workers, it was possible for Gulf states to transfer the worst impacts of the crisis onto migrant labor and—by extension—the surrounding region, with little regard for its social consequences. In essence, the spatial fix structurally embedded at the core of Gulf capitalism permitted the spatial displacement of crisis.

By early 2010, figures from the main labor-exporting states surrounding the GCC confirmed this process. In Sri Lanka, the number of male workers departing for the GCC in 2009 declined by 4.5 percent compared to the previous year—a very serious reversal for a country where one-quarter of its labor force is located in the Gulf (SLBFE 2009, p. 4). For Bangladesh, the declines were even more dramatic. Figures from the Bangladeshi labor exporters association showed a 45 percent decrease in annual overseas employment in the GCC from 2008 to 2009 (BAIRA 2010). The plunge in new employment was reflected in figures for air travel from Bangladesh to the Gulf—with industry spokespeople claiming a drop from 26,000 travelers per week in 2007 to 12,000 in mid-2009 (*Financial Express* 2009). Neighboring India also experienced a reduction of nearly 25 percent in the outflow of workers to the Gulf from 2008–2009 (MOIA 2010, p. 15). The Minister for Overseas Indian Affairs, Vayalar Ravi, told the Indian parliament on July 8, 2009 that up to 150,000 Indian workers from the Gulf countries had probably returned to the country due to the global economic slowdown. The Indian state of Kerala put in place plans to deal with an expected 200,000 workers who were predicted to return from the UAE by the end of summer 2009 (Karkouti 2009, p. 25). Further east, the Philippines saw its first decline in seven years for the number of new hires in the GCC. This was a sharp reversal of previous trends—since 2003 there affected (15 percent suffered redundancies), as well as senior executives (13 percent) (Ligaya 2009, p. b1).

While these trends raised fears of a drop in remittances to the surrounding region, several countries (including India, Pakistan, and Bangladesh) initially saw a temporary rise in flows. This was likely due to long-term migrant workers repatriating significant levels of accumulated savings in preparation for a return home.[16] Bangladeshi human rights activists noted in December 2009, for example, that they were encountering workers who lost their jobs and had sent all their savings home while attempting to work illegally for as long as possible without getting caught (Rahman and Mohaiemen 2009).[17] Not long into the crisis, however, flows of remittances began to slow in several countries. Remittance flows to South Asia as a whole declined by nearly 2 percent in 2009; while smaller than the decline in the rest of the world, this needs to be compared with annual increases of around 10 percent to many South Asian countries in the years immediately preceding the crisis (World Bank 2010). The slowdown in remittances continued into 2010. In Bangladesh, remittances during the third quarter of 2010 were nearly 2 percent less than a year earlier. Pakistan also experienced little or no growth in remittance flows during most of 2010, compared with annual double-digit increases throughout most of the previous decade (Ratha, Mohapatra, and Silwal 2010, p. 5).[18]

Alongside this spatial displacement of crisis, those workers remaining in the GCC also saw their working conditions deteriorate sharply. Journalists reported in early 2010 that thousands of workers in the UAE were stranded as companies fled the country without paying workers or returning confiscated passports. Conditions such as these led to a spike in suicides among migrant workers, with one social worker commenting to a newspaper reporter in early 2010: "[T]hey [migrant workers] think if they kill themselves the loan sharks will leave their families at home alone. But they don't. They'll still go after them" (Solomon 2010). In Kuwait during March 2010, migrant workers were committing suicide at the rate of one every two days.[19] In the rest of the GCC, arrests, deportations, and abuse of workers (including several shocking cases of torture of female domestic workers) were reported on a daily basis.[20]

Nevertheless, despite the GCC's "labor market flexibility" and the specific role it played in this crisis, the future stability and permanence of this spatial structure should not be taken for granted. Within many GCC states, high unemployment levels in the citizen population—most particularly among youth—are a noticeable trend. This dilemma is posed most sharply in Saudi Arabia, where unemployment among Saudi citizens rose to 10.5 percent in 2009, up from 10 percent in 2008 (Saudi MoPE). Among women and youth (those aged 20–24), 28.4 percent and 43.2 percent were unemployed, respectively, in 2009. Moreover, the GCC states have a very pronounced demographic bias—in Saudi Arabia, more than half the population is less than 20 years old—and the cost of maintaining the current structure will place exponentially greater demands on state revenues. Finding ways to absorb new generations into the workforce while retaining the specific characteristics of the spatial fix of the past decades is likely to provoke future policy crises in the long run.[21]

One of the suggested responses to this dilemma has been to encourage the regional movement of citizen-labor as a solution to unemployment in states such as Saudi Arabia (Badr El Din 2007, pp. 33–58). Successive GCC summits have pledged equal treatment for GCC nationals working in neighboring GCC states so that, for example, a Saudi worker in the UAE public service would be extended the same rights in housing, insurance, retirement, education, and other benefits as UAE citizens. However, while there has been a notable increase in the pan-GCC labor mobility of nationals, the levels are still low and work conditions may not always coincide with legislation.[22] Moreover, any fundamental shift in labor market composition—such as the widespread proletarianization of GCC citizenry—carries with it deep political implications precisely because of the role that the spatial structuring of class has played in the development of Gulf capitalism (and thereby the hierarchies of the world market). To a considerable extent, the development of Khaleeji Capital would not have been possible without this spatial structuring of class. To reverse this structure in any real way implies significant social dislocation and brings with it the potential development of domestic social movements that have largely been absent from the GCC over the past few decades.[23] For these reasons, the spatial fix of Gulf capitalism—amply demonstrated in this particular crisis—may precipitate a much more systemic "switching crisis" in the medium-term future.

Future Paths of Development

In short, the response of GCC states to the crisis reinforced the position of the large conglomerates and further strengthened the tendencies underlying the development of Khaleeji Capital. The core orientation of the GCC circuits of capital remains pointed toward a pan-GCC scale and, as a

Gulf region as a central element to the formation of postwar capitalism have only been accentuated in the postcrisis environment; the nature of internationalization and financialization at a global scale—and of the rivalries that these tendencies precipitate—rests fundamentally on the way that the GCC is integrated into the structure of the world market.

For the foreseeable future, the world's productive capacities remain firmly tied to Gulf oil and gas supplies. More than half of the world's energy comes from oil and gas and this proportion is unlikely to change much in the coming period (IEA 2008). It is predicted that the share of the GCC in world oil production will increase to close to 25 percent by 2030. Most importantly, the GCC is one of the few oil producing regions with the capacity to meet any future growth in oil demand.[24] These potential increases in production—particularly in Saudi Arabia but also in the UAE and Kuwait—mean that the GCC will be the main factor in increasing oil supplies in coming years and hence a critical determinant of the price of oil. Likewise, GCC production of natural gas (mostly in Qatar) is predicted to meet around one-fifth of the world's expected increase in world demand over the coming years (IIF 2009, p. 9). And, of course, it is essential to remember that the GCC is the anchor of a broader energy zone encompassing Iraq, Iran, and the Central Asian republics—a region that holds close to half of the world's total oil and gas reserves, as well as the largest areas of unexplored potential supplies.[25]

Moreover, the Gulf will take a fundamental position in the global petrochemical market. In 2009, 90 percent of the world's ethylene capacity growth was located in the Gulf as petrochemical plants closed elsewhere and relocated to the region. The CEO of one of the world's largest chemical companies, Huntsman Chemicals, remarked in 2010: "The chemical industry is leaving the United States and it won't be back. When demand picks up, they'll build new plants overseas—in the Mideast, Singapore, China" (Whitehouse 2010). A Vice President of Exxon Mobil similarly predicted that the global trade of petrochemicals would double over the next ten years with the Middle East becoming the source of 75 percent of the world's exports. Most significantly, "leading the Middle East and leading the world will be the kingdom of Saudi Arabia" (Ordonez 2010). Alongside their increasing domestic capacity, the large GCC petrochemicals firms noted throughout this book have been pursuing purchases in Europe and the

United States. In 2006, SABIC bought the UK petrochemicals division of Huntsman and in 2007 acquired General Electric's plastics unit. SABIC is now one of the five largest petrochemical manufacturers in the world. Similarly, the Abu Dhabi sovereign wealth fund, The International Petroleum Investment Company (IPIC), bought the Canadian petrochemicals producer NOVA Chemicals in 2009. This global expansion will continue to strengthen the weight of the GCC within the world petrochemicals market.

Concurrent with this continued centrality of GCC hydrocarbons to world capitalism, the region's role in financialization processes will become even more significant. Various scenarios for petrodollar flows based on the future price of oil confirm this in a striking manner. The investment firm McKinsey Global has provided one such set of estimates for a variety of different paths of development for the global economy.[26] McKinsey estimated that, by 2013, the value of foreign assets held by the GCC could increase by 77 percent to around the $3.8 trillion range if oil prices remain at the $70 level of early 2010. This would be comparable to the value of foreign assets held by China. If oil rises to around $100 by 2013 and there is a stronger global recovery, GCC foreign assets could reach $5.7 trillion by 2013, an increase of over 160 percent from 2008 levels and exceeding China's foreign assets by around $1 trillion.[27] According to McKinsey's estimates, petrodollar foreign asset holdings will exceed those of the three other "powerbrokers" (East Asia, hedge funds, and private equity) in all scenarios.[28] Whatever the precise value of GCC investments, the level of GCC petrodollars will likely remain very large—both in absolute terms and relative to other surplus countries—confirming that the future patterns of global imbalances will be strongly influenced by GCC surplus capital flows.

Furthermore, these large financial flows, reinforced by the changes in the nature of the GCC productive circuit, mean that the region is an increasingly important market for both goods and services from the rest of the world. Of noteworthy significance here are the potential profits for high-end engineering, technical and design work—as well as royalty and other types of payments for technological patents, legal and financial services—which accompany the trillions of dollars of development underway in the Gulf. One illustration of this, which perhaps also demonstrates the future East-West fault lines of geopolitical rivalry, was the announcement on December 27, 2009 that a team of South Korean firms had won a $40 billion contract to build and operate four nuclear power plants in Abu Dhabi, beating rival US and French bids. As one of the biggest energy contracts offered in the Middle East, it was the largest engineering project

. ... South Korean firms won
more projects in the Middle East in 2008 than any other country—a quarter
of all projects on offer (Salisbury and Foreman 2010, p. 20).

The Rise of East Asia?

These three broad themes that continue to characterize the GCC's role in
the global market—the increasing dependency on oil and gas imports for
all regions of the globe, the centrality of the GCC's financial flows to capitalism's financialization, and struggles over potential markets for goods and
services in the GCC—mean that the area will be a decisive factor to the
future trajectory of global capitalism. The nature of conflict between the
leading capitalist states, most specifically the evolution of any rivalry
between the United States and other potential powers, will largely pivot
around who is successful in dominating the GCC and its surrounding
region. In this context, the emerging relationship between the GCC and
East Asia assumes a world-historic importance.

Is there a growing confluence of interest between East Asian elites, GCC
states, and Khaleeji Capital at the expense of US power? Some possible
indications of this have been encountered throughout this book. Chapter 4
noted, for example, that an increasing proportion of GCC imports are
sourced from Asia, while the share of US-GCC trade is dropping (although,
it should be remembered, the EU continues to dominate exports to the
GCC). Moreover, the growing weight of Asian contractors in the Gulf's
EPC work confirms that these trends are not restricted to commodity trade
but likewise encompass the vital services sector. Strengthening links with
Asia are also evident in the GCC's energy exports. Indeed, in early 2010, a
spokesperson for Saudi Arabia's Aramco made the dramatic announcement
that the Kingdom's "eyes are focused on China" and that oil exports to
China had surpassed those to the United States (Saudi Gazette 2010).
China's (and India's) expected future growth in energy consumption means
that this trend will likely continue. In the petrochemical sector, half of
SABIC's exports were going to Asia by the end of 2009.

Similarly, there are strong indications of deepening ties between the
GCC and East Asia at the financial level. It has been noted that many GCC
states have made important strategic investments in Chinese petrochemical
plants, reciprocated with Chinese investments in the upstream Gulf

hydrocarbon sector.[29] In Malaysia and Singapore, GCC capital has made significant links through the Islamic finance sector—with key GCC banks opening branches in those countries.[30] In a rare public disclosure of its asset breakdowns, the Abu Dhabi Investment Authority (ADIA) revealed in 2010 that it had up to 20 percent of its investments in Asia (*Khaleej Times* 2010). Both the Kuwait Investment Authority (KIA) and the Qatar Investment Authority (QIA) have also stated that they plan to double the share of Asian assets in their portfolio from the current 10 to 20 percent (EIU 2008, p. 5). All of these trends indicate that GCC investment in China and other Asian countries will almost certainly increase from their post-2000 average of around 10 percent of total Gulf foreign investments. This eastwards shift has been confirmed by many of the region's political leaders and economists. Nasser Saidi, the chief economist in Dubai's International Financial Centre, remarked in early 2010 that the Gulf "will be dancing to a Chinese tune; this is a tectonic shift in economic and political power eastwards . . . this is where our future lies" (*Arabian Business* 2010, p. 34). Perhaps also indicating a potential break with US power, several GCC analysts have advocated replacing the US dollar currency peg with a trade-weighted basket that includes a higher proportion of Asian currencies or, alternatively, the establishment of a single GCC currency pegged to oil (Rutledge 2009, pp. 117–23).

Despite these trends, however, some caution is necessary in interpreting the future evolution of the GCC-US-Asia triad. Most important to note are the potential contradictions inherent in China's accumulation model and its insertion into the global political economy.[31] Although China's growth has been extremely rapid, much of this has been based upon its low-cost labor platform linked to intraregional East Asian trade, with exports ultimately aimed at the United States and other advanced capitalist markets. In this sense, China's growth and its patterns of accumulation have been tied to the evolution of the broader world market and should not necessarily be seen as opposed to US dominance. The structural features of that market described in Chapter 4 remain largely unchanged—low-cost assembly of commodities in Asia, underpinning exports to the United States, sustained by high levels of debt and global financial imbalances. Any realignment of this structure will likely generate crisis and sharp conflicts. A shift in final consumer demand to China, for example, is not simply a matter of economic fiat, but implies a precipitous drop in US living standards, the massive retooling of Chinese factories (to meet the different profile of consumer needs in China), and addressing the widening inequalities in China itself. It is certainly not clear that either US or Chinese elites have an interest in realigning this structure or, indeed, whether they economy, Martin Hart-Lindsberg, has pointed out: "Approximately half of the loans [in response to the economic crisis] have gone to finance property and stock speculation, raising incomes at the top and fuelling destructive bubbles . . . it is difficult to know how long the Chinese government can sustain this effort. Property prices and stock bubbles are worsening. Overcapacity problems are driving down prices and the profitability of key state enterprises" (Hart-Landsberg 2010, p. 290).

Given these uncertainties, there are two different scenarios for the evolution of the relationship between the leading states and the GCC, both of which hold significant implications for Khaleeji Capital, the Gulf states, and the surrounding region. The first of these scenarios is a general persistence of the status quo. US power remains dominant, and the Asian political economy continues to reproduce itself within the accumulation structures that have characterized the latest phase of the global system. The continuation of this highly unstable set of global imbalances is heavily dependent upon the GCC maintaining its role as the nodal point linking East and West, in an accumulation structure of counterdirectional movements of energy commodities and financial flows. The maintenance of this system requires the full participation and assent of the GCC and its ruling elites. At a financial level, both Khaleeji Capital and, most particularly, state-run funds and central banks need to continue to reinvest their surpluses within US financial markets and support US dollar hegemony. The GCC states must also work to provide the necessary flows of energy to all sectors of the global economy. This would need to happen at a price that is not too high that it disrupts profitability, but is high enough that the requisite financial surpluses continue to be generated to sustain both the GCC and the necessary flows to the global capital markets. In this sense, GCC capital will be increasingly drawn into a role of "superintending" the structure of global capitalism alongside the United States and other leading capitalist states (including China).[32] It takes place within a system that is highly dependent on contingent factors—unstable and prone to potential bubbles of overaccumulation and deflationary crises.

The second scenario sees a major shift in this structure. This could occur as a result of a deep systemic crisis and would be indicated by a sharpening rivalry between the leading capitalist states—an outcome that continues to be explicitly discussed (and planned for) within ruling circles. A recent US government national security report, for example, openly noted the possibility that such intercapitalist rivalry would erupt on the world stage. While this did not necessarily mean "a complete breakdown of the international system, as occurred in 1914–1918 when an earlier phase of globalization came to a halt," the report noted "the next 20 years of transition to a new system are fraught with risks. Strategic rivalries are most likely to revolve around trade, investments, and technological innovation and acquisition . . . we cannot rule out a 19th century-like scenario of arms races, territorial expansion, and military rivalries" (NICGT 2008, p. vi). In this eventuality, intercapitalist rivalries will undoubtedly manifest themselves in competitive struggles to align with and incorporate the GCC states and Khaleeji Capital into new hierarchies of global accumulation. Success in this competitive struggle over the GCC will be a key determinant of which region becomes ascendant.

The continuing tight military relationships between the United States and the GCC states—and the region's ongoing dependence on a US security umbrella—make it difficult to conceive of a fundamental shift in the GCC's allegiances away from the United States and toward an alternative power. However, in the event of any significant weakening of US hegemony at the global scale, it is possible to foresee widening conflicts, contradictions, or disputes within this relationship. The key flashpoints in the broader region— Iran, Iraq, Pakistan, Afghanistan, and Palestine—need to be viewed through this lens, particularly to the extent that China (and Russia) appears to be forging foreign policies that are somewhat independent of the United States.

Whether global capitalism continues to be dominated by the United States or a new hegemon arises, one striking fact remains—the trajectory of the global political economy and the balance of attendant geopolitical rivalries will continue to be deeply intertwined with the nature of class and capitalism in the Gulf. Class formation in the Gulf did much to underpin the ascendency of US power in the postwar era. Simultaneously, Gulf capitalism was wrought in the world market formed by this very same ascendant power and its careful assurance of the systemic drives of internationalization and financialization. Whatever the future course of world politics, there will continue to be a close interlacing of the needs and outlook of the ruling elites of the Gulf region with those of global capitalism, materialized in the ongoing growth of Khaleeji Capital and the deepening internationalization of the Gulf's own accumulation processes.

Appendix A   Khaleeji Capital Conglomerates

CONGLOMERATE	PRODUCTIVE CIRCUIT	COMMODITY CIRCUIT	FINANCE CI
SAUDI ARABIA			
KINGDOM Owned by Prince Alwaleed bin Talal bin Abdulaziz Al Saud, richest Arab in the world.	Tasnee Petrochemicals; Savola, (edible oils, dairy products, sugar, and packaging); runs a private hospital and school for 4,000 students; news-paper and media conglomerate; agricultural company in Egypt; private domestic airline in Saudi Arabia; Dana Gas, the largest private gas project in the Middle East.	Savola, (supermarkets and hypermarkets); Herfy's fast food; Licensee of SAKS Inc (handbags, jewelry, cosmetics including Dior, Cartier, Prada, Roberto Cavali, and Valentino).	SAMBA; Citigro Commercial Bar the Bank of Chi Ghana, Nigeria, PADICO and A of total shares in Kodak, Hewlett Pepsico, Procter a Disney, E-Bay, A Commercial Inve
AL RAJHI Owned by Al Rajhi family, an old merchant family that established the first foreign exchange agency for pilgrims to Mecca and Medina.	Arabian Cement Company, Al-Yamama Saudi Cement Co., the Yanbu Cement Co., the Southern Province Cement Co., Raysut Cement Co., and the Saudi Cement Co. Owns cement factories in Sudan, Syria, and Jordan; manufac-tures water coolers and air conditioning units, carpets, and fabrics in Saudi Arabia; Al Arrab Contracting Company; Al Rajhi Steel factories; largest poultry farm in the Middle East. Tabuk Agriculture and Development Co.; National Agricultural Development Co. producing wheat, dairy, fruits, and dates; transport fleet with over 1,000 trucks; Advanced Polypropylene Co.; SIPCHEM (The Saudi International Petrochemical Co.; Dana Gas; ACWA Power Projects; board of Saudi Telecom Company.	50% stake in the UAE-based Tameer Holdings. Through Tameer, al Rajhi has very extensive interests in shopping malls and commercial districts; Imports and distributes building materials such as steel beams, wood, steel pipes; Travel agency Fursan Travel; Agency for Emerson Motor Technologies (water coolers, air condition-ers, and refrigerators).	Al Rajhi Bank, B the Arab Banking Baraka Banking C Investments; Tam (UAE).

Appendix A Continued

CONGLOMERATE	PRODUCTIVE CIRCUIT	COMMODITY CIRCUIT	FINANCE CIRCUIT
AL GOSAIBI Established in the 1940s as a trading and money exchange firm in the growing oil-rich city of Al Khobar as Aramco was growing in the area. Was an early client of King Abdulaziz.	Saudi Industrial Investments Group (SIIG); Zamil Industrial Investments Corporation; Soft drink manufacture, can manufacturing, corrosion powder manufacturing; oilfield chemicals; pipe coating; cork; paper; snack food and fertilizer production; Saudi Cement; Savola; Saudi Consolidated Electric Co., the first power plant in Saudi Arabia.	National Bottling Company (bottles Pepsico beverages in Saudi Arabia); Distribution and agency rights for American Express, Sumitomo of Japan, Jeumont of France, Mirrlees Blackstone of the United Kingdom, Alstom and the US-based ShawCor.	International Banking Corporation; SAMBA; Saudi British Bank, Arab National Bank, Dar Almaal Alislami Geneva, IFA Banque Paris, and the Saudi United Bank.
ZAMIL Began as a trading firm involved in food and textiles in Bahrain. Later expanded into real estate and industrial firms.	Steel manufacturing, air conditioning, glass, bricks, blocks, fencing, paint, automatic doors, packaging materials, and ladders; Saudi Cement; SIPCHEM; Sahara Petrochemicals; the Nama Petrochemical company; Chemanol and others; National Power Company; Production of dairy and meat products; Ship building and repair, and tourism.	Imports frozen foods; exclusive licensee of manufacturing techniques in the glass and ceramic sectors; license to manufacture and distribute General Electric brand air conditioners; joint venture with Morris Cranes to manufacture and distribute under the name in Saudi Arabia; license from the Canadian Canam Manac Group (CMG) to produce and distribute steel joists and frames in Saudi Arabia	Investcorp; Shaml Bank; Bahrain Islamic Bank, Arcapita; Jadwa Investments, Capital Management House, a leading private equity firm based in Bahrain; Bank al Bilad.
OLAYAN Began as a trucking and transportation contractor for Aramco and Bechtel in 1947. In 1954, launched food and consumer trading business, and later insurance firm in Saudi Arabia.	SIPCHEM; Saudi Cement; Olayan Descon; construction and engineering services for refinery and petrochemical industries; assemble solar cells for energy companies operating in remote areas; can manufacturing plant; joint venture with Kimberly-Clark and SPIMACO to produce surgical gowns, drapes, and other operating room accessories; Dana Gas.	Agency and distribution rights for Coca-Cola, Kraft Foods, Nestlé, Kimberly-Clark, Colgate-Palmolive, Australian Rice Growers, Nabisco, Polaroid, Pillsbury, and others; Burger King franchisee for the Middle East; agent for Xerox and Toshiba; Distributor and dealer of Scania trucks, Cummins Power Generation and Power Rental, Kenworth trucks, and Amco Veba truck cranes; Carrefour hypermarket franchise.	Saudi Hollandi Bank; Saudi British Bank (SABB); LeasePlan, the world's biggest vehicle management and leasing provider; founded the Arab Commercial Enterprises (ACE), the largest local insurance and reinsurance broker in the Middle East; represented on the board of Morgan Stanley.

DALLAH AL BARAKA

Founded by Saleh Kamel as a contractor to the Saudi government in the 1960s.

Constructs aircraft hangars and spare parts stores; food supply, maintenance, and operation services at airports, military bases, and hospitals; contract to clean and maintain the Muslim holy cities of Mecca and Medina; production of dairy and meat products, sweets, ice cream, juices, edible oils, grains and spices, and honey; largest juice manufacturer in the Middle East; manufacture and distribution of cement; production of cables, pipes, and wire through its 41% stake in Arabian Steel Pipes Manufacturing Co.; owns Arab Radio and Television Network (ART), one of the largest media conglomerates in the Middle East.

Imports of paper, electrical appliances, and machinery; operates an advertising company that solicits advertising for its media network.

Albaraka Bank
subsidiary or a
countries such
Africa, Kazakh;
Bangladesh, M.
Albania, and Pa
Jazira; one of th
holders in Taml
estate developer

AL TURKI

Founded in the 1950s as a supplier of retail goods for foreigners working in the Saudi oil industry.

SIPCHEM; manufactures stationery products, customized panel boards, surface treatments, adhesives, grouts, repair compounds, sealants, and other construction-related material; civil engineering and contracting material; waste management services; ports management services; operates Saudi Aramco's private port marine services; provides services such as drilling, contracting, servicing, and equipment and tool supply for oil and gas sector.

Agents for 3M, ABB, ARW Transformers, AXIS, Adobe, Allen Bradley, Apple, Areva, Bailey Birkett, Bantex, Beamex, Bently Nevada, Broyce Control, Carboni, Cavan Industries, Chemshire, Claved, Clipsal, Dodge Mechanical Power Transmission, Durable, Epson, General Electric, Genisys Enterprise Solutions, HP, Honeywell International, IBM, J. S. Humidifiers, Kappa, Klein Tools, Max Tube, Osram, Prosoft Technology, Rockwell Automation, Sinopec, T. D. Williamson, and Weed Instruments.

Abraaj Capital; I
Investment Hold
Investment Co. (
Saudi Insurance (

Appendix A Continued

CONGLOMERATE	PRODUCTIVE CIRCUIT	COMMODITY CIRCUIT	FINANCE CIRCUIT
AL JOMAIH Established in 1936 as a foodstuffs and textile trading company. Was the grocer to King Abdulaziz and later expanded to hold agencies for key foreign firms.	Dana Gas; major shareholder of Pakistan's recently privatized electric company; Karachi Electric Supply Company; represented on the board of directors of the Bahrain Ferro Alloy Co.; bottles Pepsi soft drinks and juices and manufactures cans in Saudi Arabia; Mobily, second-largest cell-phone company in Saudi Arabia.	Largest distributor of GM in the Middle East; sole distributor of Cadillac, Hummer, Saab, and Opel in Saudi Arabia; holds agency rights for Pepsi, Shell, Yokohama, and Fiat.	Bank Al Bilad; Arcapita; founder of British Islamic Insurance Holdings; founding shareholder of the Arab Palestinian Investment Company (APIC).
ALI REZA An old merchant trading house that grew through the 1920s and won distribution and agency rights for a number of key firms. Was an early client of King Abdulaziz.	Designs and installs radio broadcasting, military communication networks, and security systems; construction and contracting company; manufactures tin, plastic, and composite containers; owns, manages, and represents shipping lines in the Jeddah and Dammam areas; owns a lubricating oil facility; designs, manufactures, and distributes sporting, leisure facilities such as pools, spas, saunas, and tennis courts; major shareholder in the agricultural company, SAVOLA.	Operates the McDonalds franchise for the western area of Saudi Arabia; exclusive representative and distributor in Saudi Arabia of Aston Martin, Ford (Mercury), Mazda, KIA, and MAN Truck; one of the largest chemical importers and distributors throughout the Middle East from Bayer, Exxon Mobil, and others; imports and distributes sanitary products for the healthcare, food processing, catering, food retail, and agricultural sectors; holds agencies for sporting equipment such as Prince, Benetton, Adidas, Rooler Blade, Nordic Track, Life Fitness, York Barbell, Cybex, and others.	SAMBA; Investcorp.
EL SEIF Established in 1951 as a trading and transport company for the oil industry.	One of the three largest construction companies in Saudi Arabia; owns and operates one of the largest private hospital networks in the Middle East and the UK; owns 50% of the National Power Company (the remaining 50% is owned by the Zamil Group).	Sole agent for a number of medical and pharmaceutical products in Saudi Arabia. These include Beckman, General Electric Medical Systems, Merck Sharp and Dohme, and Varian.	Capital Bank of Jordan; Azizia Commercial Investment Company; strategic investor in the MerchantBridge's Iraq Reconstruction Fund, a fund set up to bid for projects in Iraq after 2003.

HOKAIR

Established in 1965 as a tourism and development company. Expanded into real estate and retail activities in subsequent decades.

Engineering, procurement, and construction work in the oil and gas, petrochemical, and power sectors; building five private hospitals, 500 pharmacies, and 50 medical centers to become operational over the next seven years.

600 outlets representing more than 40 international brands: Accessorize, Adams Kids, Aldo, Ann Harvey, Bershka, Bonita, Booster Juice, Camaieu's, Cinnabon, Colony, Du Pareil au Meme, Elvi, Exit, Foschini, GrandOptical, Jack and Jones, Jennyfer, Joe Bloggs, Kekos, Kiabi, La Senza, La Senza Express, La Senza Girl, La Senza Sprit, Le Chateau, London Dairy, Marks and Spencer's, Massimo Dutti, Monsoon, Nine West, Orsay, Oysho, PriceLess, Seattle's Best Coffee, Sports City, Spring, Swensen's, Tape A Loeil, The Pizza Company, Thyme Maternity, Vero Moda, Wallis, Zara; Six malls, including: Mall of Dhahran (300+ shops), Aziz Mall (228), Khurais Plaza (175), Mall of Arabia Jeddah, Salaam Mall (100+), Sahara Plaza (55); franchise rights for Geant Hypermarket in Saudi Arabia; distributes the Chinese automobile, the Chery, in Saudi Arabia; operates four luxury hotels under the Marriot name.

Manar Finan
Services; ope
and nonlife)
venture with
founding shar
an investment
Bahrain.

Appendix A Continued

CONGLOMERATE	PRODUCTIVE CIRCUIT	COMMODITY CIRCUIT	FINANCE CIRCUIT
KUWAIT			
AL GHANIM The two key holding companies in this group are Al Ghanim Industries and Yousef Al Ghanim and Sons. The Al Ghanim are one of the original merchant families of Kuwait.	Manufactures fiberglass insulation, prefabricated steel buildings and structures; involved in design, supply, installation, and maintenance services for HVAC, electrical, plumbing, fire fighting, and technology systems; runs one of the largest freight companies in the Middle East, providing air and ocean shipping, customs clearance, packing services, overland transport, and warehousing.	First distributors of General Motors in the GCC and continue to represent them in Kuwait. The company is sole agent for Chevrolet, SABB, Hummer, and BP Lubricants; largest consumer electronics retailer in the Middle East. It has exclusive representation rights in Kuwait for Toshiba, Philips, Daewoo, Konka, Frigidaire, Whirlpool, Electrolux, Amana, Lager mania, Techno gas, Terim, Hitachi, Minolta, and also distributes other brands; imports Hitachi air conditioners as the exclusive agent; agents for Kraft Foods, Mars, Colgate-Palmolive, Nabisco; represents British Airways, Gulf Air, Cathay Pacific, Qantas, Air Arabia, Cunard, and the Australian Government for visas to Australia; the largest importer of Chinese products in the Middle East.	National Bank of Kuwait; owns the largest stake in the Gulf Bank; founding shareholder of Perella Weinberg Partners, a privately owned financial services firm; member of the Kuwait China Investment Fund in India and China; runs a consumer credit service integrated with its retail outlets; owns an insurance company; major shareholder and represented on the board of Shuaa Capital.

KHARAFI

Original merchant family in Kuwait and one of the founders of the National Bank of Kuwait. Closely related to the Kuwaiti state (one of the family members is the Speaker of the Kuwait National Assembly).

Portland Cement Company; the United Stainless Steel Company; poultry and meat processing plants in Kuwait, Saudi Arabia, and Egypt; maintenance, servicing, and project management of refineries, pipelines, power stations, water treatment plants, and other civil engineering projects; manufactures insulation materials, aluminum architectural products, steel products, pipes, mobile homes, glass, and plastic products; largest paper mill in the Middle East; Construction company with branches in Saudi Arabia, the UAE, Yemen, Egypt, Kenya, and elsewhere building airports, pipelines, hotels, roads, power plants, petrochemical facilities, hospitals, and sewage treatment plants; designs and constructs oil and gas facilities, refineries, pipelines, and other industrial work; major shipbuilder and repairer in Kuwait; manufactures and installs oil pipes; represented on the board of the National Industries Group.

Agencies for: KFC, Pizza Hut, Hardee's, TGI Friday's, Tikka, Fish Market, Saint Cinnamon, Costa Coffee, Grand Café, Baskin Robbins Samadi, Krispy Kreme's, Americana Meat, Americana Cake, Koki Chicken, California Gardens, Farm Frites, Heinz, and Cadbury; operates over 600 brand name restaurants in eleven Arab countries including Kuwait, Bahrain, Qatar, Egypt, Saudi Arabia, Oman, Jordan, and Lebanon; imports and acts as agents for computing, printing, and office equipment including the brands Kinkos, Kodak, Danka, Screen, and Reeves; operates Sheraton Hotels in South Africa and Syria.

Owns approxi...
National Bank...
Investment Hu...
holder in Al N...
company and ...
(Al Mal, in tur...
venture called ...
East that was fu...
members of the...
Intelligence. Di...
William Webste...
the CIA and the...
involved in secu...
gathering in Iraq...

BABTAIN

Founded in 1948 by an important merchant family. Later won the agency rights for a number of Japanese and European automobile companies.

IT, software design, networks, GIS, CAD, training et cetera through its subsidiary National Computer Services; owns the Kuwait Paint company; produces shopping bags, garbage bags, packing, laundry bags, disposable gloves, and packing tape; produces transport trailers.

Sole distributor of Nissan, Renault, Citroen, CMC, and JMC motor vehicles; holds agency and distribution rights for: Cheng Shin Tyres, Dacia Automobiles, Dunlop Tyres, Farabi Technologies, GS Storage Battery, Hewlett Packard, Holts Lloyd, Jiangling Motors, Legato, Mastek, NGK Spark Plugs, Network Appliance, Oracle, Citroën, China Motors.

Founding shareho...
Zumorroda Invest...
large Kuwaiti priv...
firm. Zumorroda ...
the Iraq Holding C...
in turn, is one of t...
owners of the Ban...
Zumorroda also ho...
stake in the Bank o...
Kuwait, and the Gu...
Zumorroda also ow...
Kuwaiti mortgage fi...
Finance.

Appendix A Continued

CONGLOMERATE	PRODUCTIVE CIRCUIT	COMMODITY CIRCUIT	FINANCE CIRCUIT
ESSA (SULTAN GROUP) Began as a private grocery chain in Kuwait, later expanded into logistics, real estate, and finance.	Runs a security and labor services company; provides telecommunications and fiber optics installation through several companies; major stake in Alpha Energy Company (20%), which is involved in oil exploration, drilling, and services in the oil and petrochemical industry; owns 30% of the National Real Estate Company, the fourth-largest real estate company in Kuwait.	Owns the major Kuwaiti supermarket chain, Sultan Center; holds franchises for Chi-Chi's and Tumbleweeds restaurants and a range of international fashion labels; Runs the largest GCC logistics company, Agility.	Owns an investment company, United Capital Group; on the board of the Gulf Bank of Kuwait; on the board of Bayan Investment Company.
SHAYA Large merchant family with a history stretching back to 1890. Now runs one of the largest retail chains across the Middle East.	General contract work specializing in construction using precast concrete systems, fabrication, and erection of steel items and construction of buildings, show rooms, markets, and commercial complexes; a leading electromechanical contractor; invested in the Kuwait Foundry Company, and sits on the company board. KFH is engaged in casting iron and other metals; manufacturing sanitary items and accessories for sewerage systems, and manufacturing casting joints for pipes, water valves, and pumps, electrical cable joints, electric fuse boxes, and other related products.	One of the largest retailers in the Middle East with over 40 franchises represented in over 1,300 stores in 13 countries in the Middle East and Eastern Europe. Some of these franchises include: Aramis, Ashas, Bhs, Boots, Claire's, Clinique, Coast, Debenhams, Dorothy Perkins, Elena Miro, Estée Lauder, Evans, Faith, Foot Locker, Hennes and Mauritz, Jack and Jones, Le Pain Quotidien, Limited Too, MAC, Mazda, Milano, Mothercare, Motivi, Next, Noodle Factory, Oasis, Oltre, Peacocks, Pearle Opticians, Peugeot, Pizza Express, Principles, River Island, Samosa, Sarai, Solaris, Starbucks, Stride Rite, Thai Chi, The Body Shop, The Gaucho Grill, Top Shop/Top Man, Totally Fish, Vavavoom, Vero Moda, Vision Express, Wallis; controls the largest mall in Kuwait, Avenues Mall; exclusive dealer of Mazda and Peugeot in Kuwait, as well as a Michelin tire and Mobil lubricant distribution; runs the Sheraton Kuwait and the Medina Oberoi Hotel in Saudi Arabia.	Represented on the board of Gulf Bank; one of the top five shareholders and represented on the board of directors of the Gulf Finance House; controlling shareholder of Injazzat Real Estate Company, whose investments include land investments, office tower developments, owned and operated residential properties, retail developments, mixed-use commercial developments, build-operate-transfer projects, and hospitality and entertainment properties; represented on the board of the Bahrain Financial Harbour, a real estate project in Bahrain designed to become the new financial center of the country; holds the largest private stake in the Securities House, one of the most important investment firms in Kuwait.

UNITED ARAB EMIRATES

GURG

Merchant family from Fujairah, which held many of the first agencies for the region. The group's founder is the UAE Ambassador to the Republic of Ireland.

Manufactures paints and finishing products; steel reinforcements for concrete and steel bars; building chemicals and water-proofing compounds; mechanical engineering unit and fabrication shop; automotive repair and maintenance workshop; manufactures, supplies and installs doors and windows, kitchen cabinets, wardrobes, exterior wooden items like pergolas, and wooden structures for commercial and residential complexes; industrial explosives for civil, mining, quarrying, seismic, onshore and offshore drilling projects.

Agent for British American Tobacco, Unilever, Benetton, Siemens, Osram, Armitage Shanks, Stanton, Carnic, Yorkshire Copper Tubes, Dunlop, Dulux, Electrolux, Fisher & Paykel, Forbes and Xenic and many others; imports and distributes building and plumbing-related products, architectural finishing products, water heaters, pipes, tiling, kitchen accessories and ceramics; distributes stationery and office products; holds franchises for 3M & NCR of USA, Elfen from Thailand, Rexel of UK, Nightingale of India and Durable, Elba & Pelikan from Germany.

National Bank
Banking Group
Dubai Growth

GHURAIR

Founded in 1960 in Dubai, it is now one of the largest private conglomerates in the UAE. The son of the Group's founder helped to establish Emaar and is the speaker of the UAE Federal National Council.

Construction company; largest aluminum extrusion factory in the Middle East (Gulf Extrusions); on the board of Dubai the world's largest single aluminum smelter site; packaging plant producing cardboard products for storage and shipping purposes; makes tin cans, sheets, and can ends; owns the UAE's first steel coil and galvanizing plant; owns a freight and shipping company; Emaar Properties; Advanced Polypropylene Co. and SIPCHEM (The Saudi International Petrochemical Co.); owns the second-largest flour milling company in the Middle East; owns a controlling stake in the National Cement Co.

Agents for 3D-Club, Daewoo, Edimax, Samsung, Scott Power, View Sonic; distributes IT products, cell phones, and consumer electronics as agents for LG, Samsung, Creative, and other international companies; largest trader of dry bulk cargo in the Middle East; owns four large malls in the UAE and Bahrain: Burjuman Mall (500 shops), Al Ghurair City (209), Bahrain Mall (120), Reef Mall (94).

Mashreq Bank, Sl
bank; Commercia
Gulfinance; on th
of the Dubai Gro
the first investmen

Appendix A Continued

CONGLOMERATE	PRODUCTIVE CIRCUIT	COMMODITY CIRCUIT	FINANCE CIRCUIT
MAZRUI Important Abu Dhabi-based business group run by Abdullah Mazrui. The Mazrui family has close ties to the Nahyan ruling family and has served in a number of important government positions.	Chemanol (Saudi Arabia); United Gulf Steel (Saudi Arabia); manufactures steel pipes; produces basic chemicals such as foams, stabilizers, and lubricants used in industrial processes in the Gulf region; freight transport and warehousing division; engineering and construction company; on the board of the Abu Dhabi National Industrial Projects Co. (ADNIP).	Holds agency rights for: 3M paints, Teku, Garden Leader, Plastecnic, Grupo Mago, Tournesol, Planters Technology, Ames, Mikskaar; sole agent for Spies Hecker GmbH, a manufacturer of automotive refinishing paint systems; Illy coffee systems; The One franchise for the UAE, operates seven department stores in the UAE and is agent for Calvin Klein, Chloe, Elizabeth Arden, Maytag, Kenwood Kitchen Appliances, Nippon, and others. A member of the Group chairs the board of Jashanmal; founders and chair of Aramex, a logistics company.	Investbank; Investcorp; Emirates Insurance Co.; The National Investor (TNI).
AL JABER Abu Dhabi-based group founded in 1970 by Obaid Khaleefa Jaber Al Murri with an initial focus on the construction sector.	Construction company; aluminum fabrication factory; aluminum extrusion plant; steel fabrication factory; iron and steel foundry; manufactures high precision engineering component and units; manufactures traffic, safety, commercial, and advertising signs; operates a transport division with 4,000 trucks, over 100 cranes, and a fleet of tanker vessels; major shareholder and vice-chair of the board of the Abu Dhabi National Industrial Projects Co. (ADNIP).	Sole agent for Kenworth trucks in the United Arab Emirates; sole authorized distributor for Shell lubricants in the Emirate of Abu Dhabi; agent for Reich Concrete pumps and mixers, Baldwin filters, Scope batteries, Braden winches, and Fulda tires; imports bulk bitumen from Bahrain for road construction in Abu Dhabi and neighboring countries.	Abraaj capital; The National Investor (TNI); Abu Dhabi Takaful, an Islamic insurance company in the UAE; Emirates Insurance Company.

NOWAIS

Abu Dhabi-based family with close ties to the UAE ruling family including representation on the Abu Dhabi Council for Economic Development.

Maintenance and project management company; scaffolding company; designs, installs, and manages local/wide area networks (LAN/WAN); major shareholder and on the board of the Abu Dhabi National Industrial Projects Co. (ADNIP); runs a food manufacturing company that produces chocolate, potato chips, and other snacks.

Represents over 100 companies in the supply and service of electromechanical and instrumentation equipment; supplies filters, explosive-proof electrical components, and industrial valves for onshore and offshore gas and oil activities, power generation, airports, and construction; distributes medical supplies, hospital equipment, pharmaceuticals, and consumer health products and represents around 30 international companies in this sector; holds agencies for 3Con, 3M, Aventis, Fujitsu, Daewoo, Pirelli, Cisco, Panasonic, Mitsubishi, Lucent, and Alcatel.

Investbank; Sh
Capital; Waha

QATAR

AL FARDAN

Prominent merchant family that has its origins in the pearling business, expanding into money exchange and finance in the 1970s.

Construction and Development Company; chairs the board of the United Development Company (UDC). UDC is one of the largest companies in Qatar, and acts as a holding company for other investments. These include sole ownership of the Pearl-Qatar Project, a massive real estate project involving 32 kilometers of new coastline, which will house 40,000 residents in more than 15,000 dwellings by 2011. UDC is also involved in the production of petrochemicals (the Gulf Formaldehyde Company); chairs Qatar Cool, a cooling plant that supplies chilled water for refrigeration to building and office blocks in Qatar through a network of underground pipes; vice-chair of Qatar Dredging, a company that reclaims land through dredging ocean areas.

Distributes Mini and Rolls Royce and is the sole agent of BMW, Ferrari, and Land Rovers in Qatar (set the second-highest world record of Ferraris sold in 2006); jewelry branch is the agent for Piaget, Corum, Chopard, and Harry Winston.

Commercial Ban
largest bank in Q
The United Arab
the National Ban
(Oman); Investco
Insurance Compa
exchange business
precious metals.

Appendix A Continued

CONGLOMERATE	PRODUCTIVE CIRCUIT	COMMODITY CIRCUIT	FINANCE CIRCUIT
AL MANA Founded by Mohammed Hamad Al Mana from the Al Mana family.	Runs a large engineering and contracting firm; provides cleaning and support services for large-scale companies, apartment buildings, government offices; major contractor of labor for oil and gas industries; designs and installs air conditioning units.	Agents for Konica Minolta, Project UK, Bertello, Fursys, Océ, Rexel UK, Ibico, 3M, Apple, HACER, Hewlett Packard; sole agents for Philips, Whirlpool, Daewoo, Frigidaire in Qatar; in consumer goods, is the agent for Unilever Arabia, Hindustan Lever Limited, Gillette Middle East, Pillsbury Company, Friesland Cobarco Dairy Products; represents Gulf Air, Air India, PIA, Qatar Airways, Emirate Airlines, Egypt Air, KLM, Kuwait Airways.	Major shareholder and represented on the board of directors of Qatar Islamic Bank; on the board of directors of Salam International, a major Qatari investment firm with extensive interests in the GCC and Palestine; chair of Al Ahli Bank, Qatar.
NBK Established in the early 1950s as a private conglomerate by Nasser Bin Khaled al Thani, member of the ruling al Thani family.	Owns one of the largest contracting companies in Qatar and has built the Khalifa Sports Stadium, the Central Bank of Qatar, West Bay Al Salam Plaza, Doha International Airport's Warehousing Facilities, Mesaid Police Department, the Ministry of Interior; installs heat insulation and fire-proofing for factories in the oil and gas, petrochemical, basic metals, and power generation sectors; runs one of the largest real estate firms in Qatar and is building a new city, Al Waab City, with 2,200 residential units, commercial space, and a 300-room hotel. Al Waab will provide housing for over 10,000 people.	Agent for Mercedes Benz, Spyker Sport Cars, Mitsubishi Motors, Harley Davidson, and Kawasaki; runs several chains of restaurants and bakeries in Qatar; agents for various IT firms including Momenta and 3i-Infotech; runs an extensive sporting, high-end fashion and luxury goods retail business. It is agent for Quiksilver, Antik Batik, Gloria Jeans, Tashia, Murphy & Nye, Lanvin, Elie Saab, Loewe, Nina Ricci, and Paul Smith; runs four supermarkets in Qatar; sits on the board of Spinney's Supermarkets, one of the largest supermarket chains in the Middle East; exclusive distributor of Bosch home appliances in Qatar; imports agricultural testing equipment, medical supplies, and other lab materials for government and university institutions in Qatar.	Major shareholder and represented on the board of directors of Abraaj Capital; on the board of directors of Shuaa Capital; a founding shareholder and chairs the board of Amwal Qatar; chair of the Doha Insurance Company; on the board of directors of Salam International (see above).

BAHRAIN

MOHAMMED JALAL AND SONS

Established after World War Two as a trading company and agents for a number of international firms.

Construction, contracting, and interior design; design and installation of large air conditioning systems, mechanical and electrical engineering for industrial projects such as refineries, pipelines, and petrochemical plants; engineering subsidiary in Oman; produces mineral water, ice and water dispensing machines in Bahrain; industrial catering to major industries, government bodies, hospitals, and airlines; Chemanol (Saudi Arabia); United Paper Industries.

Sole agent in Bahrain for Jaguar, Proton, Peugeot, and Suzuki automobiles; holds the exclusive franchises for Rothmans cigarettes, Cartier, and Jubilee in Bahrain; sole agent for Schindler lifts, escalators, walkways, and conveyor systems; exclusive distributor for the Trane company, one of the world's largest manufacturers of air conditioning equipment; largest distributor of stationery products in Bahrain. It is also the agent for a number of English language presses including Macmillan Books, Cambridge University Press, and Oxford University Press. Transports bulk, packed, heavy industry, and petrochemical products across the GCC and provides freight forwarding and warehouse services in the region; United Parcel Services (UPS) in Bahrain.

Al Ahli Unite owns 51% of Bahrain, a sul largest currenc

ZAYANI

Founded by Khalid Rashid Zayani in the 1970s, the company is mainly organized through Al Zayani Investments. The Zayani family has its origins in a Sunni merchant family with interests in pearling. A family dispute in the 1970s led the original family firm to be divided between different branches of the family.

Owns 50% of Midal Cables, which produces aluminum rods, steel reinforced conductors, and power transmission lines; produces bottle caps; the company is the single largest user of aluminum from Aluminium Bahrain (ALBA).

Holds agencies for Rolls Royce, Ferrari, Maserati, MINI, Land Rover, Rover, MG, Mitsubishi, and Hyundai; distributor of commercial vehicles, trucks, heavy machinery, garage equipment, and spare parts with agencies for Freightliner, Kalmar, MAHA, Mitsubishi, Nussbaum.

Investcorp; Bahrai Ta'sheelat, a credit company that is th vider of consumer in Bahrain.

Appendix A Continued

CONGLOMERATE	PRODUCTIVE CIRCUIT	COMMODITY CIRCUIT	FINANCE CIRCUIT
AL MOAYYED Established by Yousuf Khalil Almoayyed in the 1940s as agents for Ford and other retail goods. Later expanded into construction and finance. Al Moayyed is a prominent Sunni merchant family in Bahrain.	Construction company; cleaning and maintenance company that provides security guards, domestic housekeeping, cleaning of sewage lines, and pest control; designs and supplies computer networks; holds vice-chair of Aluminium Bahrain.	Bahrain Maritime and Mercantile International (BMMI), a major retail company in Bahrain that is the sole agent for Colgate-Palmolive, Henkel, Japan Tobacco, Kellogg's, Kraft Food International, MasterFoods, Red Bull, Yardley, Storck, Jergens, American Garden, and Sue Bee. It also distributes alcoholic beverages including Heineken, Johnnie Walker, Jack Daniels, Smirnoff, and Becks; holds the agency in Bahrain for Nissan, Renault, Infiniti, Ford automobiles; hold the agency for Akai, Toshiba, Westinghouse, Kenwood, Electrolux, and Akira; imports bathroom fittings, tiles, paints, and construction materials; imports construction equipment from suppliers such as Kenworth, Komatsu, Iveco, Nissan diesel; principal suppliers of office equipment in Bahrain, and distributors for major international companies such as Konica Minolta, Agfa, Hitachi; Seef properties, a large real estate company that owns several malls in Bahrain.	Investcorp; National Bank of Bahrain; TAIB Bank; Alpine Wealth Management; National Finance House, a company that provides financing to consumers for auto and other retail purchases, and real estate loans.

KANOO			
The group was established in 1890 in Bahrain and was initially involved in pearling, trade, and finance. Different branches of the Kanoo family came to be located in Oman, Saudi Arabia, and the UAE.	Shipping and travel agencies; Chemanol (Saudi Arabia); Alujain Petrochemical Corporation; provides repair and maintenance services for ships in the Gulf; engineering company for power plant engineering, project management, repair, and maintenance; two factories in Saudi Arabia that produce marine paints.	Represents firms such as Grove, Hyster, Perkins, Bobcat, Hiab, Massey Ferguson, Lincoln Electric; principal agent for many suppliers of petrochemical, oil and gas equipment including instrumentation, drilling material, valves, turbines, filtration systems, chemicals, and process control machinery; import agent and distributor for British American Tobacco (BAT); sole representative of Maersk Shipping in the UAE. Runs an air cargo and freight forwarding service throughout the Gulf.	National Bank of Bahrain; Investcorp; Abraaj Capital; First Leasing Bank; insurance joint venture with Norwich Union; Unicorn Investment Bank; Jadwa Investments.

OMAN

ZAWAWI			
Main companies making up the group are Omzest, Alawi Enterprises, Zawawi Trading Company, and Talal Zawawi Enterprises. The Zawawi family has held prominent positions in the Omani state, and the group's head, Omar Zawawi, is considered the second-richest person in Oman after the Sultan.	Two methanol plants and a formaldehyde plant in the Sohar Industrial Port area; produces paint, shoes, boots, and sandals, disposable baby diapers and female sanitary napkins; construction and engineering company; Oman Agricultural Development Company (produces milk, yoghurt, juices, and vegetable crops); Oman Textile Mills Company; Areej Vegetable Oils & Derivatives; largest detergent and soap manufacturer in Oman.	Agent and distributor for Mercedes Benz, Brother, Olivetti, Xerox, Wyef Pharmaceuticals Maersk Shipping, Avis-Rent-a-Car, Siemens, GSM handsets and cordless phones in Oman; owns a network of 120 gas stations.	Oman International Bank; Arab International Bank; National Finance; Muscat Finance Company; Muscat National Holding company, which owns the Muscat Insurance Company and the Muscat Life Assurance Company.

(continued)

Appendix A Continued

CONGLOMERATE	PRODUCTIVE CIRCUIT	COMMODITY CIRCUIT	FINANCE C
ZUBAIR Modern company originates in contracting work for the early Omani oil industry and as agents for foreign automobiles. Members of the Zubair family have served as ministers and advisors in the Omani government since the early 1900s.	Owns an oil industries service company; joint venture with Larsen and Toubro, the third-largest engineering, procurement, and construction company in the world; established the first private sector power project in the Gulf, the Manah Power Project; operates an Independent Power and Water Plant; two manufacturing units that produce fluorescent lighting, electrical power controls, motor controls and specialized electrical panels; manufactures custom made wooden furniture, upholstered items, and fitted joinery for the hospitality sector; Dana Gas; real estate division.	Agent for Audi, Bentley, Chrysler, Mitsubishi, Peugeot, Rolls Royce, Volkswagen, and Volvo in Oman; distributes Bang & Olufsen, Kenwood, JBL, Harman Kardon, Nakamichi, Sansui, Changhong home appliances in Oman; imports and sells watches and jewelry including Cerruti, Corum Daniel Hechter, Eterna, Paloma Picasso, and Tiffany & Co.; has a fully owned company operating in the Jebel Ali Free Zone (in the UAE), that acts as the exclusive agent across the GCC for international companies involved in imaging (Polaroid), car entertainment (Autosonik, Fusion), and household appliances (AFK); operates a four star hotel in Dubai under the Shangri-La International Hotels name.	Oman Interna and Investmen (Ominvest); N Company; Na Company; O
SULTAN Originates in a British-owned company, the W. J. Towell company, which worked as an importer and agent for British steamship lines in the Gulf. Later acquired by the Sultan family, which continued the company's role as agents as well as expanded into construction and contracting work.	Construction company and interior design service; chairs Oman Oil Co (OOC); manufactures orthopedic spring mattresses and beds; 10% share in Sohar Power; operates a shipping and road haulage joint venture with the Swedish Barwil Group; Oman National Dairy Company; Al Jazeirah Services (catering, housekeeping, laundry, equipment supply, and related services); extensive real estate holdings in Oman.	Agents for: Nestle, British American Tobacco, Colgate-Palmolive, Kelloggs, Bridgestone Tyres and Unilever; operates 30 retail outlets at Oman Oil fuel stations in the country; distributor of Mazda in Oman; imports and distributes industrial equipment for the oil and gas industry; supplies uniforms, stationery, glassware, tents, tarpaulin for the Omani military; imports building materials; distributes and markets food, detergents, and perfumes in the UAE.	National F Finance C Investmen a life insu

Appendix B   Ownership of the Largest GCC Ban

Bank	Ranking in the Top 100 Arab Banks 2007	Ownership	Relations to Khalee (either board memb ownership)
Saudi Arabia			
National Commercial Bank	1	Saudi government institutions 79%, Public 21%	
Al Rajhi Bank	2	Public 55%	Al Rajhi (45%)
SAMBA	4	Saudi government institutions 44%, Kingdom Holding Company 5%, Bank Melli Iran 1.24%, Public 46.19%	Kingdom (5%) Al Gosaibi (-) Saad (-) Ali Reza (board men
Riyad Bank	5	Government of Saudi Arabia 51.30%, Public 48.70%	Rashed Group (boar
Banque Saudi Fransi	9	Groupe Crédit Agricole (France) 31.10%, Public 68.90%	Rashed Group (boar
SABB	10	HSBC Holdings (United Kingdom) 40%, Saudi Investors (60%)	Al Gosaibi (-) Saad (-) Olayan (board memb
Arab National Bank	15	Arab Bank (Jordan) 40%, General Organization for Social Insurance (Saudi Arabia) 10.80%, Public 33.33%	Rashed 10% Jabr 5.90% Al Gosaibi (-)
Saudi Hollandi Bank	33	ABN AMRO (Netherlands) 40%, General Organization for Social Insurance (Saudi Arabia) 8.50%, Public 31.50%	Olayan 20%
Bank Al-Jazira	34	National Bank of Pakistan 5.83%, Public 52.87%	Rashed 22% Dallah Al Baraka Grou
Bank Al Bilad	41	Al Subeaei Group (Saudi Arabia) 21.28%, Al Mukairin Group (Saudi Arabia) 8.56%, Public 50%	Al Rajhi 15% Al Jomaih (-) Zamil (-)

Appendix B Continued

Bank	Ranking in the Top 100 Arab Banks 2007	Ownership	Relations to Khaleeji Capital (either board membership or share ownership)
Bahrain			
Arab Banking Corporation	17	Kuwait Investment Authority 28.61%, Central Bank of Libya 28.46%, Abu Dhabi Investment Authority 26.56%, National Bank of Yemen 0.34%, Public 12.03%	Al Rajhi—Saudi Arabia (4%)
Gulf International Bank	19	Saudi Arabian Monetary Agency 27.50%, Bahrain Mumtalakat Holding Company 12.10%, Government of Kuwait 12.08%, Government of Oman 12.08%, Government of Qatar 12.08%, Government of Saudi Arabia 12.08%, Government of the United Arab Emirates 12.08%	Zamil Group—Saudi Arabia (board member)
Al Ahli United Bank	27	Public Institution for Social Security 20.25%, Tamdeen Investment Company 13.20%, The Pension Fund Commission 10.10%, Salem Salah Al Naser Al Sabah (Kuwait) 5.60%, Global Express Company 5.30%, Public 45.55%	Al Ghanim—Kuwait (board member) Behbehani Group—Kuwait (board member)
International Banking Corporation	29		Al Gosaibi Group—Saudi Arabia (100%)
Awal Bank	36		Saad Group—Saudi Arabia (100%)
National Bank of Bahrain	56	Bahrain Mumtalakat Holding Company 49%, Public 49%	Kanoo Group (board member) Fakhroo Group (board member) Al Moayyed Group (board member)
United Gulf Bank	52	Kuwait Projects Company 88.30%, Public 11.70%	
Shamil Bank	63	Ithmaar Bank (Bahrain) 60%, Bahrain Islamic Bank 0.26%, Public 27.67%	Saudi Binladin Group (12.07%) Zamil Group—Saudi Arabia (board member)

Bank		Ownership	
Bank of Bahrain and Kuwait	68	Commercial Bank of Kuwait 19.12%, The Pension Fund Commission (Bahrain) 18.83%, General Organization for Social Insurance (Bahrain) 13.35%, KIPCO (Kuwait) 11.60%, Bank of Kuwait and the Middle East 6.75%, Securities Group (Kuwait) 4.15%, Kuwait Investment Authority 3.75%, Zumorroda Investment Company (Kuwait) 3.07%	Al Ghanim Group (board member)
Khaleeji Commercial Bank	87	Gulf Finance House (Bahrain) 40%, Emirates Islamic Bank (UAE) 10%, Qatar Islamic Bank (Qatar) 4.24%, MENA Real Estate Company (Kuwait) 3.75%, Awqaf and Minors Affairs Foundation (UAE) 3%, Bahrain Islamic Bank (Bahrain) 2.50%	Al Jabr Group—Sa (board member)
Bahraini Saudi Bank	99	The Pension Fund Commission (Bahrain) 10%, Mohammed Bin Fahed Bin Abdulaziz (Saudi Arabia) 8.27%, Ibrahim Jaber Hussein Al Ahmadi (Saudi Arabia) 5.82%, Al Fatah Investment (Bahrain) 5.50%, Fahed Mohammed Al Adel (Saudi Arabia) 5.38%, Capital Finance Investment (Bahrain) 5.25%, Awal Group (Bahrain) 5%, Public 54.78%	Zayani Group (boa

UAE

Bank		Ownership	
Abu Dhabi Commercial Bank	7	Abu Dhabi Investment Council 64.84%, Public 35.16%	Mazroui (board men
National Bank of Abu Dhabi	11	Abu Dhabi Investment Council (UAE) 73%, Al Qasimi Group (UAE), Public 27%	Mazroui (board men
Emirates Bank International	12	Emirates NBD 100%	Gurg Group (board r Al Majid Group (boa Lootah Group (board
Dubai Islamic Bank	13	Government of Dubai 29.80%	Lootah Group 7.20%
First Gulf Bank	14	Sheikh Tahnoun Bin Zayed Bin Sultan Al Nahyan 5.60%, Nahda Investment Company 5.12%, Public 89.28%	
Mashreq Bank	16	Public 13%	Al Ghurair Group 87%
Union National Bank	21	Government of Abu Dhabi 40.01% Abu Dhabi Investment Council 10% Government of Dubai 10%, Al Qasimi Group UAE, Public 39.99%	

Appendix B Continued

Bank	Ranking in the Top 100 Arab Banks 2007	Ownership	Relations to Khaleeji Capital (either board membership or share ownership)
National Bank of Dubai	24	Emirates NBD 100% (merged with Emirates Bank in 2009)	
Commercial Bank of Dubai	40	Government of Dubai 20%, Public 80%	Al Mulla (board member) Ghurair (board member) Rostamani (board member) Futtaim (board member)
Sharjah Islamic Bank	49	Government of Sharjah 27%, Kuwait Finance House 20%, Al Qasimi Group, Public 50%	Mazroui (board member)
Bank of Sharjah	53	Government of Sharjah (UAE) 20%, Mubarak Abdulaziz Al Hassawi (Kuwait) 9%	
Arab Bank for Foreign investment and Trade	57	Ministry of Finance and Industry (UAE) 42.28%, Libyan Arab Foreign Bank (Libya) 42.28%, Banque Extérieure d'Algérie (Algeria) 15.44%	
National Bank of Umm Al-Qaiwain	62	Government of Umm Al Qaiwain (UAE) 30%, Umm Al Qaiwain Cement Industries Company (UAE) 5.55%, Salim Abdullah Salim Al Hosni (UAE), 6.74%, Public 37.66%	Rostamani Group (20%)
Invest Bank	64	Global Private Group (UAE) 15.05%, Emirates Development Company (UAE) 6.65%, Alliance Insurance (UAE), Al Qasimi Group (UAE), Public 69.50%	Mazroui Group (6.08%)
Rakbank	65	Government of Ras Al Khaimah (UAE) 52.75%, UAE investors 36.85%, GCC investors 10.40%	Ghurair (board member) Sagar Group—Kuwait (board member)
National Bank of Fujairah	69	Government of Fujairah 43.23%, Government of Dubai 10.76%, Public 24.62%	Al Gurg Group (21.39%)
United Arab Bank	80	Commercial bank (Qatar) 14.70%, UAB Shareholders Investment Portfolio (UAE) 14.70%, Al Hosani Group (UAE) 18.10%, Al Qassimi Group (UAE) 13.00%, Public 24.60%	Juma Al Majid Group 7.80% Fardan Group (board member)

Bank	No.	Ownership	Board members
Dubai Bank	92	Dubai Financial (UAE) 70%, Emaar Properties (UAE) 30%	
Kuwait			
National Bank of Kuwait	6	Public 100%	Bahar (board meml; Kharafi (board men; Sagar (board memb; Fulaij Group (board
Kuwait Finance House	8	Kuwait Investment Authority (Kuwait) 24.08%, Public Authority for Minors Affairs (Kuwait) 10.48%, Kuwait Awqaf Public Foundation (Kuwait) 8.23%, Public 57.21%	Babtain (board men
Commercial Bank of Kuwait	31	Al Sharq Holding (Kuwait) 23.11%	
Gulf Bank	35	Expansion for Trading and Construction 11.74%, Zumuruda Holding 10.37%, Public 40.36%	Al Ghanim Group (; Behbehani Group (5; Essa Group (board n; Shaya Group (board; Fulaij Group (board; Behbehani Group (30
Al Ahli Bank of Kuwait	42	Kuwait Investment Company 9.90%, Government Debt Settlement Office 9.55%, Public Institution for Social Security 9.51%, Wafra International Investment Company 7.50%, Kuwait and Middle East Financial Investment Company 4%, Public 23.96%	
Burgan Bank	46	Kuwait Projects Company 50.24%, Public Institution for Social Security 6.11%, Wafra International Investment Company 5.72%, Public 37.93%	Bahar Group (board r
Boubyan Bank	60	Kuwait Investment Authority 20%, The Investment Dar Company 20%, Public 60%	Al Shaya Group (boar
Oman			
Bank Muscat	44	Oman government institutions 34%, HSBC (UK) 17%, Dubai Financial (UAE) 15%, Groupe Société Générale (France) 8%, Muscat Overseas Group (Oman) 9%, Public 27%	

Appendix B Continued

Bank	Ranking in the Top 100 Arab Banks 2007	Ownership	Relations to Khaleeji Capital (either board membership or share ownership)
National Bank of Oman	54	Oman government institutions 23%, United Development Company 4.46%, National Equity Fund 2.99%, Public 17.66%	Al Fardan Group—Qatar (35%) [through Commercial Bank Bahwan Group (14.74%) Sultan Group (2.42%)
Oman International Bank	70	Muscat Overseas Group Oman 7.91%, Public 73.62%	Zawawi Group (18%)
Bank Dhofar	89	Dhofar International Development and Investment Holding Company 30%, Al Aujaili 10.14%, Civil Service Employees Pension Fund 10%, Public 49.86%	
Oman Arab Bank	93	Oman International Development and Investment Company (Oman) 51%, Arab Bank (Jordan) 49%	Zubair Group
Qatar			
Qatar National Bank	18	Qatar Investment Authority 50%, Public 50%	Darwish (board member)
Commercial Bank of Qatar	26	Qatar Insurance Company 3%, Public 87%	Al Fardan Group (10%)
Qatar Islamic Bank	39	Public 100%	Al Mana Group (board member)
Doha Bank	45	Qatar Insurance Company (Qatar) 0.80%, Al Thani family	Darwish (board member) Mana (board member)
International Bank of Qatar	66	National Bank of Kuwait 30%, Al Sanad Commercial Company 24.50%, Broog Trading Company 24.50%, Alfiya Investment Company (Qatar) 10.50%, Qatar Investment and Projects Development Holding Company 10.50%.	
Ahli Bank	82	Ahli United Bank (Bahrain) 40%, Public 60%	Al Mana Group (board member)

Notes

Chapter 1

1. The First Saudi State was founded in 1744 in the Najd by the al-Saud clan, and slowly expanded to include the Hijaz in 1802. It came to an end after the Ottoman Viceroy of Egypt, Muhammad Ali Pasha, retook the Hijaz in 1803, and fully subdued the al-Saud in 1818. The al-Saud returned to power in 1824 but did not succeed in conquering the Hijaz, which remained under Ottoman control. After the defeat of the Second Saudi State in 1891 by the al-Rashid dynasty, the al-Saud regrouped and finally established modern-day Saudi Arabia in 1932. The 1915 to 1927 Darin Treaty (or al-Qatif Treaty), signed between the British and al-Saud, was in practice much looser than the control exerted by Britain over the Gulf states.
2. The nature of the precapitalist social formations in the Arabian peninsula differed greatly from the feudal societies found in Europe or Japan. One of the key features of Arabia was the constant conflict between nomadic and settled peoples, which reflected itself in repeated cycles of conquest and downfall a characteristic noted by the Arab thinker Ibn Khaldun (see Baali 1988). Another important feature of these societies was the preponderance of state-ownership of land. Arab scholars describe the nature of landownership with the term *'iqta,* under which rulers granted the right of usufruct (but not ownership) to individuals in exchange for military service.
3. This control was exerted through a Native Agent, first appointed by the British in 1825. The Native Agents were usually Muslims from India or the Iranian littoral whose job was to report on political developments and tribal alliances, and to control the entry permits into the area. The Native Agent reported to the Political Resident, located in Bushire, Iran. In turn, the Political Resident reported to the Government of British India, which was subordinate to London.
4. At the time, foreigners described Iran as "Persia" although inhabitants of the country used the name Iran. This book will use Iran as the preferred term.
5. From 1934, Bahrain was also a key administrative center of British rule. In that year, the British created a new position on the island, the Political Agent, who became the main conduit of British rule in the Gulf Arab states.
6. From 1856 to 1970, the country was known as the Sultanate of Muscat and Oman, reflecting the division between the two geographical areas of the

country. Following the separation from Zanzibar, Britain was the main source of income for the Sultanate (Townsend 1977, p. 43)

7. Kaylani (1979, p. 574) estimates that 70 percent of the armed forces were composed of Baluchi and another 20 percent were mercenaries conscripted from British dependencies.

8. Although the link is rarely made in the literature, the origins of the term "rentier-state" actually extend back to the early 1900s and debates over the nature of the world economy. With the growth of finance capital at the end of the nineteenth century, and the increasing significance of financial profits drawn from credit extended to overseas borrowers, many commentators described the leading European states as rentier-states. There is clearly a distinction with the contemporary use of the term and its focus on states that have weakly developed domestic economies, but this earlier usage has the value of highlighting the fact that externally derived financial flows have long been a key feature of the world market and need to be situated in the broader context of developments in the world economy as a whole.

9. Ross attempts to prove the rentier-state/authoritarian nexus through a statistical analysis of time-series cross-national data from 113 states between 1971 and 1997. Among many other problems with this methodology, he completely ignores the role of foreign powers in shaping "regime types." Tim Mitchell (2009) has presented a useful critique of the rentier-state claims around authoritarian states, arguing instead for an interpretation that examines the character and control of energy within the capitalist world market.

10. Lukacs is here describing the fetishism expressed by the commodity, but the same argument applies to the nature of the state.

11. The latter should not be understood solely in the sense of force, as Gramsci, among others, has emphasized. The more the state is able to project itself as a neutral body that stands above the different classes of society, the more effectively it is able to conceal its actual character as a class relation. For this reason, a key feature of the modern capitalist state is the projection of the interests of the dominant class as equivalent to the interests of all. This function relates to the *legitimacy* of the state, and is developed through an ideological representation of the "common good."

12. It is a misunderstanding of this point that leads Nazih Ayubi in his lengthy discussion of the Arab state to claim that Marx held two "potentially contradictory concepts of the state" (Ayubi 1995, p. 5). The question of relative autonomy, and much of the subsequent debate around this concept in Marxist state theory, extends the analysis of Marx's classic work *The Eighteenth Brumaire of Louis Bonaparte*. In this book, Marx provides an assessment of Bonapartism, the state-form in France following the rise to power of Louis Bonaparte, who became Napoleon III after a coup in December 1851. Marx argued that Bonaparte had risen above the contending classes in society as a mediating factor during the great social crisis of the time but nevertheless continued to act in the interests of French capitalism at a time when the bourgeoisie was unable

class-state relations in Japan, he discusses the role played by state bureaucrats who move to leading business positions after their term in the bureaucracy (a job-shift known as *amakudari,* "descent from heaven") thus blurring the lines between state and capitalist class.

14. Another pertinent example outside of the Gulf is the Egyptian state under the leadership of Muhammed Ali. Samir Amin (1985) argues that Ali played an important role in fostering the rise of a "bureaucratic bourgeoisie," in alliance with foreign powers, which was tied to the export of cotton to Europe.

15. Terry Karl (1997) raises similar criticisms over "agency-centered" approaches to the rentier-state. She attempts to overcome these problems by presenting state decision-making as being framed by "structured contingency," effectively a form of path-dependency in which the decisions of the state are shaped by the structural constraints of earlier choices. In essence, however, this approach does not fundamentally move away from a focus on institutions rather than social relations.

16. See Ross (2001) for a striking, but by no means unique, example of this approach.

17. A similar critique is made by David McNally (1981) of the main institutionalist school of Canadian history, the Staples Approach, which interprets Canadian capitalism through the lens of various staple products such as furs and timber.

18. This approach should be distinguished from theories of the "transnational capitalist class" (Cox 1987; Sklair 1995, 2001; Robinson 2004, 2007). Transnational theorists argue that a qualitative change has occurred in capitalism in which the state is "no longer the organizing principle of capitalism and the institutional 'container' of class development and social life" (Robinson 2004, p. 40). In contrast, this book employs the notion of "internationalization" articulated in the vein of Palloix, with its emphasis on the continuing salience of the nation-state and its role in reinforcing rather than undermining state formation.

Chapter 2

1. Figures provided by Robert Brenner confirm this pattern. He compares the net profit rate in manufacturing from 1950–1970 to that prevailing in 1970–1993: 12.9 percent/9.9 percent in the US, 23.2 percent/13.8 percent in Germany, 21.6 percent/17.2 percent in Japan (Brenner 2000, p. 8). See also T. Weisskopf (1992) who presents before and after tax profit rates for eight advanced capitalist countries (UK, Sweden, France, West Germany, Italy, Canada, Japan, and the United States) showing a marked decline in profit rates from the late 1960s onwards.

2. Another factor helping the US economy was the outbreak of the Korean War in 1950, which helped to generate a commodities boom and a rapid increase in industrial activity, primarily benefiting US capital and its ally Japan.

3. The period 1930 to 1960 saw the development and commercial production of polyurethane, polystyrene, nylon, Polyethylene Terephthalate (PET), polyester, polypropylene, Styrofoam, DDT, detergents, and so forth.

4. One of the preconditions for receiving US funds was the reinstatement of the Agnelli family (allies of Mussolini and original owners of the firm who had been ousted by the Italian resistance following liberation) to a position of power in the firm.

5. See the superb account by Simon Bromley (1991, especially chapters 2 and 3) for detailed discussion of these trends and the relationship between oil and US hegemony in the postwar period.

6. Allied forces consciously targeted German, Italian, and Japanese oil supplies, and this was a major factor in the eventual collapse of the latter's military machines.

7. The historical account of this process has been told by many authors. See Sampson (1976); Terzia (1985); Skeet (1988); Yergin (1991); and Bromley (1991).

8. The discussion over the reasons behind the end of the "Golden Age" is complex and cannot be given full treatment here. See Mandel (1983, 1995); Harvey (1999, 2005); and Brenner (2000) for some of this debate.

9. These companies controlled virtually all the world's oil supplies during the 1950s and 1960s. In 1966, for example, the eight IOCs controlled 76 percent of all oil outside North America and the USSR (Sampson 1976, p. 221).

10. As the role of Saudi Arabia makes clear, this does not imply that the national-ization of Gulf oil supplies was antagonistic to the interests of the United States. Simon Bromley (1991) clearly maps the common interest of Gulf producers and the IOCs that was centered on securing a steady oil supply and IOC con-trol over refining, marketing, and distribution. Moreover, a rise in the price of oil did not hurt the United States as much as it did European and Japanese rivals, which were heavily reliant on imported oil.

11. The increasing price of oil further accentuated inflationary problems and the undermining of the rate of profit in the industrial sector due to the increasing cost of energy inputs. Although it was widely argued at the time that the oil price rise was the cause of the economic crisis, it is more accurate to see the crisis as systemic, representing the exhaustion of the factors that had made the upturn in the rate of profit possible in the immediate postwar period. Indeed, the decline in the rate of profit across most of the advanced capitalist world had begun long before the rise in oil prices, and the price rise was initially used to counteract its effects through the extension of liquidity in the form of credit. See Mandel (1995) for a full treatment of this argument.

12. The interlocking of the Gulf financial sector and the Euromarkets can also be seen in the direct geographical expansion of Gulf banks into Europe. Sherbiny provides a 1983 list that shows 60 Arab banks in London, 3 of which were established before 1970, 12 during 1970 to 1975, 22 during 1976 to 1980, 16 after 1980, and the remaining 7 at an unknown time. Paris held about 39 Arab banks, 3 of which were established before 1970, 7 during 1970 to 1975, 26 during 1976 to 1980, and 3 after 1980 (Sherbiny 1986, p. 36).

13. While these are figures for OPEC as a whole (Algeria, Angola, Indonesia, Iran, Iraq, Kuwait, Libya, Nigeria, Qatar, Saudi Arabia, the United Arab Emirates, Venezuela, and Ecuador) the Gulf countries (particularly Saudi Arabia) were the dominant producers. Calculated from Gibson (1989, p. 5) and Congressional Budget Office (1981, p. 35).

14. According to a US treasury memo, in March 1978, US Treasury Secretary Michael Blumenthal secretly flew to Saudi Arabia in order to negotiate a deal with the Saudis to sell their oil solely in US dollars (Clark 2005, p. 2).

15. Gowan argues that the Nixon administration encouraged OPEC to raise oil prices a full two years before this actually happened, and to place US private banks at the center of petrodollar recycling in the emerging Euromarkets. Gowan's explanation of this process is detailed and fascinating although his argument sometimes conflates the outcome of policies with the intention of actors. He thus implies that the use of petrodollars and the oil price rise was deliberately engineered by the Nixon government in order to construct what he calls the Dollar-Wall Street Regime. It is necessary to bring into the argument the relative strength of the oil exporting countries in the context of the anticolonial movements of the postwar period. In other words, it is mistaken to understand the Gulf countries as being "forced" to undertake a rise in oil prices, rather than seeing the confluence of interest between the Gulf monarchies and US policy.

16. See Saad-Filho and Johnston (1995) and Harvey (2005) for further discussion of neoliberal ideology.

17. For an excellent analysis of the Volcker Shock and its role in the reconstitution of US finance as the dominant pole of a new global order, see Panitch and Gindin (2005).

18. On the western flank of the Middle East, the key element to US control was its embrace of Israel, which, with its origins as a settler-colonial state, was organically tied to external support for its continued viability in a hostile environment.

19. Abrahamian casts the 1953 coup as a battle between Western Imperialism and Iranian nationalism over control and distribution (not profits) of oil, rather than a US-Soviet proxy battle. He uses British Foreign Office documents to dispute the CIA version of events and shows that from the outset Britain and the United States knew quite well that Mossadegh was distrustful of the Soviet Union.

20. It should also be noted that the United States simultaneously gave support to Iran, which later came to light in the Iran-Contra Scandal.

Chapter 3

1. The Sultanate of Muscat and Oman was renamed the Sultanate of Oman in 1970 following a coup by Sultan Qaboos bin Said al Said against his father, Said ibn Taymur.

explain ...

actually creating the conditions in the periphery ...

in the first place. If the later argument of this book is correct (see in particular chapters 4 and 6), then the Gulf itself is implicated in creating the worsening poverty found in the peripheral countries, and generating the widening differential between their social conditions and the GCC. In other words, the two key themes of this book are mutually reinforcing and deeply intertwined: the GCC's central role in the development of global capitalism helps to generate the political and economic dynamics that induce labor migration to the Gulf itself.

5. A key step in this process was the 1968 Royal Decree, the Public Land Distribution Ordinance (PLDO) (Royal Decree No. 26/2, 1968), which prevented use of undeveloped lands. Instead, land was reallocated as private property to individuals, companies, and organizations.

6. Steffen Hertog notes the remarkable fact that in 1975, one-third of the employees in the Saudi Deputy Ministry of Social Affairs were illiterate (Hertog 2010, p. 106).

7. In Kuwait today, the term *bidoun* (those without) is used to describe the large numbers of Kuwaiti residents who have long been present in the country but lack citizenship rights. The issue of *bidoun* is a central question of Kuwaiti politics.

8. Heard-Bey notes that these schemes also differentiated rights according to tribal background and relationship to the ruler.

9. These figures likely underestimate the number of temporary migrant workers throughout the GCC. If workers who are living and working illegally are included, this figure would rise considerably. In the mid-2000s, Saudi Arabia was deporting around 700,000 "illegal" workers on an annual basis, more than 10 percent of the total number officially recorded as present in the country.

10. The death sentences were never carried out and the 14 were freed from imprisonment following Iraq's invasion of Kuwait in 1990.

11. Children of migrant workers were allowed back into Emirati schools in 2006, but only at the ratio of one in five pupils. Noncitizens were also required to pass entrance exams and pay tuition fees.

12. This shift should not be interpreted as diminishing the importance of the Gulf region for Arab workers. Many Egyptian, Lebanese, Yemeni, and Jordanian families are still reliant upon remittance flows from the Gulf region. It has been estimated, for example, that in 2007, 30 percent of Lebanon's labor force resided in the Gulf and the country obtained 24 percent of GDP from remittance flows.

13. This number increased dramatically following the oil boom of the early twenty-first century. By 2002, 95 percent of Bangladeshi overseas workers were located in the GCC.

...storey villa in the Naif area of Dubai and killed 13 people. Over 500 workers were found to have been living illegally in the villa.

16. In Saudi Arabia, for example, a Saudi manufacturing worker was compensated, on average, three times more than a non-Saudi worker in the year 2000. In the transport and communication sector, the difference was four times as great (Saudi MoEP 2000). A foreign manufacturing worker in Qatar received one-sixth the average compensation of a Qatari worker in 2003 (State of Qatar 2004, p. 127). In Bahrain, according to the General Organization for Social Insurance, the general average wage for 2006 in the private sector was BD377 for Bahraini workers and BD170 for foreign laborers (http://www.bahrainrights.org). An important related factor here is that national labor tends to be concentrated in the government and public sectors, which are higher paying (and with better conditions).

17. The first comment is from Majeed Al-Alawi, the Bahraini Minister of Labour and Social Affairs (Qatar Peninsula 2004) and the second from GCC Secretary-General Abdul Rahman Al Attiya (Alam 2006).

18. With the partial exception of Bahrain, where the larger proportion of poor nationals within the overall workforce, overlapping with the Shia-Sunni dynamic noted in Chapter 1, creates greater potential for anti-regime struggles.

19. Aramco originated in 1933 under the name California Arabian Standard Oil Company (Casoc) after the government of Saudi Arabia granted an oil concession to Standard Oil of California (today known as Chevron). In 1936 the Texas Oil Company (known today as Texaco) purchased a 50 percent share in the concession and in 1944 the joint venture became known as Aramco. The Saudi Arabian government acquired a 25 percent share of Aramco in 1973, increased to 60 percent by 1974, and finally acquired full control by 1980.

20. In the UAE, each of the Emirates established its own state-owned company but considerable foreign investment remained in the subsidiaries of these companies. For example, in Abu Dhabi, the Abu Dhabi Company for Onshore Oil Operations (ADCO) was 40 percent owned by foreign multinationals and 60 percent by the state-owned ADNOC. ADCO generates more than half of Abu Dhabi's oil production and is the largest crude oil producer in the southern Gulf. In Qatar, foreign companies accounted for around one-third of Qatar's oil production capacity. In Oman, more than 90 percent of oil exploration and production in Oman takes place through Petroleum Development Oman (PDO), which is a joint venture between the government (60 percent) and foreign companies (Royal Dutch Shell 34 percent, Total 4 percent, and Partex 2 percent). In Bahrain, onshore oil production is controlled by the state-owned Bahrain Petroleum Company (Bapco) while exploration concessions have been awarded to foreign investors in offshore areas.

21. Dubal grew to become the largest manufacturer in the country and the biggest single non-oil contributor to Dubai's economy.

22. The Zayani conglomerate is a massive Bahraini capital group whose investments span automobiles (agents for BMW, Rolls Royce, Mitsubishi, Ferrari, and Hyundai), finance capital (founders of Investcorp, the Bahrain Islamic Bank, and Bahrain Kuwait Insurance) as well as manufacturing. Xenel is involved in petrochemical production (the first privately owned petrochemical plant in the Middle East at Yanbu), construction, real estate, and information technology.

23. These companies were the Saudi Cement Company (1955), Qatar National Cement Company (1965), Kuwait Cement Company (1968), and, in the UAE, the National Cement Company (1968). Oman established the Raysut Cement Company in 1981 (although ownership was dominated by Saudi and UAE capital).

24. Prominent Gulf capitalist groups involved in cement include Al Rajhi, Olayan, Al Zamil, Gosaibi (Saudi Arabia); Al Rashed, Saqer, Al Kharafi, Babtain, and Boodai (Kuwait); Ghurair, Qassimi (UAE); and Al Fardan (Qatar). The UAE also leads in the related ceramics industry. The RAK Ceramic plant in the UAE is the world's largest single ceramic products plant and accounts for 5 percent of the total world production of ceramic tiles (UAEY 2006, p. 113).

25. Calculated by author from World Bank statistics.

26. Calculated by author from UNCTAD data, www.unctad.org.

27. Niblock argues that this is one piece of evidence against the thesis of Chaudhry that the rise of a new Najd bourgeoisie had displaced the dominance of the old Hijazi merchant class.

28. In the UAE, there were 6,000 commercial agencies registered at the Ministry of Economy in 2009. According to one of the country's largest holder of agencies, the Bin Hamoodah Group, the system was explicitly designed by the late Sheikh Zayed as an alternative to taxes on foreign investors (Abdel Hai 2009, p. 3). This is one further example of how the state established preferential laws that privileged citizen-owned businesses rather than the entire resident population.

29. Between 1959 and 1966 the Gulf states (again with the exception of Saudi Arabia) issued their own currency, the Gulf Rupee, which was pegged to the Indian Rupee. When the Indian rupee was devalued in 1966, the Saudi Riyal was briefly adopted as a common currency. By the early 1970s, all states had their own sovereign currency.

30. In Saudi Arabia, where oil was discovered in 1939, the Nederlands Handel-Maatschappij (NHM) (today known as ABN AMRO following a merger with the Amsterdam-Rotterdam Bank) held the country's gold stock and processed oil royalty payments. In Qatar, the Eastern Bank was established in 1950, a few months after the first oil exports. It was the only bank in the country at that time and acted as the government bank. In Dubai, BBME acted as a state bank and helped finance Dubai's first hospital and other development schemes. It also collected customs dues on imported goods on behalf of the ruling family. The Dubai manager of BBME was part of a coterie of close advisors to the

_____ agents in the early decades of the state. They con-
_____ued to control the bank until 1999, when 50 percent of the shares were sold
to the Public Investment Fund and the management changed.

32. Following a liquidity crisis in 1960 and the insolvency of Al Watani Bank,
SAMA transferred the assets of Al Watani to Riyad Bank and rearranged the
management of the latter in 1961. The crisis had arisen due to the failure of
some of the board of management to repay loans taken from the bank. In
response, the government took over the shares of the defaulters and ended up
with 38 percent ownership of the bank.

33. Champion (2003) and Chaudhry (1997) document the role of state largesse in
the development of these institutions, particularly the Riyad Bank. Riyad Bank
was owned by Najdi merchants and was given the lucrative contract to manage
government accounts at the expense of the NCB in 1967, despite the latter being
the more qualified institution. They argue that this was one marker in the transition to Najdi-dominated capitalism in Saudi Arabia (Champion 2003, p. 98).

34. In 2004, 40 percent of all loans and deposits in Kuwait were held between
Kuwait Finance House and the largest bank, the National Bank of Kuwait.

35. In Qatar, the state owns 50 percent of Qatar National Bank. In Oman, the
Royal Court owns around 20 percent of Bank Muscat.

36. Hertog has a different reading from Chaudhry of this period in Saudi Arabia,
arguing that the Saudi state acted to maintain its wider distributional mechanisms rather than business interests per se (see Hertog 2010, p. 119).

Chapter 4

1. In 1989 the US Treasury built upon this approach by proposing a new plan,
the Brady Plan (named after US Treasury Secretary Nicholas Brady), which
inaugurated an avalanche of private capital flows to the South. The Brady Plan
enabled debtor countries to switch their outstanding debt from an amount of
money they were required to pay a particular lender, into a bond that could be
bought and sold in financial markets. Brady Bonds, as they were called, carried
a slight reduction in the overall loan principal or in interest rates. In return for
receiving this discount, countries were required to implement neoliberal structural adjustment measures. Under the scheme, thousands of investors from
across the world could purchase a share in the income stream generated by these
debts simply by purchasing a bond on the financial markets. Because the price
of these bonds moved up and down depending on market conditions, investors
could also speculate on these movements.

2. The importance of this intraregional trade for Asia is shown in export figures: in
2005/2006 intraregional exports accounted for 40 percent of total Asian

manufacturing exports (for component exports the comparable figure was 60 percent) (Brooks and Changchun 2008, p. 30). Nevertheless, 61 percent of total Asian exports are eventually consumed in the United States, Japan, and the EU.

3. IMF Statistics. Accessed August 10, 2008, http://www.imf.org.

4. For a good explanation of the rise of derivatives and the role they play in "binding" and "blending" capital across different geographical spaces, see Bryan and Rafferty (2006). David McNally (2009) has also argued that the rise of derivatives represents an attempt to find a new standard of "world money" given the increasing contradictions in the role played by the US dollar in the global economy as both a universal measure of value and a domestic currency.

5. This all required a series of changes to the regulations governing US financial markets. Enticed by enormous potential profits, US banks led a sustained lobbying effort to free themselves from restrictions on their investment activities. In 1999, the US Congress passed The Financial Services Modernization Act, which repealed the Banking Act of 1933 (also known as the Glass-Steagall Act). Glass-Steagall had been passed in the wake of the Great Depression and prohibited commercial banks from engaging in investment and insurance services. It had been aimed at preventing bank deposits of ordinary Americans from being exposed to risky investments and speculative activities. The repeal of Glass-Steagall opened the door to commercial bank investments in instruments such as derivatives.

6. Iraq, Algeria, and Kuwait are also among the top Middle East oil exporters to the United States.

7. Natural gas imports are also projected to double between 2005 and 2010, and then quadruple between 2020 and 2030 as Indian demand continues to grow and domestic production peaks (IEA 2007, p. 501). Much of this demand stems from the expansion of Indian industry. After China, India is the world's second-largest producer of both cement and nitrogenous fertilizer (IEA 2007, p. 471), two industries that require large quantities of energy. India is also the world's seventh-largest producer of steel, and by 2030 around 35 percent of India's total industrial electricity demand will come from the iron and steel industry (IEA 2007, p. 469).

8. There are differences of course in the importance of these regions. While the GCC, Iraq, and Iran possess large quantities of oil and natural gas, the Afghanistan/Pakistan region holds more of a strategic significance—located in the intersection of the Gulf and Central Asia. Not only does it form the crossroads of these two energy-rich areas, but (through Pakistan) it abuts onto the Indian Ocean, which remains the primary shipping route for Gulf oil (see Kaplan 2009 for a discussion of these strategic issues).

9. There is considerable debate over the reasons for this rise in the price of oil and the relative contribution of increased demand from China, the actions of speculators and derivative markets in commodity futures, or the depletion of oil fields. There is no space to explore this debate in detail—suffice to say that the increased demand from China was certainly a major contributing factor in the oil price rise.

..., ..., ... important implications for the process of class formation (see next chapter).

12. Deutsche Bank was to estimate in 2009 that GCC countries accounted for around 45 percent of all SWF global assets.

13. Setser and Ziemba's estimate of $457 billion is probably closer to the mark and has been obliquely confirmed by ADIA spokespeople.

14. It was estimated in 2007, for example, that only 27 percent of asset purchases by Middle East oil investors (Saudi Arabia, Kuwait, Algeria, UAE, Qatar, Libya, Iran, and Oman) were identifiable (Toloui 2007, p. 5).

15. One of the reasons for this is the predominance of family-owned companies that are not publically listed and therefore do not need to provide public financial records. Individuals also include the private wealth of the ruling families.

16. For example, it is widely believed that the Saudi Arabian Monetary Authority does not use a mark-to-market method for valuing their assets (i.e., measuring value on their current fair market price) and thereby understated losses in the 2008 downturn (Setser and Ziemba 2009, p. 13).

17. These estimates broadly correspond with Toloui (2007), who notes that net private capital outflows, as a proportion of total current account surpluses, reached 36 percent for Saudi Arabia, 30 percent for Kuwait, and 40 percent for Qatar in 2007—greatly exceeding the average of 20 percent all the world's major oil producers.

18. See Lubin (2007); Setser and Ziemba (2006); Toloui (2007) for a discussion of these issues.

19. Middle East OPEC is defined as Saudi Arabia, Kuwait, Algeria, UAE, Qatar, Libya, Iran, and Oman. Lubin (2007) provides slightly different figures but with the same overall trend. He has compared the post-2000 oil price rise with that of the 1970s period. Using available statistics from the Bank of International Settlements, Lubin estimates that only 19.8 percent of the total current account surplus from 2002 to 2005 was deposited in BIS reporting banks. This contrasts to the 1977–1982 period, in which 28 percent of the surplus was deposited in these banks (Lubin 2007, pp. 5–6).

20. Toloui estimates 64 percent for the period 2002–2006. ECB figures broadly confirm this estimate (Sturm, Strasky, Adolf, and Peschel 2008, p. 42). The caveats about TIC data raised above should also be noted.

21. Toloui estimates 27 percent for 2002–2006 (of identifiable petrodollars).

22. For Credit Suisse, the two largest shareholders are Qatar Investment Authority and the Saudi Olayan Group (10 percent and 7 percent). Barclay's Bank is one-third owned by investors from the Gulf. The largest stakes in the London Stock Exchange Group—equivalent to nearly 50 percent are owned by Gulf investors (Borse Dubai and Qatar Investment Authority). With Daimler AG,

the world's largest truck maker, the two largest shareholders (holding 17 per-cent) are from the Gulf (Aabar Investments and the Kuwait Investment Authority). The Qatar Investment Authority owns stakes in J Sainsbury, NYSE, Volkswagen, and Porsche.

23. The estimate of US$420 billion in private wealth is found in SABB (2008, p. 5).

24. The Saudi British Bank (SABB) estimates only $7.5 billion returned to Saudi Arabia in the year following the attacks (SABB 2003, p. 5).

25. Author calculated from McKinsey (2009).

26. Figures calculated by author from UNCTAD. Accessed July 10–15, 2008, www.unctad.org.

27. See, for example, Zoellick's comments at a press conference in Jordan following the World Economic Forum in 2003: "[W]e could start to combine [FTAs], for example, we look towards the possibility of countries in the Gulf perhaps joining into the Bahrain Free Trade Agreement, making specialized arrange-ments for their goods and agriculture but following the basic rules, and that would have a benefit of encouraging regional integration, so that their products to qualify would not have just to come from Bahrain, but may come from Qatar or Oman or from UAE or a combination of that. So we can encourage regional integration in the process, whether in the Gulf, whether in the Maghreb or whether in other parts of the Arab world. And the ultimate goal, as the President said, would be to draw these into the Middle East Free Trade Area. That, of course, depends on the willingness of countries to undertake these reforms" (Zoellick 2003b).

28. If the negotiations are successful, the European Union-Gulf Cooperation Council FTA would represent the first ever FTA between two regional blocs.

Chapter 5

1. An earlier statement, the Unified Economic Agreement (UEA), had been signed at the formation of the GCC in 1981. The UEA was part of the broader goal of establishing "the institutions and apparatus that will make . . . economic integration and social merger a living reality" (cited in Ramazani 1988, p. 28). It aimed to lessen the ability of member states to control the movement of capital (in its various forms) across intra-GCC borders. It called for the freedom of movement, work, and residence for GCC citizens regardless of their national location, and extended national treatment in a range of economic sectors to capital investments. In 1983, as part of the UEA framework, a GCC free trade area came into operation. Nevertheless, the pace of integration moved slowly throughout the 1980s and early 1990s, with many of the stated goals of the UEA remaining rhetorical rather than real changes on the ground. Significant restrictions on the movement of capital and goods continued to exist within the GCC and national economic policy was largely uncoordinated.

2. This law removed certificate-of-origin requirements for all domestically pro-duced goods in the GCC. Previously, an elaborate procedure was required to

vastly reduce the costs placed on foreign importers to the region (in 1999 the simple mean tariff was 12.6 percent in Saudi Arabia, compared with 4.8 percent in Oman).

4. The intent of Articles 3 and 4 were summarized in the closing statement of the 26th Session of the Supreme Council in 2005: "The [economic agreement] aims at unifying the external trade policy of the GCC States, and dealing with the outside world as a single economic unit. It also calls for adopting a unified internal trade policy that would facilitate the movement of citizens, commodities, services, and means of transport" (CS26 2005).

5. The earlier 1982 agreement raised the possibility of a monetary union but no concrete steps were taken in this regard. In December 2000, the GCC Committee of Monetary Agencies and Central Bank Governors, and member states' Ministers of Finance, were mandated by the GCC Supreme Council to devise a working plan and a timetable for a single currency, which they presented to the 2001 Muscat Summit. It was included within Article 4 of the EASCC.

6. With the exception of Kuwait's dinar, which is pegged to a basket of currencies. The precise breakdown of this basket is not made public but is clearly weighted toward the US$.

7. The convergence criteria were put forward by member states in Abu Dhabi on December 18–19, 2005: a cap on the budget deficit at 3 percent of gross domestic product (GDP) when oil prices are $25/barrel or above; a ceiling on public debt of 60 percent of GDP; inflation to be kept within 2 percent of the GCC average; interest rates to be no more than 2 percent above the average of the three lowest rates; and maintenance of foreign exchange reserve coverage of four-six months of imports (MEED 2005, p. 28).

8. The countries and year of membership are as follows: Bahrain (1995), Kuwait (1995), Qatar (1996), United Arab Emirates (1996), Oman (2000), and Saudi Arabia (2005).

9. At a meeting of the Arab Business Council in December 2006, this disciplinary nature of FTAs was succinctly captured by Robert Lawrence, Professor of Trade and Investment at the John F. Kennedy School of Government, who opined that "[t]he test of a good agreement is what it gets you to do" (ABC 2007, p. 7). It should be noted that these agreements also accentuated the contradictions in the regional integration process. Bahrain and Oman's bilateral FTA agreements with the United States violated the collective negotiation position outlined in EASCC Article 2 and generated significant complaint from other GCC states.

10. Niblock argues that membership of the WTO was utilized by elements within the Saudi state as a useful pretence for enabling those reforms to move forward against the efforts of others who were opposed. Hertog examines the neo-patrimonial

structure of the Saudi state, which he characterizes as a hierarchical and vertically divided "hub-and-spoke system." As a result of deals and counterbalancing within the al-Saud family, ministries were parcellized from one another and operated as independent "fiefdoms" with strong vertical control but little horizontal communication. This pattern meant that some liberalization measures could be retarded through a de facto veto power held by each ministry. In contrast, in the case of a small emirate such as Dubai, the operation of the state was much more centralized in the individual decisions of the Ruler and his immediate family members.

11. "Extra liquidity" refers to the amount of petrodollars that these states received relative to the period preceding the oil price rise. The rate of increase of this liquidity was also accelerating in this period. According to the IMF, the current account surplus for the Gulf region in 2006 amounted to nearly one half of the cumulative surplus during the period 2001–2005 (Lubin 2007, p. 8).

12. This average obscures significant differences between GCC states. In 2008, GDP per capita ranged from $18,903 in Saudi Arabia to over $70,000 in the small Gulf country of Qatar. These figures also need to be framed by the considerable differentiation of wealth due to the very large proportion of low-paid migrant workers. For these reasons, average per capita GDP is a poor representation of the true nature of accumulation in the GCC states.

13. A caveat should be noted here regarding the transparency of data in the GCC. A 2002 IMF report estimated, for example, that the Saudi government did not disclose 20 percent of oil receipts within the budget (Rutledge 2009, p. 88).

14. By 2008, the GCC's per capita energy consumption was among the highest in the world, and electricity demand to 2015 was estimated to require $7 billion per year and a capacity increase equivalent to 80 percent of currently installed capacity (Hertog and Luciani 2009, p. 8).

15. Calculated by author from national statistics.

16. In contrast, among UAE nationals the gender profile is almost balanced at 50.7 percent males and 49.3 percent females.

17. The Compounded Annual Growth Rate (CAGR) for the construction sector from 2003–2007 was as follows: Bahrain (32.15 percent), Kuwait (13.80 percent), UAE (22.35 percent), Qatar (33.04 percent), KSA (20.51 percent), and Oman (29.52 percent). Calculated by author from national statistics.

18. The law is called "Regulation of Ownership and Investment in Real Estate by Non-Saudis," issued under the Royal Decree No M/15 dated 17/4/1421H.

19. The survey was based on the value of contracts won in 2006 and 2007. It covered contractors involved in the building and civilian sectors and did not include companies that focused on the oil and gas, petrochemicals, utilities, and industrial sectors (foreign companies dominate those sectors and are discussed below).

20. Of the entire list of 50, 28 companies are from the GCC.

21. Although strictly outside of the period examined in this chapter, inclusion of this analysis is justified due to the fact that almost all of these projects were launched in 2005–2007.

22. Author calculation from annual statistics.

24. Of course, the latter prediction depends greatly on the future scenarios of world economic growth.

25. Balexco by the Gulf Finance House, which is controlled by the Al Shaya Group (Kuwait), the Saudi Arabian Economic Development Company, Dubai Islamic Bank, Ohali Group (Saudi Arabia), QInvest (Qatar), Oman Pension Fund, and Kuwait Investment Company; and Midal Cables controlled by the Ali Reza Group (Saudi Arabia) and Al Zayani Group (Bahrain).

26. The GCC's relative advantage in petrochemical production arises because it uses ethane as a feedstock, rather than naptha, which is typically used elsewhere. Ethane in the Gulf is captured as a byproduct of crude oil production (it is extracted from the associated gas produced alongside crude oil), whereas naptha is distilled from oil and hence linked to the oil price. The cheap supply of ethane in the GCC is indicated in the price differential natural gas is offered to domestic producers at US\$ 0.75/mmbtu compared to US\$3-8/mmbtu elsewhere in the world. Because the price of naptha is linked to the price of oil, in periods of high oil prices there is even greater cost benefit for ethane-based petrochemical production.

27. The impetus for this shift has been reinforced by the increasing cost of oil (and hence the relative advantage of GCC-based production) for global petrochemical companies such as Shell, Exxon, Union Carbide, Mitsubishi, Hoechst, and Dow.

28. A manager of Shell's joint venture plant at Nanhai, which supplies China's special economic zones with petrochemicals, confirmed this shift: "In 2000, about 25% of our chemicals assets were in the Middle East and Asia-Pacific. By 2010, the aim is to have just over a third in these two regions, to take feedstock advantage opportunities and to be positioned to meet demand in the area of highest growth potential. The bulk of Shell's future chemicals capacity additions will be in these two regions. In the Middle East, we have two production joint ventures in Saudi Arabia, one producing ethylene, styrene monomer, EDC, MTBE and crude industrial ethanol, the other producing benzene. We are also planning a joint venture world-scale gas-based cracker and derivatives complex in Qatar" (McKendrick 2007, p. 11).

29. A key signal of this was a visit by then Chinese President Jiang Zemin to Saudi Arabia in 1999, which resulted in an agreement to open up the Chinese refinery sector to Saudi investment, in return for allowing Chinese companies to invest in Saudi hydrocarbon exploration and development. As a result of this agreement, the Chinese state-owned oil company Sinopec won the bid for a natural gas project in a northwestern block of Saudi Arabia's Rub al-Khali gas fields in 2004 the first time in 25 years that the area had been opened up to foreign firms.

30. If basic infrastructure costs are also included, the sector constitutes around 55 percent of the total megaproject bill. Examples of these megaprojects in

Saudi Arabia include a $10 billion Aramco-Sumitomo Chemical refining and petrochemical joint venture called Petro-Rabigh, a $6 billion Aramco-Total export refinery, a $6 billion Aramco-ConocoPhillips export refinery, and the US$8 billion Saudi Kayan Petrochemicals plant.

31. It should be noted that despite LBC-Rotana's relatively small share, it is the most diversified of all the media conglomerates. Owned by Saudi Arabia's Prince Bin Talal Al Waleed, it controls the largest music label in the Middle East, six music TV stations, and two Lebanese newspapers. It is also the third-largest shareholder in the global conglomerate, News Corp.

32. This internationalization of capital within the media sector bears significant cultural implications within the Arab world. Despite Gulf-dominated ownership and the apparent conservatism of the Gulf societies, TV programming is heavily westernized and music videos often portray women in ways that are strikingly at odds with typical Gulf norms. It is also now commonplace for Lebanese and Egyptian performers to include *khaleeji*-style music on their recordings, or to film videos within the Gulf, in order to cater to the Gulf consumer market. In this sense, the internationalization of Gulf capital is provoking a broader cultural transformation through the Middle East.

33. A second local company, DU, entered the UAE market in 2007. The Omani market is dominated by a local company, Omantel, and a Q-tel subsidiary, Nawras Telecom. In September 2010, Etisalat made a non-binding offer to purchase 46 percent of Zain, an acquisition that would strongly confirm the pan-GCC internationalization tendencies characterizing this sector.

34. One illustration of the strong outlook toward broader internationalization in this sector was an estimation by the Chief Executive of Q-Tel, Nasser Marafih, that as much as 90 percent of Q-Tel's revenues would come from international revenues by 2014 (George-Cosh 2009, p. 6).

35. With the sole exception of 1996–1997. Calculated by author from United Nations Statistics Database. Accessed June 2008, http://comtrade.un.org.

36. Calculated by author from United Nations Statistics Database. Accessed June 2008, http://comtrade.un.org.

37. Calculated from United Nations Commodity Statistics Database. Accessed June 2008, http://comtrade.un.org.

38. Calculated by author from UN Comtrade figures. Accessed April 2007.

39. Over 3,000 companies reside within UAE FZs, the majority of which are located in Dubai and involved in warehousing and repackaging of goods before they move to their final destination. Dubai's integration in these regional flows is indicated in figures released by the Dubai Chamber of Commerce in 2009, which show the GCC accounted for 46 percent of total exports of DCC members and was the largest export market for the Emirate. Iran, India, and Egypt are other important non-GCC export markets (KT 2009).

40. A prominent franchising industry magazine argues, for example, that Dubai is "a 'window to world.' It provides a soft landing for international franchise systems to test product and brand acceptability against a diverse cultural and

_____ Bahrain and Oman for 2005.

_____ 2009, Agility was suspended from bidding for US government contracts on claims that it overcharged the US military by $60m over a 41-month period on $8.5bn worth of food supply contracts.

44. Futtaim also operates hotels, a property development company, a financial services firm, and an indoor energy-use and facilities company.

45. A striking example of this was the Qatargas II project, the world's largest LNG project and, in 2004, the third-largest project financing in history (behind the Channel Tunnel and a Taiwanese high-speed rail financing). According to the law firm that represented Qatar Petroleum and Exxon in the negotiations for the financing, it took forty-eight commercial banks, one Export Credit Agency, six Islamic banks, and one ExxonMobil Lender to finance the $12bn project (White and Case 2004).

46. Figures calculated by author from Bank of International Securities database. Cross-border bank loans refer to BIS reporting banks, mostly headquartered in North America, Europe, and Japan.

47. Calculated by author from Central Bank reports. Changes in banking policies helped to facilitate this credit growth. The initial steps taken in this regard through the 1990s involved an end to central bank controls on interest rates, and removing ceilings on individual or aggregate credit in the banking sector. By 2003, the traditionally strict ceilings on credit had been completely eliminated across the GCC and only minor administrative restrictions on loans remained.

48. Of course these markets later retreated in the wake of the global crisis. In the course of 2008, the Dubai Financial Market decreased by 72.42 percent, followed by the Saudi Stock Exchange (56.49 percent), Abu Dhabi Securities Exchange (47.49 percent), Muscat Securities Market (39.78 percent), Kuwait Stock Exchange (38.03 percent), Bahrain Stock Exchange (34.52 percent), and Doha Securities Market (28.12 percent) (BSE 2008b, p. 18).

49. In 2008, international investors were allowed to buy local equities through swap agreements with local companies, giving them indirect ownership.

50. UAE owns 82 percent and GCC citizens 9 percent (DFM 2008, p. 25).

51. From 2001 to 2007, the GCC represented just over 60 percent of all global *sukuk* value, with the UAE making up 36 percent of global issuance (GIH 2008d).

52. It should be noted that while estimates of total GCC debt market size vary across different sources, the overall trends remain constant. The issuance of *sukuk* dropped dramatically in 2008 and 2009 as a consequence of the global financial crisis (see Chapter 7).

53. "Corporate" does not necessarily mean private as it includes massive state-linked companies. Over the 2006–2008 period, for example, the largest conventional bond in the GCC was issued by the ports operator DP World, worth US$1.74

billion. DP World is government-controlled yet is considered a corporation under NCB definition. Likewise, the largest *sukuk* was offered by Nakheel, another "corporate" state-run entity.

54. By the end of December 2009, the value of *sukuk* listings on Bursa Malaysia totaled $17.6 billion, compared to Nasdaq Dubai ($15.7 billion), The London Stock Exchange (GBP6.5 billion), Luxembourg Stock Exchange ($7.3 billion), and Bahrain Stock Exchange ($2.18 billion). In mid-2009, Saudi Arabia launched a *sukuk* market on Tadawul with five *sukuk* (three of which were issued by SABIC).

55. Of this amount, around $9 billion was invested, leaving $11 billion still to be deployed by early 2010.

56. Information on Abraaj is taken from Abraaj Website. Accessed June 2008, http://www.abraaj.com.

57. Investcorp's investments in this regard include the luxury brand companies Gucci and Tiffany's both of which were bought by the company and subsequently floated.

58. Global Investment House, Shuaa Capital, and Gulf Capital are representative examples.

59. The EDB is composed of four teams that are tasked with developing the macroeconomic strategy for Bahrain, mapping out the detailed economic changes that the government should take, seeking foreign investments and articulating an ideological justification for these measures to the Bahraini public (Accessed August 2008, http://www.bahrainedb.com). The WTO has remarked on the pace of neoliberal change in Bahrain, noting that the country "has shown significant change in terms of economic transformation, but the next 6 years are projected to be nothing short of remarkable" (WTO 2007, p. 5).

60. The 2009 conflict between Saudi Arabia and the UAE around the establishment of the GCC Central Bank (see Chapter 7) is one indication of this contradiction.

Chapter 6

1. The full text of these orders is available at http://www.iraqcoalition.org/regulations/. Accessed October 5, 2009.

2. It should also be noted that many commentators overlooked the fact that Iraq's economy had begun moving away from state-dominated ownership in the 1980s and during the decade of sanctions in the 1990s, (see Parker and Moore 2007).

3. See, for example, the 2005 interview by *Democracy Now* with Hassan Juma'a Awad al-Asade, President of the General Union of Oil Workers in Iraq. Accessed 10 October 2009, http://www.democracynow.org/2005/6/13/iraqi_oil_workers_fight_privatization_and.

4. A fourth company, the UAE-giant Etisalat, also announced plans to enter the market in early 2010.

5. These ANIMA figures confirm the conclusions of the World Bank data cited above. It should be noted, however, that the World Bank utilizes a different

_____ prone to cancellation than other types of investment (de Saint-Laurent 2009, p. 3).

6. In the Maghreb countries (Algeria, Tunisia, Morocco, Libya), GCC FDI is also highly significant despite the fact the region has traditionally been closely linked to Europe. The GCC constituted 29 percent of total FDI to the Maghreb from 2003–2008 (compared to 46 percent from Europe) (ANIMA 2009 p. 23).

7. Calculated by author from analysis of Amman Stock Exchange data.

8. Indeed, even in many of apparent instances of "noneconomic" investment flows, a closer examination reveals that these investments actually act to further deepen the penetration of regional economies by GCC capital groups.

9. Beyond the geographical scope of this chapter, but nevertheless important to note, is the recent rash of Gulf acquisitions of huge tracts of prime agricultural land in Asia and Africa for both food production and biofuels. These investments have included the purchase and leasing of 1.6 million acres in Indonesia (by a consortium of 15 Saudi firms), 800,000 acres of farmland in Pakistan (UAE), 250,000 acres in Philippines (Qatar), and 124,000 acres in Cambodia (Kuwait).

10. See Timewell 2009 for the full list.

11. Among the GCC banks, Saudi Arabia tops the list with just over 27 percent of the total Tier 1 capital of all 100 banks on the list. Saudi dominance is being challenged, however, by the UAE, which has more banks in the top 100 (17 compared to Saudi Arabia's 11) and has 23 percent of the list's total Tier 1 capital. Kuwait has 7 banks in the top 100 and Bahrain has 11, and make up around 10 percent and 9 percent of total capital, respectively. Qatari and Omani banks together hold another 10 percent of the total capital in the top 100.

12. The Arab Bank was initially established by the Shoman family (of Palestinian origin, based in Jordan) and consistently ranks as one of the largest in the Arab world. It has the largest Arab banking branch system worldwide, with 400 branches across 29 countries in 2007. The influence of the Shoman family has dropped considerably over recent years to around 5 percent of ownership.

13. The 1993 Oslo Accords established the Palestinian Authority, which was described as a self-rule Palestinian government in the key towns of the West Bank and Gaza Strip. It was constituted by returning members of the Palestine Liberation Organization (PLO), and dominated by the PLO's leading faction Fatah. The PA has led the negotiations process with Israel since that time, although the Fatah faction lost control of the Gaza Strip in 2006. The following analysis concentrates on the West Bank.

14. Information taken from ASTRA Corporate profile. Accessed March 2007, http://www.astra.com.sa/.

15. In addition to the Masri Group, a significant proportion of CAB is held by the Talhouni family (12 percent), a prominent Jordanian business group with close

ties to the Jordanian state. The Masri and Talhouni groups are closely linked through the jointly owned Zara Holdings, which operates luxury hotels throughout Jordan.

16. Another example of a major Palestinian-owned conglomerate enriched through activities in the Gulf is the Consolidated Contractors Company (CCC). The company was established by Sa'id Khoury and Hasib Sabbagh in 1952, and built its initial fortune through contracting work in the Middle East for the largest engineering company in the US, Bechtel. CCC is one of the largest construction companies in the Middle East, and the thirteenth-largest engineering contractor by revenue in the world. Although headquartered in Athens for regulatory reasons, many of CCC's largest projects are based in the GCC and much of its staff are located in Dubai. In 2006, Sa'id Khoury was estimated to be worth US$6 billion and was listed as the eleventh-richest Arab in the world by *Arabian Business*. Khoury was also the Governor of the Arab Monetary Fund.

17. This "Palestine Investment Conference" (PIC) was convened in Bethlehem from May 21–23, 2008, with Munib Al Masri a keynote speaker at the opening panel. The conference was organized with the strong backing of the Israeli and US governments, and formed the major point of discussion at a summit convened in Jerusalem on March 30, 2008, between Condoleeza Rice, Israeli Defence Minister Ehud Barak, and Palestinian Authority Prime Minister Salam Fayyad. The main aim of PIC was to showcase the PRDP as "good for business" and an attractive reason to invest in the Palestinian economy.

18. Hasib Sabbagh and Sa'id Khouri were also founding shareholders.

19. One final indication of the role that Gulf-related capital plays in the West Bank is shown in the finance sector. The Palestinian banking system is overwhelmingly dominated by the Jordanian banks listed in Table 6.1, which, as the analysis above demonstrated, are closely related to GCC capital. These banks include the Arab Bank, CAB, The Housing Bank for Trade and Finance, Jordan Kuwait Bank, Jordan Islamic Bank, Union Bank for Savings and Investment, Jordan Ahli Bank, and Jordan Commercial Bank (in 2005, for example, the Arab Bank and CAB alone held around 60 percent of total customer deposits between them). The main exception to this is the Bank of Palestine, which was established in Gaza in 1960 and later expanded to the West Bank. The main shareholders are Palestinian investors (such as the Shawa family). Other Palestinian-based banks include the Palestine Investment Bank and the Al Quds Bank for Development and Investment. Both of these banks show a strong connection with Khaleeji Capital groups (the former through the Qatari Salam Group and the latter through Kuwait's Global Investment House).

Chapter 7

1. From 2007 to 2009, the current account balance as percentage of GDP fell in Bahrain (15.8 percent to 3.7 percent), Kuwait (44.7 percent to 29.4 percent), Oman (8.4 percent to −0.5 percent), Qatar (30.4 percent to 10.8 percent),

... dollar, low US interest rates, ... in the Gulf, many speculators believed that the GCC would not be able to hold its peg to the dollar. They thus placed funds in the region (and local Gulf residents brought their capital home) in expectation of making a profit when the currency was revalued. This currency appreciation did not occur because of the financial crisis and the strengthening of the US dollar.

4. In the case of Dubai, some companies had originated asset-backed securities similar to those issued in the United States. These securitizations were backed by mortgages that lost significant value during the crisis. In November 2008, Tamweel, one of the two largest home lenders in the UAE, ceased operations due to financial difficulties arising in part from asset-backed securities derived from mortgages on the Nakheel Palm Jumeira project. Prices for apartments and villas on the Palm dropped by 60 percent from their peak.

5. Although the plan was supported by at least half of the 50 elected legislators it was eventually scrapped and replaced with a more targeted assistance scheme.

6. The budget also included a public sector wage increase, further example of the privileging of citizenship given the overwhelming concentration of national labor in this sector.

7. This is the first development plan passed by Kuwait's parliament since 1986, an indication of the particularly fractious relationship between the parliament and the Kuwaiti ruling family that is peculiar to the country.

8. In Kuwait, for example, 200,000 square meters of office space was available in the city center in early 2010 while annual demand for 2003–2009 was only 40–60,000 square meters. An additional 425,000–450,000 square meters will be available by 2013. Rents in the city center have almost halved as a result of overaccumulation of office space (MEED 2010, p. 21).

9. For example, Bahrain's BBK had planned to merge with Shamil Bank (eventually postponed) and, in Kuwait, the National Bank of Kuwait gained central bank approval to acquire 40 percent of Boubyan Bank in order to gain access to the latter's Islamic banking capacities (Chawdhry 2009, p. 46).

10. These tendencies predated the crisis. In March 2008, the Commercial Bank of Qatar (CBQ) acquired a 40 percent stake in the UAE-based United Arab Bank. CBQ also has a 35 percent stake in the National Bank of Oman. In August 2008, Qatar National Bank—Qatar's largest bank with 47 percent of the country's total bank assets—acquired a 24 percent stake in the Commercial Bank of Dubai, one of the ten largest banks in the UAE.

11. A related development was the call—particularly expressed in the wake of the extensive cross-border liabilities arising from the collapse of the Saad and Gosaibi conglomerates—to establish a pan-GCC institution to exchange information on corporate and consumer debt.

12. Credit default spreads on debt from across the GCC particularly Qatar, Bahrain, and Abu Dhabi—soared in the wake of Nakheel's imminent default. Another indication of the regional view in which this was perceived was the sharp fall in share prices of European companies in which GCC investors held large stakes. Share prices of the London Stock Exchange, UK supermarket J Sainsbury, and German carmakers Porsche and Daimler dropped in the fear that Dubai's default would mean other GCC states would pull back their foreign investments in order to meet obligations at home.

13. In 2005, the UAE's construction contracts were worth over ten times that of Saudi Arabia ($28.7 billion compared to $2.4 billion). By the first three months of 2009, Saudi construction contracts were worth $15.7 billion compared to the UAE's $4.1 billion. (MEED 2009, p. 21).

14. Arabtec formed its joint venture with the Saudi Bin Ladin Group.

15. See, for example, the comments by Mohammed bin Obaid Al Mazroui, Assistant Secretary-General for economic affairs at the GCC general secretariat, who described the railway project as "a strategic one intended to achieve economic integration" (Roberts 2007). A related example of the economic incentives toward transport integration is found in the aviation industry, where a number of companies have called for the creation of a single GCC aviation market. Jazeera Airways, a Kuwaiti company controlled by the Boodai Group, noted prior to the 30th GCC Summit in Kuwait, that "[u]nder a single market, all commercial restrictions for GCC carriers flying within the GCC, such as the restrictions on routes, the number of flights and fare, will be removed to allow the aviation industry to reach its full potential" (Emirates Business 2009b).

16. World Bank figures for India show remittance flows nearly doubled during 2008 (US$51 billion compared to $27 billion in 2007). In Pakistan, the year-on-year growth of the three-month moving average of remittances averaged more than 20 percent for each month of 2009.

17. Rahman and Mohaiemen also note that there are no timely official Bangladeshi statistics on the number of workers losing their jobs and returning home (only outgoing migrant numbers). They argue that anecdotal observations from low-cost carriers confirm a large number of Bangladeshi workers returning home after being deported.

18. Remittance statistics should be treated with some caution. First, much of the geographic specificity of remittance data can be misleading as it is common for various cities to route remittances through correspondent banks in the United States. Since banks attribute the origin of funds to the most immediate source, the United States appears to be a larger source of remittance flows than it actually is. Moreover, much of the remittance flows to South Asia from the GCC do not show up in official figures because they happen through informal channels rather than licensed money exchanges or the banking system. This is particularly true in the case of Pakistan where the informal *hawala* money transfer system is highly popular and almost impossible to track. In this system, a customer approaches a broker in one city and gives them a sum of money to

assessment of the impact of any drop in remittances needs to differentiate on a subnational basis as labor flows to the Gulf tend to be drawn from specific regions within countries. Remittances, for example, represented over 30 percent of the Indian state of Kerala's net domestic product in 2008, whereas they only represented around 2 percent of total Indian GDP (Zachariah and Irudaya 2008, p. 13).

19. Documentation of these deaths was not widely covered in the media; the Website migrant-rights.org was the only online source that drew attention to these deaths.

20. In mid-November 2010, Saudi newspapers reported the torture of a young Indonesian woman who had been brought to the country to work as a maid. Her body had been burned, fingers broken, and skin removed from her face. Also in November, a Sri Lankan maid in Kuwait had nails hammered into her body by her employees whenever she requested to be paid. Because of their dependence on sponsors and virtually complete isolation from the rest of society, domestic workers are particularly vulnerable to this type of abuse in the GCC.

21. To date, most Gulf states have responded to this tension with "Gulf-ization" programs that offer incentives or set quotas for businesses in the hiring of Gulf citizens. These programs, however, have had little real efficacy and have not substantially altered the structure of the labor force.

22. This point was stressed to the author in a 2010 interview with a member of the UAE Foreign Ministry who wished to remain anonymous.

23. As this book was coming to press a series of uprisings across the Arab world seemed to confirm this analysis. Despite some isolated calls for democratic reform, the GCC states appeared to remain relatively insulated from these uprisings. It was only in Bahrain, where the larger component of poorer Bahraini citizens intersected with Shia grievances against the Sunni al-Khalifa rulers, that significant protests occurred.

24. In Saudi Arabia, for example, investments in productive capacity raised the country's oil production capacity to 12.5 mbd in 2008, which meant a record 4.3 mbd of spare capacity (IIF 2009, p. 10).

25. According to estimates by international oil companies, in 2005 the Caspian Sea region held proven oil reserves equivalent to about 4 percent of total world reserves (48 billion bbls)—far exceeding that of the United States (29 billion bbls). Likewise, proven gas reserves constituted 4 percent of world reserves. Most significant is the fact that many areas of the Caspian Sea basin remain unexplored. It is estimated that additional crude oil reserves approach the amount now held by Saudi Arabia (reaching about 15 percent of total world

reserves), and that natural gas reserves potentially exceed Saudi deposits (Gelb 2006, p. 3).

26. These estimates obviously depend on a variety of factors including the price of oil, the amount of money spent domestically, asset appreciation/depreciation, and the pace and shape of any global recovery. See McKinsey (2009) for a full discussion of different scenarios.

27. Chinese estimates given in McKinsey (2009, p. 46).

28. These estimates for foreign asset accumulation as well as the potential for expansion of development plans depend a great deal on the future oil price. In general, the "break-even" price for oil to keep budget spending at 2008 levels is estimated to range from a low of $35 in Qatar to around $75 in Oman, with Saudi Arabia and Kuwait at around $50. If the price drops below $50 for an extended period of time, some foreign asset sales may be necessary to cover expenses (IIF 2009, p. 14).

29. In this respect, it is interesting to note that in early 2010 China was the largest investor in Iraq's oil and gas sector, winning around 20 percent of the reserves auctioned in the 2009–2010 period.

30. In Malaysia, for example, Al Rajhi Bank, Kuwait Finance House, and Dubai Islamic Bank all operate Islamic finance subsidiaries. In Singapore, the Islamic Bank of Asia was established in 2007 as a partnership between one of the largest banks in Asia, DBS, and investors from the GCC.

31. Clearly this is a complex question and only broad themes in relation to the Gulf can be raised here. For more on the contradictions in China's accumulation model see Li (2008) and Hart-Landsberg and Burkett (2005).

32. This phrase, and the accompanying conception of US dominance, is drawn from Panitch and Gindin (2005).

References

Abdel-Fadil, M. 1987. "The Macro-Behaviour of Oil Rentier States in the Arab Region," in *The Rentier State: Nation, State and the Integration of the Arab World*, ed. H. Beblawi and G. Luciani. London: Croom Helm.

Abdel Hai, M. 2009. "Seventy Agency Deals Cancelled This Year," *Emirates Business*, 27 December, p. 3.

Abed, G., ed. 1988. *The Palestinian Economy: Studies in Development under Prolonged Occupation*. New York: Routledge.

Abrahamian, E. 2001. "The 1953 Coup in Iran," *Science and Society*, Summer, Vol. 65, No. 2.

Achcar, G. 1998. "The Strategic Triad: The United States, Russia, and China," *New Left Review* I/228 (March-April): 91–126.

———. 2002. *Clash of Barbarisms: September 11 and the Making of the New World Disorder*. New York: Monthly Review Press.

Alam, M. 2006. "Dreaming Big." *Oman Economic Review*, March.

Albo, G. 2003. "The Old and New Economics of Imperialism," in *Socialist Register 2004: The New Imperial Challenge,* ed. C. Leys and L. Panitch. London: Merlin.

———. 2005. "Contesting the 'New Capitalism,'" in *Varieties of Capitalism, Varieties of Approaches,* ed. D. Coates. New York: Palgrave Macmillan.

Altvater, E. 1993. *The Future of the Market: An Essay on the Regulation of Money and Nature after the Collapse of "Actually Existing Socialism."* London: Verso.

Anderson, L. 1987. "The State in the Middle East and North Africa," *Comparative Politics,* Vol. 20, No. 1 (October).

ANIMA. 2009. "Foreign Direct Investment Towards the Med Countries in 2008: Facing the Crisis," *Anima Investment Network Study*, No. 3, 20 April.

Arabian Business. 2009. "News in Numbers," Vol. 10, No. 10, 13.

Arab Business Council (ABC). 2007. "2006 Annual Meeting Report, United Arab Emirates," World Economic Forum Insights, Geneva: ABC/WEF.

Arab Investment Company (AIC). 2010. "Monthly Roundup," Vol. 2, No.13, January.

Armstrong, P., A. Glyn, and J. Harrison. 1991. *Capitalism since World War II.* Cambridge, MA: Basil Blackwell.

Ayubi, N. 1995. *Over-Stating the Arab State: Politics and Society in the Middle East.* London: I. B. Tauris.

Baali, F. 1988. *Society, State, and Urbanism: Ibn Khaldun's Sociological Thought.* Albany, NY: State University of New York Press.

Badr El-Din, I. 2007. *Economic Cooperation in the Gulf.* New York: Routledge.

Badre, A., and S. Siksek. 1959. *Manpower and Oil in Arab Countries.* Beirut: Economic Research Institute, American University of Beirut.

Bahrain Stock Exchange (BSE). 2008a. *Annual Trading Bulletin.* Available at http://www.bahrainstock.com. Accessed 5 November 2009.

———. 2008b. *Annual Report.* Available at http://www.bahrainstock.com. Accessed 5 November 2009.

Baldwin, H. 1959. "Oil Strategy in World War II," *American Petroleum Institute Quarterly—Centennial Issue.* Washington D.C.: American Petroleum Institute.

Beblawi, H., and G. Luciani, eds. 1987. *The Rentier State: Nation, State and the Integration of the Arab World.* London: Croom Helm.

Booz Allen (BA). 2005. *Strategic Review of the Television Broadcasting Sector in the Middle East.* Beirut/Dubai: Booz Allen Hamilton.

BP. 2007. "Annual Statistical Review." Accessed June 2008, http://www.bp.com.

Brenner, R. 2000. *The Boom and the Bubble: The US in the World Economy.* London. Verso.

Bromley, S. 1991. *American Hegemony and World Oil.* Cambridge: Polity Press.

———. 2005. "The United States and the Control of World Oil," *Government & Opposition.* Spring, Vol. 40, Issue 2, pp. 225–55.

———. 2008. *American Power and the Prospects for International Order.* Cambridge: Polity Press.

Brooks, D., and H. Changchun. 2008. "Asian Trade and Global Linkages." *ADB Institute Working Paper,* No. 122, December. Tokyo: Asian Development Bank Institute.

Bryan, D., and M. Rafferty. 2006. *Capitalism with Derivatives: A Political Economy of Financial Derivatives, Capital and Class.* Basingstoke and New York: Palgrave Macmillan.

Brzezinski, Z. 1997. *The Grand Chessboard: American Primacy and Its Geostrategic Imperatives.* New York: Basic Books.

Business Monitor International (BMI). 2007. "Saudi Arabia Business Forecast Report; 2007 2nd Quarter." Accessed April 29, 2008, http://www.business-monitor.com.

Callinicos, A. 2005. "Iraq: Fulcrum of World Politics," *Third World Quarterly,* Vol. 26, Nos. 4–5.

Champion, D. 2003. *The Paradoxical Kingdom: Saudi Arabia and the Momentum of Reform.* New York: Columbia University Press.

Chapman, K. 1991. *The International Petrochemical Industry: Evolution and Location.* Oxford: Blackwell.

Chaudhry, K. 1994. "Economic Liberalization and the Lineages of the Rentier State," *Comparative Politics,* Vol. 27, No. 1 (October 1994), pp. 1–25.

———. 1997. *The Price of Wealth: Economies and Institutions in the Middle East.* New York: Cornell University Press.

Chawdry, R. 2009. "GCC: The Banks Urge to Merge," *The Middle East,* February: 45–48.

Output, Prices, and Exchange Rates in the United States and Other Industrialized Countries," Washington, D.C.: CBO.

Cox, R. 1987. *Production, Power, and World Order: Social Forces in the Making of History*. New York: Columbia University Press.

Credit Suisse. 2009. "Potential Dubai Impact More Than Fully Priced into European and US Banks, Yet Contagion Could Become an Issue," *Equity Research*, 27 November. Zurich: Credit Suisse.

Crystal, J. 1995. *Oil and Politics in the Gulf: Rulers and Merchants in Kuwait and Qatar*. Glasgow: Cambridge University Press.

Davidson, C. 2008. *Dubai: The Vulnerability of Success*. New York/London: Columbia University Press/Hurst.

De Saint-Laurent, B. 2009. "Investment from the GCC and Development in the Mediterranean." Paper presented to the IAI Seminar, *The Mediterranean Opportunities to Develop EU-GCC Relations?* Rome, December 10–11. Available at www.animaweb.org. Accessed 20 December 2009.

Dubai Financial Markets (DFM). 2008. "Annual Bulletin 2008." Available at www.dfm.co.ae. Accessed 9 July 2009.

Downstream Today. 2008. "Project Snapshot: Fujian Venture," 10 September, http://www.downstreamtoday.com. Accessed 9 May 2009.

Dubai International Financial Centre (DIFC). 2009. "DIFC Calls for Uniform Legal and Financial Frameworks and Common Payment Systems in Light of Imminent GCC Common Currency." Press Centre, 5 May. Available at http://www.difc.ae. Accessed 3 October 2009.

Duménil, G., M. Glick, and D. Levy. 1992. "Stages in the Development of U.S. Capitalism: Trends in Profitability and Technology since the Civil War," in *International Perspectives on Profitability and Accumulation,* ed. F. Moseley and E. Wolff. Aldershot, UK: Elgar Publisher.

Dun and Bradstreet. 2008. "UAE Private Equity Report," Industry Perspectives. Dubai: Dun and Bradsheet.

Dunia Frontier Capital (DFC). 2009. "Private Foreign Investment in Iraq." Accessed 29 October 2009, http://www.dfcinternational.com.

Economic and Social Commission for Western Asia (ESCWA). 2008. "Foreign Direct Investment Report," Technical Paper 1, 3 September, New York: United Nations.

Economist Intelligence Unit (EIU). 2008. "Near East Meets Far East: The Rise of Gulf Investment in Asia," New York: Economist Group.

Emirates Business. 2009a. "Top 10 players of Mideast TV Business Grab 70% of Ads," 29 April.

———. 2009b. "Jazeera Wants GCC to Have a Single Market," 15 December.

Engels, F. 1972. (1877). *Socialism: Utopian and Scientific.* New York: Pathfinder Press.

———. 1884. (1972). *The Origin of the Family, Private Property and the State*. New York: International Publishers.

———. 1990. (1890). "Foreign Policy of Russian Tsardom," in *Marx/Engels Collected Works*, Vol. 27, pp. 11–29. London: Lawrence & Wishart.

European Commission (EC). 2000. "Green Paper—Towards a European Strategy for the Security of Energy Supply." Luxembourg: Office for Official Publications of the European Communities.

Farsakh, L. 2005. *Palestinian Labour Migration to Israel: Labour, Land and Occupation*. New York: Routledge.

Fattah, H. 1997. *The Politics of Regional Trade in Iraq, Arabia, and the Gulf 1745–1900*. Albany, NY: State University of New York Press.

Fattouh, B. 2007. *OPEC Pricing Power: The Need for a New Perspective*. Oxford: Institute for Energy Studies.

Fauri, F. 1996. "The Role of Fiat in the Development of the Italian Car Industry in the 1950's," *The Business History Review*, Vol. 70, No. 2, 167–206.

Fergany, N. 2001. *Aspects of Labor Migration and Unemployment in the Arab Region*. Cairo: Almishkat Center for Research.

Ferraro, V., and M. Rosser. 1994. "Global Debt and Third World Development." In *World Security: Challenges for a New Century*, ed. M. Klare and D. Thomas. New York: St. Martin's Press.

Field, M. 1984. *The Merchants: The Big Business Families of Saudi Arabia and the Gulf States*. Woodstock, NY: Overlook Press.

Financial Express. 2009. "Travel Trade in Jeopardy as Manpower Export Falls," Tuesday, April 2, 2009, p. 1.

Ford, N. 2006. "Marubeni Powers Up in the Gulf," *The Middle East*, 1 December.

Foreman, C. 2008. "Global Heavyweights Arrive in Force." *Middle East Economic Digest*, Vol. 52, Issue 5, pp. 34–38.

Freedman, L., and E. Karsh. 1993. *The Gulf Conflict: 1990–1991*. Princeton, NJ: Princeton University Press.

Furey, T. 2007. "Franchising in the Middle East, Dubai and Beyond," *Franchising World*, Vol. 39, Issue 1, January.

Gambard, M. 2009. "Advocating for Sri Lankan Migrant Workers," *Critical Asian Studies*, Vol. 41, Issue 1.

Gause, G. 2005. "The International Politics of the Gulf," in *International Relations of the Middle East*, ed. L. Fawcett, 2005. Oxford: The University Press.

GCC Secretariat General. "Monetary Union and Single Currency." Available at http://www.gcc-sg.org/eng/index.php. Accessed 9 October 2009.

———. 2010. *GCC: A Statistical Glance, 2010*. Riyadh: GCC Statistical Department.

Gelb, B. 2006. "Caspian Oil and Gas: Production and Prospects," Washington, D.C: Congressional Research Services.

George-Cosh, D. 2009. "Telecoms Go Long Distance," *The National*, December 17.

Ghose, G. 2010. "Market Volatility Affects Gulf Bonds Issuance," *Gulf News*, March 6.

———. 2008b. "GCC Telecom Sector: Ringing All the Way," Research Report, August. Kuwait: Global Investment.

———. 2008c. "GCC Steel Sector." Kuwait: Global Investment.

———. 2008d. "Sukuks—A New Dawn of Islamic Finance," January. Kuwait: Global Investment.

———. 2008e. "Saudi Arabia." Kuwait: Global Investment.

———. 2009. "UAE" April. Kuwait: Global Investment.

Gluffrida, A. 2010. "Qatari Diar and Binladin Join Up," *The National*, Wednesday, March 3.

Goma, E., and R. El Gamal. 2009. "Gulf Banks Urged to Merge in Crisis Aftermath," November 2, Reuters.

Gowan, P. 1999. *The Global Gamble: Washington's Faustian Bid for World Dominance.* London: Verso.

Grimwade, N. 2000. *International Trade: New Patterns of Trade, Production, and Investment.* New York: Routledge.

Gulf Capital Group (GCG). 2008. "GCC Industry Report, Manufacturing the Future," January.

Gulf Daily News (GDN). 2007. "UK Exports to UAE Reach £3.6bn," July 15.

Gulf Organization for Industrial Consulting (GOIC). 2006. *Gulf Industrial Bulletin*, Vol. 6, Issue 73, August.

Hajrah, H. 1982. *Public Land Distribution in Saudi Arabia.* London: Longman.

Halaoui, H., G. Hasbani, M. Mourad, and K. Sabbagh. 2008. "The Content End Game: Capturing the Benefit of Media and Telecom Convergence in the GCC," Beirut/Dubai: Booz Allen Hamilton.

Hanieh, A. 2008. "Palestine in the Middle East: Opposing Neoliberalism and US Power," in MRzine, 19 July. Accessed October 5, 2008, http://www.monthlyreview.org/mrzine.

———. 2009. "Hierarchies of a Global Market: The South and the Economic Crisis," *Studies in Political Economy*, Vol. 83, Spring, pp. 61–84.

———. 2010. "Temporary Migrant Labour and the Spatial Structuring of Class in the Gulf Cooperation Council," *Spectrum: Journal of Global Studies*, Vol. 1, No. 3, pp. 67–88.

———. 2011. "The Internationalization of Gulf Capital and Palestinian Class Formation," *Capital & Class*, Vol. 35, No. 1, 81–106.

Harrison, R. 2008. "Retail Boom Needs Smooth Supply Chain," *Emirates Business.* 23 January.

Hart-Landsberg, M. 2010. "China, Capitalist Accumulation and the World Crisis," *Marxism 21*, Vol. 13.

Hart-Landsberg, M., and P. Burkett. 2004. "China and Socialism," *Monthly Review*, July-August, Vol. 56, No. 3.

———. 2005. *China and Socialism: Market Reforms and Class Struggle*. New York: Monthly Review Press.

Harvey, D. 1985. "The Geopolitics of Capitalism," in *Social Relations and Spatial Structures,* ed. D. Gregor and J. Urry. London: Macmillan.

———. 1999. *The Limits to Capital.* London: Verso.

———. 2001. *Spaces of Capital: Towards a Critical Geography.* Edinburgh: Edinburgh University Press.

———. 2005. *A Brief History of Neoliberalism.* Oxford: Oxford University Press.

Heard-Bey, F. 1982. *From Trucial States to United Arab Emirates.* Abu Dhabi: Motivate Publishing.

Henderson, C. 1998. *Asia Falling: Making Sense of the Asian Crisis and Its Aftermath.* New York: McGraw-Hill.

Hertog, S. 2010. *Princes, Brokers, and Bureaucrats: Oil and the State in Saudi Arabia.* New York: Cornell University Press.

Hertog, S., and G. Luciani. 2009. "Energy and Sustainability Policies in the GCC," Kuwait Programme on Development, Governance and Globalisation in the Gulf States, Center for the Study of Global Governance, No. 6, November.

HSBC. 2005. "Cement Industry in the GCC," January. Riyadh: HSBC Industry Research.

———. 2007. "SABIC Company Profile," April. Riyadh: HSBC Global Research.

Ibrahim, S. 1982. *The New Arab Social Order.* Westview: Croom Held.

Ijtehadi, Y. 2007. "Growing Pains—Private Equity Industry in MENA," *Arab News,* May 5.

Ikeda, S. 1996. "The World-Economy and Its Production System," in *The Age of Transition: Trajectory of the World-System 1945–2025,* ed. T. Hopkins and I. Wallerstein. London: Zed Books.

Institute of International Finance (IIF). 2007. "Gulf Cooperation Council Economic Report," January 16.

———. 2008. "Summary Gulf Cooperation Council Countries," November 6.

———. 2009. "GCC Regional Overview," September 28.

———. 2010. "Capital Flows to Emerging Market Economies," January 26.

Inter-Arab Investment Guarantee Corporation (IAIGC). 2005. *Investment Climate in the Arab Countries.* Abu Dhabi: IAIGC Studies & Investment Promotion Unit.

International Energy Agency (IEA). 2007. *World Energy Outlook 2007: China and India Insights.* Paris: IEA.

International Energy Agency (IEA). 2008. *World Energy Outlook 2008.* Paris: IEA.

International Monetary Fund (IMF). 1997. *Financial Systems and Labor Markets in the Gulf Cooperation Council Countries.* Washington, D.C.: International Monetary Fund.

.... A Closer Look at Dubai's Debt, Morgan Stanley, December 10.

Jensen, N., and L. Wantchekon. 2004. "Resource Wealth and Political Regimes in Africa," *Comparative Political Studies,* Vol. 37, No. 7, 816–41.

Jolly, D. 2008. "ArcelorMittal to Cut Steel Output," *New York Times,* Wednesday, November 5.

Jones, D., and J. Womack. 1985. "Developing Countries and the Future of the Automobile Industry," *World Development,* Vol. 13, No. 3, pp. 393–407.

Jones, G. 1986. "Banking in the Gulf Before 1960," in *The Gulf in the Early 20th Century: Foreign Institutions and Local Responses,* ed. J. Dewdney and H. Bleaney. Occasional Papers Series, No. 31, Centre for Middle East and Islamic Studies. London: University of Durham.

———. 1987. "The Imperial Bank of Iran and Iranian Economic Development, 1890–1952," *Business and Economic History,* 16.

Jones, J. 1955. *The Fifteen Weeks.* New York: Viking Press.

Juhasz, A. 2004. "Ambitions of Empire: The Bush Administration Economic Plan for Iraq (and Beyond)," *Left Turn Magazine,* 12 (February/March), 27–32.

Kapiszewski, A. 2004. "Arab Labour Migration to the GCC States," in *Arab Migration in a Globalized World,* Volume 2003 International Organization for Migration and League of Arab States.

Kaplan, R. 2009. "Center Stage for the Twenty-First Century," *Foreign Affairs,* Vol. 88, No. 2 (March/April): 16–32.

Karkouti, M. 2009. "Workers Go Home," *The Middle East,* No. 43, August/September, p. 25.

Karl, T. 1997. *The Paradox of Plenty: Oil Booms and Petro-States.* Berkeley: University of California Press.

Katzman, K. 2006. "The Persian Gulf States: Issues for U.S. Policy," Washington D.C.: Congressional Research Service, Library of Congress.

Kawach, N. 2010. "Combined Arab Debt to Global Banks Rises by 18%," *Emirates Business,* January 19.

Kaylani, N. 1979. "Politics and Religion in 'Uman: A Historical Overview,'" *International Journal of Middle East Studies,* Vol. 10, No. 4.

Kazim, A. 2000. *The United Arab Emirates AD 600 to the Present: A Socio-Discursive Transformation in the Arabian Gulf.* Dubai: Gulf Book Centre.

Khaleej Times (KT). 2009. "DCCI Members' Exports Surpass 2007 Record," November 20.

———. 2010. "Abu Dhabi ADIA Sees Substantial Risk to Global Economy," January 11.

Khan, S., and Arnold, T. 2009. "Gulf Due for Central Credit Body," *The National,* October 25.

Kharboush, M. 2006. "Key Challenges for the Petrochemical Industry," SABIC keynote address to Elite Conferences 8th International Conference of Indian Petrochemical Industry, November 6.

Khouja M., and P. Sadler. 1979. *The Economy of Kuwait—Development and Role in International Finance.* London: Macmillan.

Khuri, F. 1991. *Tribe and State in Bahrain: The Transformation of Social and Political Authority in an Arab State.* California: University of California Press.

Klare, M. 2004. "The Bush/Cheney Energy Strategy: Implications for U.S. Foreign and Military Policy," *Journal of International Law and Politics,* Vol. 36, Nos. 2–3 (double issue).

Kobrin, S. 1985. "Diffusion as an Explanation of Oil Nationalization: Or the Domino Effect Rides Again," *The Journal of Conflict Resolution,* Vol. 29, No. 1, pp. 3–32.

Kogler, U., F. Majdalani, and S. Kuge. 2009. "Not Too Late Finding Opportunity in Middle East Logistics." Beirut: Booz and Company.

Kotilaine, J. 2009. "Rebalancing via Deleveraging," *GCC Economic Monthly.* NCB Capital, October.

Kuwait China Investment Company (KCIC). 2009. *The New Silk Road Asia and the Middle East Rediscover Trade and Investment Opportunities.* Available at http://www.kcic-asia.com. November 11. Accessed 5 February 2010.

Kuwait Financial Centre (KFC). 2009. "GCC Bond Market Survey H1 Highlights," August.

Lebanese Ministry of Finance (LMF). 2007. "International Conference for Support to Lebanon, Paris III, Third Progress Report," September.

Lefebvre, H. 1991. *The Production of Space.* Oxford: Basil Blackwell.

Legrenzi, M. 2008. "Did the GCC Make a Difference?" In *Beyond Regionalism? Regional Cooperation, Regionalism and Regionalization in the Middle East,* ed. C. Harders and M. Legrenzi. Aldershot: Ashgate.

Levinson, M. 2006. *How the Shipping Container Made the World Smaller and the World Economy Bigger.* Princeton, NJ: Princeton University Press.

Li, M. 2008. *The Rise of China and the Demise of the Capitalist World-Economy.* London: Pluto Press.

Ligaya, A. 2009. "Job Losses Add up to One in 10 in Region," *The National,* December 9.

Lindsey, B. 2003. "The Trade Front Combating Terrorism with Open Markets," *Trade Policy Analysis,* No. 24, Cato Institute, August 5.

Looney, R. 2003. "The Neoliberal Model's Planned Role in Iraq's Economic Transition," *Middle East Journal,* Vol. 57, No. 4 (Autumn), pp. 568–86.

Lubin, D. 2007. "Petrodollars, Emerging Markets and Vulnerability," *Economic and Market Analyses,* March 19. London: Citigroup.

Luciani, G. 2006. "From Private Sector to National Bourgeoisie: Saudi Arabian Business," in *Saudi Arabia in the Balance: Political Economy, Society, Foreign Affairs,* ed. P. Aarts and G. Nonneman. London: Hurst and Company.

Mahdavy, H. 1970. "The Patterns and Problems of Economic Development in Rentier States: The Case of Iran," in *Studies in the Economic History of the Middle East*, ed. M. Cook. London: Oxford University Press.

Mandel, E. 1975. "The Industrial Cycle in Late Capitalism," *New Left Review*, I/90, March-April.

———. 1983. *Late Capitalism*. London: Verso.

———. 1995. *Long Waves of Capitalist Development*. London: Verso.

Marglin, S. 1991. "Lessons of the Golden Age: An Overview," in *The Golden Age of Capitalism: Reinterpreting the Post-War Experience*, ed. S. Marglin and J. Schor. Oxford: Oxford University Press.

Marx, K. 1844. "Critical Notes on the Article 'The King of Prussia and Social Reform. By a Prussian,'" in *Vorwarts!* No. 63, August 7. Available at http://www.marxists.org. Accessed 5 September 2010.

———. 1977. (1859). *A Contribution to the Critique of Political Economy*. Moscow: Progress Publishers.

———. 1973. *Grundrisse*. Harmondsworth: Penguin Books.

———. 1992. *Capital: Volume 1*. London: Penguin Classics.

Massey, D. 1984. *Spatial Divisions of Labour: Social Structures and the Geography of Production*. London: MacMillan Education.

———. 1988. *Global Restructuring, Local Responses*. Worcester, MA: Graduate School of Geography, Clark University.

McCormick, T. 1987. *America's Half-Century: United States Foreign Policy in the Cold War*. Baltimore: Johns Hopkins University Press.

McKendrick, C. 2007. "Developments in China's Ethylene Cracker Projects and Markets, from an International Perspective," Speech at China Petrochemical Focus, Shanghai, China, May 24–25. Available at http://www-static.shell.com. Accessed 24 February 2008.

McKinsey Global Institute (McKinsey). 2009. *The New Power Brokers: How Oil, Asia, Hedge Funds, and Private Equity Are Shaping Global Capital Markets*. Available at http://www.mckinseyquarterly.com. Accessed 8 June 2010.

McNally, D. 1981. "Staples Theory as Commodity Fetishism: Marx, Innis and Canadian Political Economy," *Studies in Political Economy* Vol. 6, Autumn: 35–64.

———. 2009. "From Financial Crisis to World-Slump: Accumulation, Financialisation, and the Global Slowdown," *Historical Materialism*, Vol. 17, No. 1, pp. 35–38.

Middle East Economic Digest (MEED). 2005. "GCC Leaders Agree Monetary Union Criteria," Vol. 49, No. 51, p. 28.

———. 2006a. "The $1 Trillion Project Market," April 21.

———. 2006b. "Developer Rankings Inside the Halls of Power," October 27.

———. 2009a. "Private Equity's $11 billion Cash Pile," May 21.

———. 2009b. *MEED Yearbook 2010*, December 24.

———. 2009c. "Dubai Reviews Plans as Population Falls," March 20–26.

———. 2010. "Bidders Line Up to Build SAMBA Headquarters," March 5–11.

Ministry of Overseas Indian Affairs (MOIA). 2010. *Annual Report 2009–2010*. New Delhi: Government of India, Ministry of Overseas Indian Affairs.

Mitchell, T. 2009. "Carbon Democracy," *Economy and Society*, Vol. 38, Issue 3, August, pp. 399–432.

Mohieldin, M. 2008. "Neighborly Investments," *Finance and Development*, Vol. 45, No. 4. Available at http://www.imf.org. Accessed 19 August 2009.

Molyneux, P. 2005. *Banking and Financial Systems in the Arab World*. New York: Palgrave Macmillan.

Morgan Stanley. 2006. "Recycling Petrodollars Boosts Global Markets, Says Morgan Stanley," *Fund Strategy*, December.

Muscat Securities Market (MSM). 2008. *Annual Statistical Bulletin*. Muscat: MSM.

Nasdaq Dubai. 2009. "Listing Debt on Nasdaq Dubai." Available at http://www.nasdaqdubai.com. Accessed 10 January 2010.

Nashashibi, H. 1984. "An Arab Capital Market: The Next Step for Arab Bankers?" *The Banker*, Vol. 134, No. 77, 5.

National Energy Policy Development Group (NEPD). 2001. *National Energy Policy: Reliable, Affordable, and Environmentally Sound Energy for America's Future*. Washington D.C: US Government Printing Office.

National Intelligence Council Global Trends (NICGT). 2008. *2025: A Transformed World*. Washington, D.C.: US Government.

National Investment Commission (NIC). 2009. "Investment Overview of Iraq," Republic of Iraq.

NCB Capital. 2009. "GCC Debt Capital Markets: An Emerging Opportunity?" *Economic Research*, March.

Nexant Chem Systems. 2004. "Outlook for the Petrochemical Industry: Good Times Ahead." Argentina: Instituto Petroquimico Argentino.

Niblock, T. 1980. *Dilemmas of Non-Oil Economic Development in the Middle East*, London: Arab Research Center.

———. 2007. *The Political Economy of Saudi Arabia*. London and New York: Routledge.

Nijim, B. 1985. "Spatial Aspects of Demographic Change in the Arab World," in *The Middle East: From Transition to Development*, ed. S. Hajjar. Leiden, Netherlands: Brill.

Ollman, B. 2003. *Dance of the Dialectic: Steps in Marx's Method*. Illinois: University of Illinois Press.

Ordonez, I. 2010. "Exxon VP: Global Petrochemical Trade to Double in 10 Years," *Dow Jones Newswire*, April 29.

Palloix, C. 1977. "Conceptualizing the Internationalization of Capital," *Review of Radical Political Economics*, Vol. 9, No. 2, 17–28.

, ̶ ̶ ̶ ̶ ̶ ̶ ̶ ̶ ̶ and C Leys. London: Merlin Press.

———. 2005. "Superintending Global Capital," *New Left Review* 35, September/October.

Parker, C., and P. Moore. 2007. "The War Economy of Iraq," *Middle East Report,* No. 243, Summer.

Peterson, J. E. 2004. "Oman's Diverse Society: Southern Oman," *Middle East Journal,* Vol. 58, No. 2, Spring, pp. 254–69.

Poulantzas, N. 1978. *Classes in Contemporary Capitalism,* London: Verso.

Qatar Peninsula. 2004. "Gulf Ministers Okay Steps to Cut Reliance on Foreign Labour," 13 October.

Rahman, J., and N. Mohaiemen. 2009. "Remittances: Behind the Shiny Statistics," *The Daily Star,* December 27.

Rahman, S. 2006. "Dubai Represents 23% of Gulf's Retail Sector," *Gulf News,* April 18.

Ramazani, R. 1988. *The Gulf Cooperation Council: Records and Analysis.* Charlottesville, VA: University of Virginia.

Ratha, D., S. Mohapatra, and A. Silwal. 2009. "Migration and Remittance Trends 2009: A better-than-expected Outcome So Far, but Significant Risks Ahead," *Migration and Development Brief 11.* Washington D.C.: World Bank.

———. 2010. "Outlook for Remittance Flows 2011–12: Recovery After the Crisis, But Risks Lie Ahead," *Migration and Development Brief 13.* Washington D.C.: World Bank.

Rattner, S. 1979. "Volcker Asserts US Must Trim Living Standards," *New York Times,* Page A1, October 18.

Redfern, B. 2008a. "Labour Shortage Delays Development," *Middle East Economic Digest,* February 1.

———. 2008b. "Private Developers Drive Boom," *Middle East Economic Digest,* February 1.

———. 2010. "Debt Stalls Hopes of Recovery," *Middle East Economic Digest,* January 29–February 4.

Roberts, L. 2007. "GCC Rail Project on Doha Agenda," *Arabian Business,* December 3.

Robinson, W. 2004. *A Theory of Global Capitalism: Production, Class and State in a Transnational World.* Baltimore: Johns Hopkins University Press.

———. 2007. "The Pitfalls of Realist Analysis of Global Capitalism: A Critique of Ellen Meiksins Wood's 'Empire of Capital,'" *Historical Materialism,* Vol. 15, 71–93.

Rosdolsky, R. 1977. *The Making of Marx's Capital.* London: Pluto Press.

Ross, M. 2001. "Does Oil Hinder Democracy?" *World Politics,* Vol. 53, No. 3 (April), 325–61.

Roy, S. 1995. *The Gaza Strip: The Political Economy of De-Development.* Washington, D.C.: The Institute for Palestine Studies.

Rutledge, E. 2009. *Monetary Union in the Gulf.* New York: Routledge.

Saad-Filho, A., and D. Johnston. 1995. *Neoliberalism: A Critical Reader.* London: Pluto Press.

Saez, E. 2008. "Striking It Richer: The Evolution of Top Incomes in the United States," Working Paper Series, Institute for Research on Labor and Employment, UC Berkeley.

Saidi, N. 2009. "Local Currency Debt Markets in the Middle East," Dubai: DIFC.

Salisbury, P., and C. Foreman. 2010. "Seoul Opens Up a New Silk Road," *Middle East Economic Digest,* January 22–28.

Samara, A. 2001. *Epidemic of Globalization: Ventures in World Order, Arab Nation and Zionism.* Glendale, CA: Palestine Research and Publishing Foundation.

Sampson, A. 1976. *The Seven Sisters the Great Oil Companies and the World They Made.* New York: Bantam.

Saudi American Bank (SAMBA). 2006. *The Saudi Economy at Mid-Year 2006.* Riyadh: Samba Financial Group.

———. 2009. "GCC Economic Update," October. Riyadh: Samba Financial Group.

Saudi Arabia British Bank (SABB). 2007. *Saudi Arabia—Thinking Big,* Fourth Quarter Report. Riyadh: Saudi British Bank.

———. 2008. "Saudi-US Trade Relations: The Ties that Bind," Research Notes, January. Riyadh: Saudi British Bank.

Saudi Arabian Monetary Agency (SAMA). 1999. "Development and Restructuring of the Saudi Banking System," in *Bank Restructuring in Practice,* ed. J. Hawkins and P. Turner. Bank for International Settlements Policy Paper No. 6. Basel: BIS.

———. 2009. "Quarterly Statistical Bulletin, 4th Quarter." Riyadh: SAMA.

Saudi Gazette. 2010. "Aramco: China Overtakes US as Largest Customer," April 6.

Scott, M. 2007. 'New Market for Middle East Clean Technology," *Financial Times Surveys,* February 26.

Secretariat-General (SG). 2001. *The Economic Agreement Between the GCC States: The Cooperation Council for the Arab States of the Gulf.* Accessed 9 September 2009, http://library.gcc-sg.org/English/Books/econagree2004.htm.

Sell, C. 2008. "Mushrif Trading & Contracting," *MEED Middle East Economic Digest,* 16 December.

Setser, B., and R. Ziemba. 2006. "Petrodollar Watch: October 2006," *Roubini Global Economics.* Available at http://www.rgemonitor.com. Accessed 17 March 2008.

———. 2009. "GCC Sovereign Funds: Reversal of Fortune," Washington, D.C.: Council on Foreign Relations Working Paper, January.

Sherbiny, N. 1985. *Oil and the Internationalization of Arab Banks.* Oxford: Oxford Institute for Energy Studies.

Strange Geographies of Emerging Markets," *Transactions of the Institute of British Geographers*, NS, Vol. 25, No. 2, pp. 187–201.

Skeet, I. 1988. *OPEC: Twenty-Five Years of Prices and Politics.* Cambridge: Cambridge University Press.

Sklair, L. 1995. *Sociology of the Global System.* Baltimore: Johns Hopkins University Press.

———. 2001. *The Transnational Capitalist Class.* Oxford: Blackwell.

Skocpol, T. 1982. 'Rentier State and Shi'a Islam in the Iranian Revolution," *Theory and Society,* Vol. 11, No. 3, pp. 46–82.

Smith, S. 1999. *Kuwait 1950–1965: Britain the al-Sabah and Oil.* Oxford: Oxford University Press.

Solh, K. 2008. "The Emergence of Regional and Global Investment Leaders Out of Abu Dhabi." Paper presented on behalf of Gulf Capital to the Abu Dhabi Economic Forum 2008 Emirates Palace, Abu Dhabi, February 3–4.

Solomon, E. 2010. "Migrant Workers Collateral Damage of UAE Slump," *Reuters,* July 20.

Spiro, D. 1999. *The Hidden Hand of American Hegemony Petrodollar Recycling and International Markets.* Ithaca, NY: Cornell University Press.

Spitz, P. 1988. *Petrochemicals: The Rise of an Industry.* New York: John Wiley.

Sri Lankan Bureau of Foreign Employment (SLBFE). 2009. *Annual Statistical Report of Foreign Employment 2009.* Koswatta: Sri Lanka Bureau of Foreign Employment.

Standard and Chartered. 2007. "Middle East Focus," August. Accessed 24 November 2008, http://www.standardchartered.com/.

Sterngold, J. 2008. "Journal of a Plague Year: Faith in Markets Cracks Under Losses," *Bloomberg,* December 31.

Stokes, D. 2007. "Blood for Oil? Global Capital, Counter-Insurgency and the Dual Logic of American Energy Security," *Review of International Studies,* Vol. 33, 245–64.

Stork, J. 1975. "US Strategy in the Gulf,' *MERIP Reports,* No. 36. (April).

———. 1980. "The Carter Doctrine and US Bases in the Middle East," *MERIP Reports,* No. 90, September, pp. 3–14, 32.

———. 1985. "Prospects for the Gulf," *MERIP Reports,* No. 132, May, pp. 3–6.

Stork, J., and M. Wenger. 1984. "US Ready to Intervene in Gulf War," *MERIP Reports,* No. 125/126, The Strange War in the Gulf, July–September, pp. 44–48.

Sturm, M., J. Strasky, P. Adolf, and D. Peschel. 2008. "The Gulf Cooperation Council Countries, Economic Structures, Recent Developments and Role in the Global Economy," *European Central Bank, Occasional Paper Series,* No. 92, July.

Sturm, M., and N. Siegfried. 2005. *Regional Monetary Integration in the Member States of the Gulf Cooperation Council.* European Central Bank Occasional Paper, No. 31.

Tadawul. 2006. *Annual Report 2006.* Riyadh: Tadawul.

Teicher, H. 1995. "Statement to the U.S. District Court, Southern District of Florida." Available at http://www.gwu.edu/~nsarchiv/NSAEBB/NSAEBB82/iraq61.pdf. Accessed 23 August 2009.

Terzian, P. 1985. *OPEC, the Inside Story* (translated by M. Pallis). London: Zed Books.

Thomson, S. 2006. "Year of the Hypermarket," *RetailME,* January/February.

Timewell, S. 2009. "Top 100 Arab Banks," *The Banker,* November 1.

Tolui, R. 2007. "Petrodollars, Asset Prices, and the Global Financial System," *Capital Perspectives.* Newport Beach, CA: PIMCO.

Townsend, J. 1977. *Oman: The Making of the Modern State.* London: Croom Held.

Tschoegl, A. 2002. "Foreign Banks in Saudi Arabia: A Brief History," *Transnational Corporations,* Vol. 11, No. 2 (August).

United Arab Emirates Central Bank (UAECB) 2009. "UAE Monetary Developments—1st Quarter," Abu Dhabi: UAE Central Bank.

United Arab Emirates Yearbook (UAEY). 2006. London: Trident Press.

United Nations Conference on Trade and Development (UNCTAD). 2007. *World Investment Report 2007.* Geneva: United Nations.

United Nations Children's Fund (UNICEF). 1989. *The State of the World's Children.* New York: Oxford University Press.

———. 1999. "Iraq surveys show 'humanitarian emergency'," 12 August, http://www.unicef.org/newsline/99pr29.htm

United States Department of State. 1945. *Foreign Relations of the United States: Diplomatic Papers 1945. Volume VIII. The Near East and Africa.* Washington, D.C.: Government Printing Office. Accessed 28 August 2009, http://bit.ly/9z8FFF.

United States Department of State (WMEAT). 2003. *World Military Expenditures and Arms Transfers 1995–1996,* Washington, D.C.: US Government Printing Office.

United States General Accounting Office (GAO). 1996. *Military Exports: Offset Demands Continue to Grow,* Report to Congressional Requesters. April. Washington, D.C.: Government Printing Office.

United States Embassy Saudi Arabia. 2004. "Economic Trends May 2004." Riyadh: Embassy of the United States Government.

Vassiliev, A. 1998. *The History of Saudi Arabia.* London: Saqi Books.

Vitalis, R. 2007. *America's Kingdom: Mythmaking on the Saudi Oil Frontier.* Stanford: Stanford University Press.

Walter, N. 2009. "Arabtec Won't Put All Eggs in the UAE Basket," *Property Weekly,* March 18.

Waters, M. 1995. *Globalization.* London: Routledge.

Weisskopf, T. 1992. "A Comparative Analysis of Profitability Trends in the Advanced Capitalist Economies," in *International Perspectives on Profitability and Accumulation,* ed. F. Moseley and E. Wolff. Aldershot, UK: Edward Elgar.

..., D. 2007. "The Crimes of Neo-Liberal Rule in Occupied Iraq," *British Journal of Criminology*, Vol. 47, No. 2, 177–95.

Wilson, R. 1983. *Banking and Finance in the Arab Middle East*. New York: St. Martin's Press.

Winham, G. 2005. "The Evolution of the Global Trade Regime," in *Global Political Economy*, ed. J. Ravenhill. Oxford: Oxford University Press.

Winning, D. 2007. "Exxon, Sinopec, Aramco Complete $4 bln Financing for China JV," *Market Watch*, September 6.

Wolf, M. 2007. "The Brave New World of State Capitalism," *Financial Times*. October 16.

Woods, N. 2006. *The Globalizers: The IMF, The World Bank, and Their Borrowers*. Ithaca, NY: Cornell University Press.

World Bank. 1989. *World Development Report: Financial Systems and Development*. Washington D.C: World Bank and Oxford University Press.

———. 2008. *World Development Indicators*. Accessed 5 February 2009, http://www.worldbank.org.

———. 2009. *From Privilege to Competition Unlocking Private-Led Growth in the Middle East and North Africa*. Washington, D.C.: World Bank.

———. 2010. *Global Economic Prospects Crisis, Finance, and Growth*. Washington, D.C.: World Bank.

World Trade Organization (WTO). 2007. *Bahrain Trade Policy Review*, June 13.

Yergin, D. 1991. *The Prize: The Epic Quest for Oil, Money, and Power*. New York: Simon & Schuster.

Zachariah, K., and R. Irudaya. 2008. "A Decade of Kerala's Gulf Connection," *Migration Monitoring Study*. Kerala: Center for Development Studies.

Zahlan, R. 1998. *The Making of the Modern Gulf States*, London: Ithaca Press.

Zoellick, R. 2003a. "Global Trade and the Middle East: Reawakening a Vibrant Past," Remarks at the World Economic Forum Amman, Jordan, June 23. Accessed 4 July 2007, http://www.usinfo.state.gov.

———. 2003b. "Transcript of Joint Press Conference: Secretary of State Colin Powell, Jordanian Foreign Minister Marwan Muasher, US Trade Representative, Jordanian Minister of Trade Salah Bashir," Movenpick Hotel, Dead Sea, June 23. Accessed 4 July 2007, http://www.usinfo.state.gov.

Websites

Amman Stock Exchange: http://www.ase.com.jo/.

Bahrain Center for Human Rights: http://www.bahrainrights.org.

Bangladesh Association of International Recruiting Agencies (BAIRA): http://www.hrexport-baira.org/.

Bangladesh Ministry of Expatriates Welfare and Overseas Employment, Government of the People's Republic of Bangladesh: http://probashi.gov.bd/publication/publication.php.

Gulf Cooperation Council (GCC): http://www.gcc-sg.org.

Gulf Investment Corporation (GIC): http://www.gic.com.kw/.

International Monetary Fund Statistics Database: http://www.imf.org.

International Iron and Steel Institute (IISI), Major Importers and Exporters of Steel, 2005: http:// www.worldsteel.org/.

Saudi Arabia Supreme Economic Council: http://www.sec.gov.sa.

Saudi Arabia Ministry of Finance and Industry: http://www.commerce.gov.sa/.

Saudi Arabian General Investment Authority (SAGIA): http://www.sagia.gov.sa.

Saudi Ministry of Economy and Planning: http://www.mep.gov.sa/.

US Energy Information Administration (USEIA): http://www.eia.doe.gov.

Arabic Language

Al-Nasrawi, A. 1990. *al-Qita' al-'amm w'al-qita' al-khas fi al-watan al-'arabi* [The Public and the Private Sectors in the Arab Nation]. Beirut: CAUS.

Amin, S. 1985. *azamat al'mujtama' al'arabi* [Crisis of Arab Society]. Cairo: Dar al-Mustabal Al-'Arabi.

Dahir, M. 1986. *Al-Mashriq al-'arabiya al- mu'asir min al badawa ila al-dawla al-haditha* [The Contemporary Arab Levant from Nomadism to the Modern State]. Beirut: Ma'had al-Inma 'al- 'Arabi.

Shamsi, M. 2006. *Ta'qiym siyassay al hijra f'il dawla majlis attawan alkhaleeji,* [Evaluation of Labour Policies in the GCC]. United Nations Expert Group Meeting on International Migration and Development in the Arab Region. Beirut: Department of Economic and Social Affairs United Nations Secretariat.

Sharara, W. 1980. *Howl Ba'd mushakel Al Dawla f'il mujtamaa wal thaqafa Al-Arabiyeh* [On Some Problems of the State in Arab Society and Culture]. Beirut: Dar Al-Hadatha.

———. 1981. *Al-ahl wa al-ghanima muqawimmat asiyassat fi al-Mamlakah al-'Arabiyah al sa'udiyah* [Kin and the Booty: The Foundations of Politics in the Kingdom of Saudi Arabia]. Beirut: Dar Al Talia Publishers.

State of Qatar. 2004. *Al Nashra Sanawiyya Al Ihsayaht Al Taq'a wa al San'aeya* [Annual Statistical Bulletin on Energy and Industry], Vol. 23. Doha: General Secretariat for Development Planning.

Yusha', A. 2003. *'Awlamat al-iqtisad al-Khaliji : qira'ah lil-tajribah al-Bahrayniyah* [Globalizing the Gulf Economies—the Case of Bahrain]. Beirut: al-Mu'assasah al-'Arabiyah lil-Dirasat wa-al-Nashr.

Index